ACTS OF DARKNESS

Also by John L. Hill

Pine Box Parole: Terry Fitzsimmons and the Quest to End Solitary Confinement & Other True Cases

ACTS OF DARKNESS

JOHN L. HILL

Foreword by

Salvatore Caramanna

DURVILE & UpRoute

DURVILE IMPRINT OF DURVILE PUBLICATIONS LTD.

CALGARY, ALBERTA, CANADA

DURVILE.COM

DURVILE & UpRoute

DURVILE.COM

DURVILE PUBLICATIONS LTD.
DURVILE IMPRINT
CALGARY, ALBERTA, CANADA
DURVILE.COM

LIBRARY AND ARCHIVES CATALOGUING IN PUBLICATIONS DATA

Acts of Darkness
Notorious Criminals, Their Defenders, Prosecutors, and Jailers

Hill, John L.: Author
Caramanna, Salvatore: Foreword

1. True Crime | 2. Criminology | 3. Canadian Justice
4. True Crime | 5. Canadian Media | 6. Wrongful Conviction

Book 13 in the Durvile True Cases Series
Series Editor, Lorene Shyba PhD
ISBN: 978-1-990735-75-2 (pbk)
978-1-990735-79-0 (audio) | 978-1-990735-80-6 (e-pub)

Cover photo is by Austin Andrews.
"In Memorium" was originally published in *Law 360 Canada.*

Printed in Canada | First edition | Second printing 2025

Canada Alberta Government

Product of Canada
Authors, Publisher, Printers

Durvile Publications acknowledges the financial support of the Government of Canada through Canadian Heritage, Canada Book Fund and the Government of Alberta, Alberta Media Fund.

With gratitude, we acknowledge the traditional land of the Treaty 7 Peoples of Southern Alberta: the Siksika, Piikani, and Kainai of the Niisitapi (Blackfoot) Confederacy; the Dene Tsuut'ina; and the Goodstoney, Chiniki, and Bearspaw Stoney Nakoda First Nations. We also acknowledge the Homeland of the Otipemisiwak Métis Government of the Métis Nation within Alberta.

Durvile & UpRoute is committed to protecting our natural environment. This book is made of material from well-managed FSC-certified forests and other controlled sources.

To my wife, Roxann
On the occasion of our
thirtieth wedding anniversary

CONTENTS

CONTENTS

SALVATORE CARAMANNA

FOREWORD

Salvatore Caramanna

Velvet-Glove Persuasion

The laws of this country ... apply to us whether one is a prime minister or a murderer. It is not the judge's fault for applying the law to a fact situation before him. The true victims, if the judge had decided in the opposite way, would have been the law-abiding taxpayers of Canada, who would have been deprived of compensation should their legal rights be ignored in favour of high-handed officials.

— John L. Hill, Op-Ed in the *Ottawa Citizen*, 2009

FEW LAWYERS can speak about a legal career as robust, challenging, and rewarding as John Hill's. As you read through this gripping first-hand insider account of legendary Canadian legal sagas, you will be left in admiration, wondering what this man has not done in his four-decades-plus career fighting for criminal justice in Canada. He has taken on battles that most would fear to tread and won. He has worked with the who's who of the Canadian criminal justice scene, making him part of that elite group. I have a deep sense of gratitude that John memorialized the achievements and lessons he learned throughout his illustrious legal career, creating a truly fabulous book that is accessible to all. For anyone interested in the inner workings of the criminal justice system and a no-holds-barred, behind-the-scenes look at what defending some of the most dangerous and notorious defendants Canada has ever seen. I am honoured that he asked me to write this foreword.

I first met John in 2004, in my seventh year as a lawyer, when we represented two young women accused of knowingly importing cocaine hidden in their luggage after a week-long Caribbean getaway. I had heard much about John before meeting him from the co-defendants' counsel in the Gladiators trial that you will read about in this book, the late Edward Sapiano and Douglas Usher. I began my legal career at the firm where Edward and Douglas practiced. I was in the office when Douglas was defending the Gladiators trial with John and Edward. They told me about John's legendary reputation as a prison law lawyer and his exceptionally fine skills as a criminal defence counsel. By the end of the importing trial with John, I was compelled to upgrade him to superb.

As a young lawyer steeped in the belief that juries always do the right thing and can always be trusted, John provided a fresh perspective in that case. You will read about John's insights into juries in this book, especially in the chapters "Gladiators" and "Collateral Damage in the Pursuit of Justice." Our clients' defence was knowledge: they did not know that cocaine had been secretly sewn into their suitcases the night before they left for Canada. They were unwittingly used as blind mules to transport cocaine into Canada, likely by rogue hotel staff who had their personal information about where they resided in Canada. On their last night, after they had packed, a hotel employee treated them to a night on the town. With hindsight, this ruse gave the cohorts-in-crime at the hotel the chance to plant the cocaine into the luggage lining.

Credibility was going to be the key issue in the trial. The orthodox view on juries amongst the lawyers I trained and worked with to that point was that you never elect judge-alone on an importing case where knowledge is the issue. Judges were simply too jaded and had seen too many far-fetched blind mule tales that they could not be trusted to impartially judge a knowledge defence. The only choice was a jury trial. John challenged my unwavering belief on the day of the trial by raising the idea of re-electing to a judge-alone trial when he found out the judge assigned to our case. I was taken aback.

John's reasoning was unassuming: we have a good case with two very credible clients whose accounts supported each other, and most importantly, he trusted this specific judge to do the right thing. The latter point directly conflicted with everything I believed about judges and juries at that point in my career. Why gamble our clients' fates on one man's opinion when we could have twelve impartial people make the decision? It just made no sense to me, but I kept an open mind. We discussed the issue at length. The tipping point for me was John's vast experience, coupled with his ability to explain himself with lucid clarity and calmness. You will see that innate talent as you read this book.

There is nothing more effective in an advocate than the ability to persuade with a velvet glove: without yelling and fist-pounding theatrics, let the force of the advocate's words and arguments become the pounding fist that lands the knockout blow. That is the best description of John as an advocate that I can conjure for you. It is one that I tried to emulate thereafter. An op-ed that John wrote to the *Ottawa Citizen* is an example of John's velvet glove advocacy. It is scintillating to read—I have chosen to include an excerpt as the opening epigraph to this foreword.

John explained that he knew this judge very well from his days as a lawyer. Lawyers can and often change when they become judges, but John said he knew this man's core values about fairness and believed he would remain true to them, making him an ideal jurist to judge this case without a jury. Critically, John did not oversell his hand, speaking plainly and even-handedly. He was fine with either course, but a judge-alone trial with an inherently fair judge would be simpler and cleaner and, most importantly, would eliminate the risk of finding a zealot on the jury that might sway the rest to an unjust verdict. He convinced me.

We then advised our clients, and they agreed to judge alone. The rest is history. The clients were resoundingly acquitted. John had taken an axiomatic concept about juries and shown that there was another equally viable perspective to consider.

As an aside, the respect and admiration that the judge had for John during the trial was palpable and was undoubtedly to our clients' benefit. It is a basic reality of the adversarial process that the stature of the lawyer, be it defence or prosecution, can make a difference. It did in that case.

Fast forward over twenty years later, and I find myself reading John's manuscript about some of the darkest and most disturbing cases he has seen and been personally involved in. I confess that as a seasoned defence lawyer, I winced at various points at the acts of darkness described in this book—the details of depravity, sadism, and violence in a few of the chapters are profoundly disturbing.

Make no mistake, however, these incredible chapters are not only about that type of darkness. As you continue to read, you will discover how darkness manifests itself in every corner of the justice system. You will be struck by the harsh and painful reality that the darkness does not always emanate from the defendants. Sometimes, the acts of darkness are perpetrated by players you would least expect to commit injustices: a prison warden, a police officer, correctional authorities, government officials, the media, archaic drug laws, and sadly, even us, the public at large.

When I finished reading John's manuscript, I was plagued by a sense that these chapters were not simply about the acts of darkness but were also about exploring the ripples created by the wave of impact initiated by these acts. Did John write this book just to entertain us with graphic, thrilling stories of crime and punishment? Or is there a bigger, more hopeful lesson that we are to glean from it all? The question was impossible for me to ignore, compelling me to read the chapters again to confirm my suspicion.

I concluded that, as much as this work is about acts of darkness, it offers considerably more—a thoughtful and deft exploration of the duality inherent in darkness itself. Does every act of darkness inevitably lead to a corresponding act of redemption? This exposé challenges readers to contemplate the validity of this dichotomy, true or false. Evidence of jailhouse conversions and numerous instances of grace under pressure, exhibited by people marginalized and ostracized from society, provides ample material for reflection and may even inspire a sense of hope. These accounts are simultaneously illuminating, gut-wrenching, and heartwarming, presenting narratives the average person might never imagine associating with the term "convicted criminal."

It is this complexity and density that make these chapters—now a book—such a masterful piece of writing. It is a pleasure to read and impossible to put down. With these opening words, I leave you to your reading.

—Salvatore Caramanna, B.Sc. (Hons), LL.B.
Toronto, Ontario, 2025

JOHN L. HILL

PREFACE

John L. Hill

Examining the Underbelly

My journey began in elementary school, where I would eagerly rush home to catch my favourite television show. The opening scene was always the same—a crowd of people, their eyes fixed on the sky. And then, the voices would call out, "Look! Up in the sky! It's a bird! It's a plane! No, it's Superman!" The hero, a "strange visitor from another planet with powers and abilities far beyond those of mortal men," was on a mission to preserve 'Truth, justice, and freedom."

As I grew older and became a member of the Bar of Ontario, I admit that my goals as a litigator were often similar to those of my boyhood hero. My mission in court was to secure truth and justice and preserve the liberties we share in a democratic society. But unlike the superhero, I did not possess superior powers and abilities. Over time, I realized there was no universal "truth." Court cases devolved from finding a universal truth into siding with a version of the fact most societally accepted. The general public often saw justice as a synonym for "Lock 'em up." The rights and liberties guaranteed by the Constitution frequently competed for precedence. In this moral fog, where even well-intentioned advocates could unwittingly participate in acts of darkness—choices or compromises that, though legal, clouded the light of fairness.

While I never doubted that the legal profession played an essential role in the peaceful operation of society, I had to disabuse myself that lawyers were social superheroes. For every case where I felt I was on the side of a morally sound, justified, and acceptable position, opposing counsel tried to convince the court to accept another viewpoint.

Nevertheless, I believe our criminal and disciplinary systems, despite their imperfections, are fundamentally workable. Yet, we must keep our eyes open to spot the flaws. Sometimes, this is difficult because we live in an imperfect world, but it may be time to identify some of the faults that create imperfection in our institutions.

One of the most prevalent concerns is our willingness to dehumanize individuals. It is easy to see lawbreakers as less than human to justify cruel and unusual treatment. Dehumanization is rampant in the way Canadian society has, in the past, treated our Indigenous populations. We need to look no further than the treatment of Indigenous children in residential schools and the length of time this abuse continued to realize that we sometimes treat some segments of the population differently, which leaves survivors of the mistreatment scarred in later life. Our method of dealing with dehumanization is to ignore the process and pretend it didn't happen. When we treat some people as though they were animals, we are creating a caste system within a country that supposedly abhors such differentiation. These, too, are acts of darkness—systemic, often invisible, but no less damaging.

Although the focus in the accounts that follow centre on the criminal and correctional systems, the concept that social mores and norms can and do change over time is suggested by our attitudes toward slavery. Although the presence of slavery has not been abolished—indeed, it has been said it is more prevalent in the world today than in the nineteenth century—there is a tendency to sanitize our history rather than learn from it.

Another area for improvement is our absolute belief in majority rule. Just because our democratically elected representatives pass a law does not necessarily mean the enactment is proper. There is merit in allowing expertise to prevail. Yet, there is also merit in keeping a close watch over the experts to ensure they stay within their authority. Our society values obedience as its ultimate goal. Historically, obedience was directed toward the Church; today, obedience to the State is frequently considered the pinnacle of citizenship. Those who disobey the rules are tortured or banished. Can we not accept that all of us can contribute to the common good even if past behaviour indicates that a few have broken the rules?

The great English poet John Milton (1608–1674) questioned how he could be obedient to God if, halfway through his life, he became aware of his impending blindness. How could he continue doing good works and contribute to his faith and fellow man if his physical ability to perform was constrained? His answer lies in the closing line of Sonnet 19, "On His Blindness," where he concludes, "They also serve who only stand and wait."

As one who has worked with prisoners for nearly half a century, I've realized that Milton's words, written nearly half a millennium ago, remain largely unaccepted. We still cannot believe that imprisoned individuals can contribute to our social good when their past behaviours have offended the social norm of obedience to the rules of society, sometimes violently. We define them by their acts of darkness, and in doing so, we too often deny the possibility of their redemption.

Every year, experts in law and psychiatry attend international conferences to discuss proper and humane ways to treat lawbreakers in society. I have attended several such get-togethers and have presented papers at some. My point has been that there needs to be improvement in the conditions and approaches we consider advisable. I suspect my efforts to discuss the imperfections in our criminal and correctional systems with academics and practitioners have been somewhat like preaching to the choir. For real change to occur, the general public must become involved, assessing our institutions with a realistic understanding of what happens once a person is accused of wrongdoing.

A law professor once claimed that examining legal theory in isolation is too dull and would rarely help advocate reform. He suggested that instead of writing and delivering academic papers to like-minded academics, a better approach would be to go to the general public and use SMUT—the story-telling method for understanding theory.

Each of the following chapters contains stories from my legal career and my retirement career as a writer and columnist for an online newspaper for the legal profession that examine many concerns that trouble me with our criminal and correctional systems. I hope many will find this a more entertaining way of understanding the theories I am trying to advance.

It has been said that one can only know a city once one examines its underbelly. Likewise, one can never see a society until one examines the commonly accepted attitudes—the good, the bad, and the ugly. If we can see some of ourselves in the following tales, we will not need to look up in the sky for a superhero to advance truth and justice and uphold our freedoms. We will have to look at and to each other.

1

Vito Buffone and Jeffrey Kompon

Collateral Damage in the Pursuit of Justice

Better that ten guilty persons escape
than one innocent suffer.

—Sir William Blackstone

NOT EVERY ACT OF DARKNESS begins with violence or bloodshed. Some are quieter, disguised in boardrooms or courthouses, hidden beneath layers of bureaucracy or stitched into the fabric of ordinary life. Vito Buffone and Jeffrey Kompon are serving life sentences in prison.

They insist—and have always insisted—that they are innocent of the offences for which they were convicted. Their story raises unsettling questions: Did a monstrous act of darkness on the part of the judicial system condemn two men to a lifetime behind bars? If so, what if the very institutions meant to protect justice instead ensured its failure?

Vito Buffone appeared to be living the Canadian dream. In 2003, he purchased what some news outlets called a mansion. He had a loving wife, three children, and a live-in nanny. As the founder and CEO of SLM Logistics Corporation, he built a thriving salvage and recycling business from scratch, a company that would eventually be valued in the millions. Buffone's journey, from humble beginnings to publicly traded success, seemed to embody entrepreneurial excellence and community respect.

Why, then, would a man of such standing end up sentenced to life for drug importation?

Jeffrey Kompon, too, saw himself as a builder, a man who turned ideas into businesses. Raised in a middle-class, entrepreneurial family, he first made a name for himself in competitive darts. As a youth, he was a successful darts player coached by an experienced senior player, Edward Oliver (Oliver would later become his co-accused). At just sixteen, he was setting records and building a brand around signature dart products. Later, he joined his family's restaurant business, then pivoted to the digital frontier, launching an email-based advertising company from his basement. That company and another of his ventures would eventually go public, further proof of his adaptability and business acumen.

When the internet era approached, Jeffrey, working from his basement, designed a method for businesses to advertise their products by email. That business expanded and became one of two companies he founded to be taken public. Jeffrey's digital marketing innovation and ability to adapt to changing technologies demonstrated his forward-thinking approach and resilience.

Jeffrey Kompon and Vito Buffone were more business associates than partners. Jeffrey's parents bought salvage goods from Vito's warehouses to resell in local flea markets. Jeffrey also helped facilitate deals with regional retailers, and eventually, he and Vito co-devised a trade workaround that enabled Canadian goods to reach Cuba without violating US sanctions. Their relationship was practical—occasional collaborations shaped by commerce and convenience.

In 2014, that all changed. On September 22 of that year, both men were arrested as part of a sweeping police operation known as "Project Roadmaster"—an investigation that would ultimately be hailed for achieving the largest cocaine bust in Canadian history.

But amid the accolades and headlines, a quieter question lingered: Had justice been served, or had two men been caught in the undertow of a prosecutorial triumph?

Jeffrey, then 43, was living a comfortable life in Welland, Ontario. He and Vito had been acquainted for a decade before their arrest. Both were convicted, and all appeals have since been exhausted. Although they are now housed in a minimum-security facility, the gravity of their situation remains unchanged. They may never freely embrace their families again.

And still, they maintain their innocence.

What if the system got it wrong? What if greed, prejudice, and imprecise testimony—not criminal intent—led a jury to convict? What if the justice system, in its pursuit of results, committed its own act of darkness?

Vito's business, unconventional in its time, may have appeared suspicious to those unfamiliar with cross-border salvage logistics and Latin American trade routes. But appearances can be deceiving—and damaging—especially when law enforcement is under pressure to deliver results. Before examining how a multi-agency task force reached its conclusions, it's worth first understanding the shape of the investigation.

The Unusual Business

We are all familiar with the three Rs for a greener environment: reduce, reuse and recycle. Vito Buffone's business was a variation of these principles. His business could be summarized in these three Rs: Review, Refurbish, and Recycle. Vito's company, SLM Logistics Corporation, was incorporated in Ontario in 2004 and was dedicated to managing consumer and retail store returns of defective and problematic electronics.

Large retailers relied on SLM to repair and return merchandise for resale, or to salvage and recycle defective goods. The source of the defects would be communicated to the manufacturer for quality assurance purposes. These defective goods could be purchased cheaply from the manufacturer and resold abroad. Vito's company used its background in consumer service, dealing with many major electronics brands, making it profitable. They provided a valuable service to retailers by managing returns and contributed to a more sustainable electronics lifecycle through innovative recycling practices.

The rapid expansion of the cell phone market presented a significant shift in consumer electronic sales. Vito's company, quick to adapt, saw this as a new opportunity and successfully expanded its operations into this market, contributing to the company's overall growth.

In 2006, Vito's company hired Raul Bulhosen (sometimes referred to by the surname Bulhosen Rios), a Mexican national with permanent Canadian status. Raul operated his own business, BVP International Trading, where he was the sole director and officer. His role was to act as a conduit between Vito's enterprise and the Mexican subsidiaries of global giants like Walmart and Costco. Raul's value to Vito was clear—his deep-rooted contacts could expedite legal clearances and streamline the importation of goods into Mexico.

But with opportunity often comes a shadow. Raul also introduced Vito to IQ Electronics Mexico, the largest electronics service provider in Latin America, employing over a thousand people across five countries. It was a connection that seemed to promise only growth. With Raul as the bridge, Vito's company expanded its reach, reinforcing its global commitment to sustainability—or so it appeared on the surface.

The ventures proved profitable. By 2007, they had established a joint enterprise in Nuevo Laredo, Mexico, and by 2013, another in Houston, Texas. Raul remained a key broker until 2014, moving product, building relationships, and—perhaps—masking other intentions.

For buried beneath the surface of this commercial success was an allegedly dark act. In *The Wolfpack*, journalists

Peter Edwards and Luis Horacio Nájera suggest that Raul Bulhosen may have had ties to the Sinaloa cartel. Their theory is chilling: that Raul's position within a legitimate Canadian firm provided a discreet entry point for one of the world's most violent criminal organizations. With the death of Montreal mafia godfather Vito Rizzuto, a void opened in Canada's underworld. And into that void, through the cracks of legitimate business, stepped a darker force—silent, strategic, and possibly invisible to Vito Buffone and Jeffrey Kompon, who maintain they were wholly unaware of any criminal infiltration.

Vito Buffone's entrepreneurial journey had begun with SLM Logistics Corporation, which had gone public on the Toronto Stock Exchange in 2013 through a reverse takeover of Penfield Capital. Subsequently, SLM was rebranded as Sentinel Exchange Corporation (SEC), and established operations in Delaware to expand into the US market. SEC acquired TRC Corporation, which specializes in electronic repairs and point-of-sale equipment servicing, with partnerships including Fujitsu and National Cash Register. This move bolstered Vito's company's reputation and profitability significantly. Supported by fundraising efforts from Jeffrey and Raul, Vito's businesses expanded to three locations by 2013, employing over 150 staff across Ontario and Tennessee. Plans included further expansion throughout Canada, the US, and Latin America.

As Vito's business grew, he looked for opportunities in Mexico. His primary contact had, of course, been Raul Bulhosen. While working with Latin American business contacts, Raul encountered Borja Vilalta-Castellanos. Vilalta-Castellanos was never an employee of Vito's company. He was Spanish and could communicate easily with suppliers in Central and South America. Vilalta's linguistic and regional experience complemented Vito's efforts to penetrate the non-English-speaking market. Raul's job was to find customers for Vito in the Spanish-speaking market. Sinaloa cartel connections could be easy for Raul and Vilalta. Vilalta's brother, José, was a respected accountant for the Sinaloa cartel in Spain and Mexico.[1]

Vito also set up a retail arm to distribute his company's products. Although most goods were sold wholesale or exported, a subsidiary company, T.O. Bargains, was established to run auctions, pop-up sales, and events to raise funds for charities and non-profit organizations. Vito was delighted that his endeavours were assisting the charitable works of deserving causes, especially the two closest to his heart: Caritas, a men's mental health charity and Shining Through, an autism school located in Vaughan, just outside Toronto. Vito's commitment to philanthropy through T.O. Bargains exemplified his dedication to giving back to the community and supporting meaningful causes.

Working with charities brought Vito into contact with Edward Oliver, Jeffrey's former dart coach. Ed had worked with Variety Club Canada for over five years and had become chairman of the charitable organization. He was looking for a full-time opportunity to help the charity and purchased wholesale goods from Vito's company. Ed's non-availability at times due to health and family issues frustrated Vito, but Vito wanted to continue working with him and trusted his expertise in charitable works. Vito was adamant that his good business fortune should also benefit the less fortunate. The Saturday before his arrest, September 20, 2014, Vito, his wife, his daughter and his sister-in-law attended a Sick Kids Hospital charity event in Toronto.

1 Money laundering involved Mexican government officials and was heavily tracked by undercover US Customs agents. See Tim Golden's Special Report, Cold Pursuit "Top Mexican Off-Limits to U.S. Drug Agents," published in the *New York Times*, March 16, 1999.

As Project Roadmaster, a sweeping police operation, gained momentum, the Niagara Regional Police filed an Information to Obtain (ITO) a warrant to wiretap Ed Oliver's phone. Ed, then in his late sixties and struggling with health issues, had emerged as a person of interest and soon became a primary target.

Wiretaps captured frequent calls between Ed and his young, fit employee, Dean Brennan. Ed had hired Dean because he could do the heavy lifting Ed no longer could. But Dean brought more to the table than muscle. From the outset, Dean made it clear he understood Ed's line of work—cocaine trafficking—and wasn't shy about pitching himself as a valuable asset. In one intercepted conversation, Dean told Ed, "Yeah, but if you're in the cocaine business, one of the first things you're gonna need is a pilot." Dean, who held a pilot's licence, had clearly done his homework before approaching Ed. His ambition and calculated approach showed a sharp understanding of the drug trade.

Yet, notably, for all Dean's initiative, his dealings were solely with Ed, not Vito Buffone the alleged head of the operation. If Vito truly ran the show, why didn't Dean go straight to him?

The wiretaps showed that Ed Oliver referred to an individual as the "big boss." Ed also referred to "Vito" and that he was close to this person. He said he had breakfast, lunch, and many dinners with him. He also spoke of several movements of four hundred kilos at a time. The disparity between Ed's claims and the evidence collected highlights potential inaccuracies in the allegations against Vito.

Was Ed Oliver exaggerating? The police constantly snooped on multiple suspects, yet police tracking confirmed only one meeting between Ed and Vito.

The police also intercepted another of Ed Oliver's calls on April 26. It was later in the afternoon when Ed Oliver spoke with a man identified by his alias of Tony Ambrosia. Ed said he had breakfast with the "big boss." Police surveillance showed that Ed never had a breakfast meeting with Vito. Police tracking confirmed only one meeting between Ed and Vito. That occurred on April 26, 2014. Ed had telephoned Vito the previous day, asking to meet. Vito suggested a 1:00 p.m. meeting at Vito's office. A meeting did occur. It lasted for fifteen minutes.

Again, in August, Ed called Dean and told him of dinner meetings with the "big boss" and discussed large quantities of cocaine. At the time, Vito was on a family vacation to Europe and could not have had the dinner meetings that Ed recounted. The timing of Vito's vacation provides a clear alibi, further questioning the validity of Ed's claims.

On April 28, 2014, the police conducted a covert operation on a stash house located inside an office complex in Vaughan, Ontario. Ed Oliver rented one of the offices that contained the stash house. The police set up cameras within Ed's office to record what was happening at that location. While the installation progressed, police found a room they regarded as the place where drugs were concealed. Inside that room, police videotaped a banker's box containing six bricks of cocaine. There were other banker's boxes that the police estimated contained 60 to 80 bricks of cocaine. The police seized only one of the bricks and left the remaining quantities to avoid disturbing the office setting.

It did not take long for Ed to discover the break-in. The next day, Ed called Dean, advising him that someone had entered the office and made off with one of the bricks of cocaine. He also said that the only other person with a key to the stash house was the "big boss."

Ed Oliver stated he was determined to find out who had taken the quantity of cocaine he found missing. Yet, no calls were made to Vito, throwing doubt on the notion that Vito was the person Ed called the big boss. The absence of any direct communication between Ed and Vito regarding the missing cocaine further undermines the credibility of the accusations against Vito.

Ed was never called at trial to identify the big boss. In the 110 telephone calls intercepted by police, the only discussion of drugs and money were the calls between Ed and Dean. Could it be that Vito was not the big boss the police believed him to be?

At Vito Buffone's bail hearing in October 2014, the Crown stated they found a key in Vito's desk as potentially damning evidence: a key, they claimed, that unlocked the door to a stash house. If true, it would suggest Vito wasn't just involved in the operation, he might be its boss. But by the time the case went to trial, that narrative had shifted. An RCMP officer testified that while a key found in Vito's desk did fit the lock on the stash house door, it did not actually open it.

It was in 2012 that Tony Ambrosia entered Vito Buffone's world. Ambrosia was looking to source merchandise for his flea market retail business and quickly became a familiar face among Vito's employees. That was the name everyone knew him by, Tony Ambrosia—a name that appeared even on his driver's licence. But Ambrosia's real identity was Marco Cipollone,[2] a fact that didn't come to light until his arrest in 2014. In the meantime, Tony had brought numerous contacts into Vito's retail operations, especially after the 2013 opening of the T.O. Bargains store in Brampton, Ontario.

Vito was initially intrigued by the investment opportunities that Tony presented, which included mortgages, property purchases, and high-end automobiles. Tony also promised to connect Vito with venture capitalists, potentially significantly increasing the company's service volume. However, these plans

2 It may have been useful for Cipillone to use an alias. An October 1, 2010, CP24 news report named Marco Cipillone as one of four men arrested and charged with the theft of a $200,000 diamond ring and a pair of diamond earrings following a police investigation in Toronto.

never materialized, and the two men had no social interactions beyond their business dealings. Meetings were rare, and Tony only occasionally showed up to buy products for resale at a Pickering flea market.

Besides this outlet, Vito also owned a business called the Trading Post. It was another method of selling repaired equipment processed through SLM. None of Vito's co-accused ever had dealings with this business.

Vito's business ventures were diverse, but one of the most notable was Premium Products and Distribution Ltd. Established in 2001, it quickly gained traction and expanded across Central America. The company's success in Panama, where it distributed SLM products, significantly boosted its visibility and reputation.

The heart of the operation was Vito's company, SLM. It provided accountable management of returns from receiving products for repair to resale or recycling with quality assurance testing, factory servicing of returns, resale of returns through non-traditional channels, and recycling of non-saleable products to support a closed-loop, first-tier distribution process. SLM was unique because it could fully recycle the non-saleable returns it received, thereby allowing customers' return processes to have a meagre environmental impact. SLM has had independent Waste Audit Reports completed, which show SLM was able to achieve waste diversion rates as high as 99.7%. Companies working with SLM's processes could divert 99.7% of their product from landfill sites. Many multinational companies wanted to ride the bandwagon of environmental accountability and increased their involvement with SLM.

Businesses facing product recalls could send questionable material to SLM. If Vito's company could permanently fix the defective goods, the material could be refurbished. SLM sometimes bought quantities of faulty products, made repairs, and sold the material in South America. This led to warehouses opening in the Southern United States and Latin America. Goods that could not be repaired and resold would be recycled locally.

Vito remained adamant that with the size and scope of his operations, he would have been unable to consider drug importation and trafficking in his endeavours and that he did not do so. Nevertheless, with the number of employees working for and under him, it was impossible to ultimately oversee any misdeeds they might pursue. He could not understand that anyone would risk losing an exceedingly profitable business to dabble in drug trafficking. His protestations may not have convinced the general public that he would not import drugs, but it intensified his resolve to defend himself against the accusation as forcefully as possible.

The Investigation

Vito Buffone had been arrested and charged with criminal conduct as a youth. The imposition of fines punished his misdeeds. However, with maturity, he stayed compliant with the law and was never troubled by the police. In the community, he held the reputation of a law-abiding businessman. Nonetheless, his name was added to a list of suspects when Project Roadmaster was established. He headed a corporation where several of the people targeted initially were employed. The police were under pressure not to arrest only mid-level operators. The greatest glory would come from eliminating the importation scheme and punishing those involved. The three-year investigation began in 2010. Project Roadmaster started locally and expanded to become an international venture.[3]

3 That is not to say that the NSA did not tip off local authorities. Intercepted telephone calls played a major role in convicting the Sinaloa cartel's head of international operations. *United States v. Zamprano,* 974 F. 3d. 774 (8th Cir. 2020). Sharing of information continues. The US also alerted the government of Russia of a pending attack by Isis K on a Moscow arena in 2024.

Eight different law enforcement agencies cooperated in Project Roadmaster, including the Royal Canadian Mounted Police (RCMP), the Canadian Border Security Agency (CBSA), the Ontario Provincial Police (OPP), the Toronto, Niagara, and Peel Regional Police Services, the United States Drug Enforcement Agency (DEA), and the Department of Homeland Security (DHS) in the United States. The investigation was massive, involving police obtaining more than 100 judicial authorizations, including wiretaps, tracking orders and production orders. Covert surveillance had been ongoing during the three years leading up to the raids. The reason why the multi-agency investigation was established has never been explained. Still, suspicion was that it had to do with American operations and the hunt to stamp out the Sinaloa drug cartel.

Police executed search warrants at nearly 30 locations on September 22, 2014, and seized narcotics, cash, weapons, vehicles, laptops, and cell phones, including encrypted devices. Two cell phones capable of sending encrypted messages were, police claim, found in Vito's office drawer along with a key suspected as being able to open the door to the room where the cocaine was located in Ed Oliver's office. The accused faced charges of conspiracy, money laundering, possessing, importing, and distributing narcotics, and participating in a criminal organization. The raids occurred in the Greater Toronto Area (GTA) and the Niagara Region. The raids involved over two hundred police officers from the seven law enforcement agencies. Vito Buffone was 50 years old and living in Caledon when arrested.

Most middle-class homeowners can scarcely imagine, let alone endure, the violence and humiliation that accompanied the police raid on Jeffrey Kompon's home in Welland, Ontario. He was 43 years old in September 2014 when heavily armed officers descended on his modest house on Colbeck Drive. It was an ordinary neighbourhood, not the sort of place where acts of darkness usually unfolded in broad daylight.

Kompon and his live-in girlfriend, Chandra Furney, had no idea what awaited them. Police smashed through the front door with weapons drawn, flooding their home with shouted commands and raw aggression. What followed went beyond any reasonable show of force. Both Jeffrey and Chandra were subjected to strip searches by the all-male raiding team. At one point, Chandra was thrown against a wall and threatened with arrest if she failed to cooperate. When she asked to use the toilet, she was told she could, but only if a male officer stood and watched her urinate.

To Chandra Furney, this wasn't policing, it was degradation. She later lodged a formal complaint, appalled that male officers had stripped her naked and supervised her private moments. In 2016, the official response was chilling and dismissive: police acknowledged that it was an oversight not to have assigned a female officer to the raid.

But if such an obvious violation of dignity could be dismissed as an oversight in a meticulously planned police operation, one is left to wonder: what other dark and indignant acts were sanctioned, overlooked, or quietly buried beneath the official record?

A Staff Sergeant with Niagara Regional Police was quoted extensively about the raids. Not mentioned in the news releases was that the Staff Sergeant had developed a relationship with Jeffrey Kompon's former wife. That woman often expressed her dislike for Chandra Furney. Jeffrey continues to feel that the treatment he and Chandra received was connected with the police sergeant's connection with Jeffrey's ex-wife.

Raul Bulhosen, 32 years old and living in Toronto, was at home when police raided his house, pointing laser-aimed guns at his body. They also pointed the weapons at Bulhosen's young nephew and niece. The two stayed with him at his home the morning of the take-down. There were no weapons in his house, and Bulhosen never carried one. There was never any information in Bulhosen's past that would indicate a likelihood to resort to violence. There was no reason suggested why such use of force was necessary. However, the force used by police would be consistent with the narrative that police would claim was the reason for the bust: a high-level drug organization was connected to the cartel and importing vast quantities of drugs into Canada. The use of force confirmed the narrative the police were trying to peddle.

The raids were the culmination of the undercover police operations that had started with the 2011 investigation by the Niagara Regional Police Department three years earlier. The investigation uncovered evidence of cocaine importation and trafficking, money laundering and participating in a criminal organization. Said Niagara Police Staff Sgt. Shawn Clarkson:

> This investigation has had a significant impact on the cocaine trafficking and associated organized crime groups in Southern Ontario....Seized in the raids were narcotics, cash, weapons, vehicles, laptops, cell phones, and encrypted devices. This led to charges of conspiracy, money laundering, possessing, importing and distributing narcotics, and participating in a criminal organization for Vito Buffone, 50, Raul Bulhosen, 42 of Mississauga, Jeffrey Kompon, 43 of Welland, Borja Vilalta-Casellanos, 29 of Toronto, Marco Cipollone (aka Tony Ambrosia), 38 of Toronto, John Edward Oliver, 67 of Toronto, Dean Brennan, 38 of Toronto, Victor Lucero, Laurence Aiello, 61 of Fort Erie, Guy Caputo, 69 of Fonthill, Herman Jones, 45 of Brampton, Luis Garcia, 30 of Toronto, Patricia Pinkerton, 29 of Toronto, and Jamie Ortiz-Sieiro, 29 of Mexico City, Mexico.

After the arrests, personalized "Substantive Event Summaries" were sent to each accused. These reports particularized the charges and disclosed intercepted communications, surveillance photographs, and witness evidence as it applied to each accused arrested. It was alleged that, from 2011 to 2014, the group was responsible for concealing thousands of kilograms of cocaine inside granite boulders, shipping them from Brazil into Canada, and then extracting and trafficking the contents in the Greater Toronto and Niagara areas.

The raids confiscated two ocean shipping containers holding three large granite boulders. It took police three days to break down the boulders into rubble; despite the theory that the boulders were used to hide the imported drugs, no cocaine or traces of cocaine were found within these boulders.

Twenty-two shipments of quarry stone came from Mexico. In February of 2012, six flatbeds of rectangular rocks arrived at a warehouse on Nugent Road in an industrial area near Port Colborne, Ontario. Each of the stones weighed over 15,000 kilograms. This material was imported by Vito's company SLM from Mexico for sale to an enterprise in Welland. The Welland buyer used the quarry stone by breaking the rocks into large slabs for flooring in an auditorium under construction in Hamilton. These rock slabs were quite different from locally available rock. They would pulverize easily when struck with a heavy object. These shipments were known to Vito Buffone but were quite different from granite boulders. Vito's company had documentation for the quarry stone, but police could not provide documentation for importing granite boulders.

It became difficult for police to link Vito to importing the granite boulders. Police were required to reveal an audio intercept of a call with Marco Cipillone in June 2014. That call confirmed that Vito did not know of any granite boulders and was not interested in dealing with them.

Nonetheless, when charges were laid, it was the responsibility of the Crown to prove beyond a reasonable doubt that Vito and his cohorts imported over two tonnes of cocaine in forty-seven shipments of granite boulders, employed meticulous record-keeping from a reservoir of shell companies, false identities and fraudulent documents to lend legitimacy to their operation. Even with the constant surveillance before the takedown, one would have expected a plethora of evidence showing how such a large quantity was moved under a veil of secrecy. Besides law enforcement speculation, no evidence was produced, and no statements were taken to implicate anyone charged with this scheme.

Court Challenges

Identifying the procedures involved in drug importation and proving the masterminds behind the operation would create publicity of national interest. Police could benefit substantially in the public eye by using such a takedown to enhance their reputation as the safeguard of the public. However, the situation can turn ugly for police if they fail to get a prosecution.

In Project Roadmaster, the Crown laid charges against the accused. The average member of the public would think that once charges are laid, the prosecution is ready to proceed. Such was not the case.

As usual in criminal prosecutions, proceedings commenced in the Ontario Court of Justice. Bail was considered for those who had been arrested. It was time for the Crown as prosecutor to release the information that would be used at trial to convict those before the court. The Crown must turn over this material, known as "disclosure," promptly. December 2014 saw the Crown producing its "first wave" of disclosure, consisting of more than 240,000 documents and 100,000 intercepted communications.

It was not unusual in a case such as this that the Crown would request case management. Justice Joseph Nadel was tasked with overseeing the proceedings. The initial case conference was held on February 24, 2015. The Crown proposed an alternative to the procedure for the preliminary hearing to expedite the hearing as per Section 540(7) of the *Criminal Code.*

Ordinarily, the preliminary hearing is the first phase in the judicial process and allows an accused to hear the evidence from Crown witnesses and cross-examine the witnesses. A record is kept that can later be used at trial to point out any variations in a witness's testimony. The procedure takes place in open court. This speedier proceeding proposed to replace a preliminary hearing, required the Crown to tender witness statements and make any deponents available for cross-examination as counsel for the defence might require. This would occur not in open court but in an office, with the answers taken down by a court stenographer for later use at trial. Lacking the formality of an open court and being able to arrange a date for such an examination can speed up the time it takes to ready the matter for trial.

Then, on March 30, 2015, the Crown advanced a second wave of redacted documents known as Informations to Obtain ("ITO"). These are the affidavits filed supporting the judicial authorizations of the raids. Another case management meeting was held on June 18, 2015. Defence and Crown counsel were ready to finalize dates for the preliminary hearing. Justice Nadel set aside 21 days between December 2015 and June 2016 to determine if the Crown had some evidence that could justify the matter proceeding to trial.

However, there was a glitch. The Supreme Court of Canada held that there was a limit on the time it should take from the time of arrest to the completion of the trial (*R v. Jordon,* 2016). This time limit was set as 30 months. The aim was to protect the accused's right to a speedy trial as guaranteed by section 11(b) of Canada's *Charter of Rights and Freedoms,* part of the Canadian constitution. The Crown counsel became so concerned that the case might be thrown out for infringement of the *Charter* right that it opted for an alternate route. Having to wait, possibly until June 2016, to complete the first phase, even if done outside a courtroom and in a court stenographer's office, could lead to exceeding the time limit for a speedy trial. On October 16, 2015, the Director of Public Prosecutions consented to prefer a direct indictment against the accused under a *Criminal Code* provision allowing proceedings to be transferred to the Superior Court of Justice to face trial without a preliminary hearing or the alternative of the out-of-court procedure.

Following the transfer of the matter to the Superior Court, the Crown petitioned for case management, appointing Justice Joseph P. Henderson to oversee proceedings. A meeting occurred in February 2016. During the case conference, the Crown estimated that the trial would take six months. Justice Henderson scheduled the trial to begin on February 27, 2017, and end on August 27, 2017. Calculations were quickly made. The estimated period of 35 months from arrest to trial completion was above the presumptive 30-month ceiling for Superior Court proceedings.

By November 2016, half of the original group of 14 co-accused had pleaded guilty. There are many reasons why an accused person would plead guilty and not have the matter tried in court. Sometimes, the Crown will propose a penalty that could be less stringent than if the matter went to trial and a guilty finding is made. Another reason is that an accused person may have made a deal with the Crown to offer substantial evidence or even testify against another co-accused in return for a lower sentence.

It is also possible that the police may offer to assist in mitigating a punishment by agreeing to help an accused when the Parole Board later hears the guilty plea results in a conviction and the matter. Another reason is that the accused person is, in fact, guilty and prefers not to waste time and money on lengthy and expensive court proceedings.

With half the original group pleading guilty, the remaining co-accused, Raul Bulhosen, Jeffrey Kompon, Vito Buffone, Vilalta-Castellanos, Dean Brennan, Marco Cipollone (AKA Tony Ambrosia), and Edward Oliver, remained. These became known as the "Bulhosen Group." They reasserted their rights for a speedy trial and brought an s.11(b) *Charter* application, alleging a breach of their right to be tried in a reasonable time. Justice Henderson heard their motion.

The Supreme Court's decision in *Jordan* held that an acquittal could result if the right to a speedy trial were breached. However, Justice Henderson found that the Supreme Court's *Jordan* decision was not rigid. It allowed enough wiggle room for the Crown to claim that unexpected delay should not be held to defeat the prosecution. Applying the *Jordan* framework, as Justice Henderson interpreted it, the application was dismissed. Henderson's finding withstood an appeal to the Ontario Court of Appeal.[4]

During the appeal, a complex legal argument was presented. It was contended that when the Crown opts to proceed without a preliminary hearing, the presumptive delay should be reduced to eighteen months, a proposition that challenged the established thirty months in the Jordan decision. However, the Court of Appeal swiftly refuted this argument, which pointed out that the Supreme Court of Canada had already deliberated and ruled on this matter in a case brought before it approximately eleven months after the Jordan case had been handed down (*R. v. Cody*, 2017).

4 R. v. Bulhosen, 2019 ONCA 600. The July 15, 2019, decision of the Court of Appeal held that the Crown brought the seven alleged co-conspirators in an international cocaine trafficking network to trial in a reasonable time. The presumptive 30-month *Jordan* ceiling yielded to the complexity of the evidence and issues in the proceedings. The piecing together of documentary, wiretap, and surveillance evidence to prove a conspiracy, map out an organized crime structure, and construct a web of relationships and transactions justified an estimated turnaround period of 35 months.

Ultimately, the Crown brought Bulhosen, Vilalta-Castellanos, Oliver, and Cipollone to trial within 27 months, Dean Brennan within 27 1/2 months, and Vito Buffone and Jeffrey Kompon within 32 1/2 months.

The accused parties endure significant emotional and financial strain in many of these prosecutions. They often make deals to accept a lighter sentence than they might receive if convicted after trial. This was the case for Messrs. Bulhosen, Vilalta-Castellanos, Oliver, and Cipollone, who, under the weight of the narrative implicating them in the drug importation scheme, pleaded guilty before Justice Henderson by December 20, 2016. By January 30, 2017, Dean Brennan also succumbed and pleaded guilty. These accused were then handed penitentiary terms ranging from 8.25 to 18 years. Mexican nationals Raul Bulhosen of Toronto and Borja Vilalta-Castellanos of Mississauga received prison terms of eight and seventeen years, respectively. Jaime Ortiz-Siero, of Mexico City, had been deported due to his misrepresentations to immigration officials.

The remaining defendants, Vito Buffone and Jeffrey Kompon, opted to be tried by judge and jury. It has yet to be made clear why these two agreed to be tried by judge and jury rather than by judge alone when the latter option would have afforded a speedier trial. Some people charged with a serious offence think their chances of acquittal are better if the Crown has to convince 12 people instead of one, the judge, of their guilt. That is a common presumption many people who are not used to courtroom tactics accept. The downside is that a jury can never be questioned about how it arrived at its decision. A judge making a finding of guilt must clearly outline the reasoning and how the law was applied to arrive at guilt lest an appeal court reconsider the matter. Most people must know that trial counsel has tactics to influence a jury, and jurors can be deliberately misguided. The prosecution and the defence must come into the trial with a clearly defined theory of the case and not allow one side or the other to distract the jury to the detriment of the opposing side.

With the anticipated trial length so long, the number of possible judges to sit in the Welland courthouse was limited. The Crown was probably delighted that the field of possible jurists was limited and that Justice James A. Ramsay could sit throughout the duration.

Ramsay was sometimes called a "hanging judge" because of his perceived conservative leanings. Before his appointment to the bench, Justice Ramsay had been a prosecutor, including in the high-profile Paul Bernardo murder trial.

Vito Buffone and Jeffrey Kompon stood trial before Justice James A. Ramsay, sitting with a jury. Ostensibly, this was a drug importation case.

The defence's theory ought to have been that drug importation occurred, but neither Jeffrey Kompon nor Vito Buffone was involved. The Crown's theory was to show that Buffone and Kompon were the masterminds of a drug importation scheme.

Yet, during the trial, the prosecution provided no evidence of importation by the two men on trial other than its theory and guesswork substantiated by scraps of paper that originated with Bulhosen, which the Crown admitted later during the sentencing did not add up. Nonetheless, the jury deliberated for only four hours before announcing its finding of guilt for the two men on trial. By September 28, 2017, Justice Ramsay convicted and sentenced Vito Buffone to years of imprisonment.

It may have been the numbers that raised judicial eyebrows. At trial, it was shown that more than a tonne of cocaine in less than two years had been brought into Canada. More damning was the assertion that the operation included associates of the Sinaloa crime cartel in Mexico.

The police surveillance and seizures did result in the takedown of a drug importation network. The police networks had seized $250,000 worth of cannabis; $430,000 in cash; watches and other jewellery valued more than $400,000, a handgun, and two shotguns. Thirteen high-end vehicles, including a Ferrari and a Porsche, were also seized. Yet, none of the evidence has linked Jeffrey Kompon or Vito Buffone with this material.

Police had become convinced that the drug smuggling involved cutting open granite boulders. At least, that was the police speculation up until trial. At trial, the narrative was put forward suggesting drugs were embedded into the boulders by cylinders filled with cocaine. It was a good theory. Yet, convictions supposedly require evidence to support the theory. No traces of cocaine were ever found on any boulder, nor was any evidence elicited of how the cocaine came to be brought into the country. Speculation does not support proof beyond a reasonable doubt.

Jeffrey Kompon and Vito Buffone were in the "upper echelon" of the business, where many of the accused individuals who had admitted involvement in the importation scheme were involved and likely presumed to have been guilty. Vito Buffone was initially sentenced to 22 years minus a year for pre-sentence custody and restrictive bail. Jeffrey Kompon was initially sentenced to 20 years minus 18 months' credit for restrictive bail and pre-sentence detention. Jeffrey Kompon, then 46, and Vito Buffone, then 53, had pleaded not guilty in the Superior Court of Justice to possession of cocaine for trafficking, trafficking cocaine, and conspiracy to import. The trial lasted more than three months. Both Vito and Kompon were dumbfounded that a jury could find that they instigated or collaborated with the others who had taken a plea admitting their involvement in the drug importation matter.

But that was not the end of the matter. The two accused appealed their conviction, and the Crown appealed the sentences imposed (*R. v. Buffone*, 2021). These two southern Ontario men convicted of drug trafficking were hit with life sentences after being convicted in the largest cocaine bust in Ontario history.

The conviction appeal was based on four objections to the judge's instructions delivered to the jury: the drug analyst's evidence; the explanation of conspiracy; the inferences drawn from Chandra Furney's withholding a cell phone when Jeffrey Kompon was arrested; and the judge's instructions on substantive counts. The appeal court was not advised that the appellants had provided further explanations and evidence their lawyers failed to use. That contention would likely have failed in any event. It would require a motion to the Appeal Court to introduce new evidence. It would likely have failed since, by the appellant's admission, it was available at the time of trial.

Vito Buffone and Jeffrey Kompon were each sentenced by the Appeal Court to life in prison following an appeal decision in November 2021. The Crown's appeal of the 2017 sentences stressed that these men were convicted of running a sophisticated ring that moved two tonnes of cocaine into Ontario between 2011 and 2014[5].

On further appeal, this time brought by the accused men to the Supreme Court of Canada, the sentence appeal of life imprisonment for the men was denied.

5 *R. v. Buffone and Kompon*, 2021 ONCA 825. The Court of Appeal admitted that in terms of parole eligibility, a life sentence would be indistinguishable from the determinate sentence. He would be eligible for parole after seven years. The difference is that the life sentence would have no warrant expiry date. That meant that he would be under state control for the rest of his days.

Next Steps

Most people would expect that having a life sentence would drain one's spirits to push on—however, the harsher the punishment for those wrongly convicted, the greater the resolve to seek exoneration. Vito Buffone never gave up trying to make the public see what he knew in his heart as accurate—he's innocent. Jeffrey Kompon would agree. The problem for Vito and Jeffrey was finding the point at which Project Roadmaster went off the rails. They would have to contemplate several theories. DNA is often used in murder cases or as evidence that the evidence has been fabricated. This is not such a case where forensic evidence can prove a wrongful conviction took place.

Despite the adversity they faced, Vito and Jeffrey never lost hope. Their determination became a beacon of resilience, showcasing the human spirit's capacity to endure and fight against overwhelming odds. The journey through the labyrinth of legal challenges also revealed the strength of community support—people who believed in their innocence and rallied behind them, offering support.

One positive aspect of their struggle is the growing awareness and attention to wrongful convictions. Through their case, more people can become educated about the flaws in the judicial system and the importance of continuous advocacy for justice reform. The best hope for showing a judicial error is to set forth a plausible alternative theory. There are three possible explanations to suggest how a miscarriage of justice may have occurred: Stereotypical Thinking, Misinformation, and International Pressure.

Stereotypical Thinking

There seemed to be no caution given to prospective jurors or a challenge to jurors to shield against what might be called the "Soprano effect." Whenever there is an accused with a surname ending in a vowel and possessing large amounts of cash, an unspoken bias of underworld connections may be raised. The famous television show *The Sopranos* featured an Italian American mobster, Tony Soprano, who was engaged in horrific crimes,

One would have thought that specific cautionary instructions would have been given before jury selection or immediately afterward, that it would be wrong to believe one or both of the accused men before the court may have ties to a foreign organized crime group because of the ancestry of one of the accused parties.

Even government agencies have been criticized for this type of inference. An inmate named Coscia was questioned at his parole hearing and accused of mafia connections or ties to organized crime without ever having been convicted of such associations. It took a Federal Court judgment that was later unsuccessfully appealed by the Department of Justice in the Federal Court of Appeal for a decision to be approved that it was inappropriate to question an offender at a parole hearing about organized crime ties unless that person had been convicted of having such ties (*Attorney-General of Canada v. Coscia*, 2005). In jury trials, suspicion can be as damning as a proven conviction.

Misinformation

Could it be that the courts had been misled? It would be a crushing embarrassment for the multi-force Project Roadmaster investigation to come up empty. Such an investigation aims to root out the brains behind the operation and not stop with someone at a low level when the prize would be to arrest the main organizer. This seemed to be the operating drive for the multi-force investigation. It would not stop at a mid-level manager if more people higher up could be dragged into the net. After all, the praise given to police operations that convicted the heads of New York's mafia crime families in the 1980s was an incentive not to stop at mid-level players when the capture of the top brass could be achieved. Perhaps Canadian police could be given similar adulation.

Police could readily prove that drug trafficking was taking place. Recall that during a covert search of Ed Oliver's workplace, police found several wrapped blocks of cocaine in a storeroom. Police tested the substance and verified it to be cocaine. The police left the storeroom largely undisturbed since they did not want to alert those involved in the illegal trade that they had been discovered. Nonetheless, police did seize one of the wrapped packages to be used for evidence later. With this find, Ed Oliver became a primary suspect, and police were extremely concerned about documenting all associations Ed would have with others.

Could it be that people the police believe who are lower down in the chain could sell information, real or imagined, in exchange for the promise of more lenient treatment? Could people like Ed Oliver or Vilalta-Castellanos cause the police to suspect that there may be "higher-ups," and those names could be divulged for a sweet deal on sentence? It is not unusual for a police investigation to lay charges hoping that people arrested at the lower end of a criminal organization may "flip" and give up information to implicate people higher up the criminal ladder. Especially if one sees an opportunity to get a better "deal," such as having police put in a good word at a parole hearing, might lead to a person willing to name others even if the accusation is false but seems imaginable.

At Vito Buffone's October 2014 bail hearing, the Crown claimed that a key found in his desk opened the stash house door—damning evidence if true. But at trial, an RCMP officer clarified that while the key fit the lock, it did not unlock the door.

One way to spot illegality would be using the methodology of "follow the money." If Vito and Jeffrey were engaged in multi-million-dollar drug importation, we would have evidence that they "cooked the books" or were handlers of suspicious amounts of cash. The two men had accountant-verified statements that all money received was legitimate, and there was no evidence of their dealing with ill-gotten gains. Someone else may have had such access.

Borja Vilalta-Castellanos was 36 years old when he was convicted in 2017 of conspiracy to commit an indictable offence, trafficking in a scheduled substance and laundering the proceeds of crime on behalf of the Sinaloa drug cartel. His arrest came about after early morning raids on September 22, 2014. Could he be profiting on his own, pretending to be a key decision-maker for Vito's business and using his connections with the Sinaloa cartel to advance his ends financially? If so, it would be to his advantage to name Vito Buffone as the mastermind. It mattered not that Vito had no interest in importing granite boulders.

Plea bargaining becomes a strong possibility when examining Vilalta-Castellanos's case before the Parole Board of Canada. Though described as "a Mississauga-based senior manager for the Sinaloa Cartel," he was released for deportation after serving less than four years of a 13.5-year sentence. He gained parole at the earliest opportunity through accelerated parole review, eligible after serving just one-sixth of his sentence.

The Parole Board decision noted that Vilalta-Castellanos was denied bail during his court case and had a supervisory role in the Sinaloa cartel's Canadian operations. Parole decisions are often critical of inmates who demonstrate violence while in custody. The decision in his case includes the following statements:

> While in pre-trial custody, you were involved in incidents of threatening and assaulting others. You admitted slapping another offender and trying to stop an altercation.

When the Parole Board mentions violent conduct in its decision, it is usually followed by a listing of steps to show measures taken to avoid aggressive behaviour in future. After all, even when the inmate will be deported, the Board can authorize release only when the risk to society, even a foreign society, is manageable.

The Board went on to outline the offender's role in the drug bust:

> The judge noted that your role was supervisory, but you were not the leader and that while you did not plead guilty, you did not contest the facts. You described that your business had gone bankrupt, and you became involved in the drug importation through a man you already knew who had introduced you to tax evasion in Mexico.

This statement indicates that Vilalta-Castellanos was the initiator and mastermind of the activity and not a mere pawn in the trafficking operation.

> You also recruited a childhood friend to participate. You began with small shipments as you wanted money, and as the quantity increased, you felt trapped and unable to distance yourself or walk away completely.

The Parole Board decision understood that Vilalta-Castellanos was required by the cartel to extract cocaine from a compartment hidden inside large boulders that were shipped by truck into the Niagara Region. The board went on to say:

> The drugs were then forwarded to the prearranged source, and you then arranged for couriers to transport payment. You denied any violence or weapons. Police and court documents support this claim.

Vilalta-Castellanos was born in Spain and acknowledged his privileged childhood as a wealthy family member. the Parole Board decision stated:

> You completed school [in Spain], had several businesses, travelled between Spain, Canada and Mexico, and led a partying lifestyle. After the failure of your concert business, you began your criminal activity to keep up your lifestyle and appearance of success.

Because of the nature of his offence and his not being a Canadian citizen nor being permitted to work in Canada, the Canada Border Services Agency ordered his deportation. In prison, he was classified as a minimum-security inmate and upgraded himself academically while in custody. The Board then dealt with his release plan:

> You had private family visits with your wife regularly and visits with other family members who came from overseas.

They also noted that he is the father of a newborn child. The Parole Board decision says his release plan was that he be deported to Spain and live there with his mother. They added:

> Your wife intends to follow you there. You describe that family members will support you while you seek employment and save for entrepreneurial pursuits and your own home. You provided support letters from numerous family members and friends to the Board, including from your wife, mother, and potential employer(s).

Despite assumptions, parole eligibility does not guarantee release. The Parole Board of Canada denies full parole to roughly 70 percent of applicants at their first hearing. The Board holds broad discretion, weighing public safety risks.

For deportable offenders, parole conditions are unenforceable abroad, so rehabilitation must be clearly demonstrated. The Board must believe the individual no longer poses a threat, even to a foreign society. It is, necessary to ensure that the inmate is fully rehabilitated and will not be a threat once released and deported.

Sometimes, when an accused knows that a prosecution is inevitable, a decision is taken to "flip," and an agreement is made to offer evidence against parties considered more substantial in exchange for the promise of a lighter sentence or favourable representations to the paroling authority. The fact of Vilalta-Castellanos' ultimate success before the Parole Board does not prove he manufactured false evidence to receive a lighter penalty. It is just a factor in support of that inference.

International Pressure

It would be yielding to a conspiracy theory to believe that an international police investigation would be targeting Vito Buffone or his corporations. How could Vito make an appearance on law enforcement radar?

The United States was mainly concerned with drugs being brought into the United States by the Sinaloa cartel. Early in the 21st century, the cartel operated in more than 50 countries and was most dominant in the United States.[6] The cartel was responsible for most illegal drugs smuggled into the United States from Mexico. By 2015, US officials claimed that

6 Throughout much of the period, the Mexican government and U.S. cooperated to control drug imports. On March 30, 2021, Reuters reported: "U.S. efforts to combat powerful drug cartels operating from inside Mexico stalled since January, as strained bilateral relations halted attempts to target drug kingpins, according to senior officials." Until recently, both sides cautiously shared intelligence on major cases. However, in December, Mexico enacted a law requiring U.S. agencies to report their contacts in the country to the Mexican government, which many American investigators deem corrupt. This policy has led both sides to pause cooperation, fearing that disclosure rules could jeopardize cases or endanger informants and officials.

Sinaloa controlled the drug markets in almost every state. Its annual revenue was estimated from $3 billion to $39 billion. The US government was particularly interested in the capture and imprisonment of the cartel leader, Joaquín Guzmán Loera, who was known as El Chapo ("Shorty").

The American authorities had a potent weapon to identify threats to the country's national security: The Foreign Intelligence Surveillance Act (FISA). Section 702 of the FISA allows the National Security Agency (NSA) to receive data directly from US companies such as Facebook and Google and capture and collect the contents of foreign targets' emails, texts, videos, photos, and chats. Collections of electronic communications were affected through methods termed "Prism" and "Upstream." Prism, in particular, allowed the agency to access unencrypted communications directly from tech providers.

In Canada, the *Canadian Security Establishment Act* formalized the creation of the Communications Security Establishment (CSE). The CSE was formed during World War II but remained secret until its existence was exposed on the CBC program *The Fifth Estate*. As a member of the Five Eyes alliance—alongside the US, the UK, Australia, and New Zealand—Canada receives and shares intelligence, including on its own citizens.

Intelligence could be gathered from abroad, but the evidence to support it must be obtained locally. The NSA could monitor a Canadian firm with operations in Mexico, and any suspicions of wrongdoing passed along to Canadian police services. In effect, the NSA pins a target on the back of an individual or group, and it is the responsibility of the police to adhere to the law in bringing the named parties to justice. It would be the police investigation that would be subject to scrutiny for violations of fundamental freedoms and privacy rights, not the NSA nor the CSE.

Vancouver Sun reporter Kim Bolan recently reported on a three-month investigation undertaken by Postmedia on transnational links in organized crime. Her investigation offered insight into the Vito Buffone/Jeffrey Kompon situation. She identified groups: the Hells Angels, the United Nations gang, the Sam Gor syndicate, the Sinaloa cartel, and Middle Eastern networks collaborating to smuggle massive drug shipments. The report notes that the City of Delta BC mayor, George Harvie, hired Peter German to prepare a report on port security. Peter German, a consultant, lawyer, and retired RCMP deputy commissioner, prepared a report about the current state of security. German noted a glaring flaw in prosecuting international criminals—the 1991 Supreme Court of Canada decision of Stinchcombe (*R. v. Stinchcombe,* 1991). That ruling mandates that the Crown must disclose all relevant information to the defence. Evidence gathered by police is not simply theirs to use to secure a conviction, it is considered public property to ensure justice. This principle creates a dilemma when international intelligence is involved.

The police's targeting of transnational organized crime involves receiving and sharing intelligence with the Five Eyes intelligence-gathering alliance. Disclosure of investigative techniques and the methods used to gather sensitive and often private information cannot be put on paper lest the Canadian recipient be forced to share the document. It would be sufficient for US authorities to advise a Canadian police force that something was amiss in Vito Buffone's organization. Still, the reporting agency would be loathe to turn over the paperwork lest that material end up in the hands of defence counsel through the disclosure processes mandated by *Stinchcombe*.[7]

7 In *Henrie v. Canada (Security Intelligence Review Committee),* [1988] 2 F.C. 229, Justice Addy recognized that information related to National Security ought not to be disclosed. It has been said that the *Henrie* case went too far. In an article for *Vice*, "How Canada's Spy Agencies Cozied Up to the NSA," dated November 7, 2014, reporter Justin Ling wrote," Pulling in the American National Security Agency to intercept Canadians' communications is 'the norm' according to Canada's spy agencies. Revelations like that, which came out of a series of court cases over the last year, prove that the Five Eyes are quickly becoming one big cyclops, and Canada doesn't give a damn if you don't like it."

The result is that the Canadian police would not simply target the bad apples in the Vito Buffone operation; they would likely feel international pressure to act and target everyone in the group.

Once a target is identified, a police force would be obliged to obtain search warrants to back up the information they have received from the spy agencies. Supposedly, the investigations should also try to confirm the data that illegal activity was ongoing. However, it is human nature to wear blinders and only accept a version of the story supportive of wrongdoing, especially in large-scale law-breaking cases. Police believed that cocaine had been smuggled inside granite boulders, requiring heavy-duty saws to extract it. To obtain a search warrant, the police photographed Jeffrey Kompon moving a large piece of equipment that police identified as a saw.[8] This was used to prove there were grounds for obtaining the search warrant. The problem, however, is that the item being moved was not a saw, but rather, it was Kompon moving his Bowflex Revolution exercise machine.

The misidentification of the evidence resulted in increased surveillance of Kompon, a search warrant of his home, and, ultimately, his arrest. The case went to trial. If one existed, the actual saw was never produced. It was implied that equipment used in Vito's recycling and construction businesses was used to sever the granite boulders that hid the cocaine. In theory, failure to substantiate the boulder-concealment theory should have derailed the case. But when investigators adopt tunnel vision, it's often full steam ahead.

8 During a surreptitious police entry into the Nugent Road warehouse on April 17 and 18, 2014, police Officer Hodges collected multiple swabs later to be tested on an ion scan from work areas, work clothing, work gloves and from a large-scale saw. The swab sample taken from the saw did not prove positive for cocaine. It was also admitted that the warehouse manager was taking the drug Effexor, which can give a false positive for cocaine. An earlier entrance by the police into the warehouse on April 8, 2014, when swabs were also taken, showed no positive results for cocaine.

Recall that the Niagara Regional Police tap on Ed Oliver's phone disclosed that during his calls, Ed referred to the "big boss" and mentioned having lunch with "Vito," supposedly the only person with a key to the stash house. Yet, no surveillance ever confirmed Vito dining with Ed—Vito was known to avoid restaurants entirely. Despite ongoing surveillance, no meeting between the two men was observed.

Wearing blinders, one can readily appreciate how a third party listening with the preconceived idea that Vito Buffone is a significant player in the drug importation scheme in the conversation could conclude that this was the identification of "the big boss." Indeed, if we appreciate that Vito Buffone was the owner of a company that had dealings with Ed Oliver, it could also be understood that connecting Vito to drug importation was not necessarily true.

Encryption technology became another focal point. Both Buffone and Kompon were found with PGP-encrypted phones—ordinary smartphones using encryption software similar to WhatsApp. For many businesses, encryption is a security tool, not a criminal signal. Yet, the presence of such devices was treated as suggestive of illicit activity.

Could the PGP phones have been in the accused's possession without their involvement in a drug smuggling operation? Kompon testified that the phone found at his residence had been handed to him by Ed Oliver, who hoped that Vito Buffone's company could repair it. There was no evidence that Kompon ever used the device. The Crown had hoped that the production of encrypted phones could link Vito and Ed to the drug importation operation.

A note in materials turned over as disclosure read: "PGP Blackberry found in Mississauga with email Acrobat, used by Buffone." The officer who supposedly found this evidence was said to have turned the device over to lead investigator Gomez.

Police must keep accurate notes on what evidence is found and how it is handled. Yet, neither the police officer who found the Blackberry nor Officer Gomez had any notes recording the phone or its transfer. The issue of finding this phone was never brought up at trial.

This omission was highly irregular. BlackBerry phones designed for encryption could be split into two parts—one storing data, the other the device ID. Proper evidence handling requires each part to be sealed and documented. But here, the evidence bags lacked descriptor entries, and no officer's notes tracked their transfer. The breakdown in this "chain of custody" undermines the credibility of the evidence.

Making matters worse is that one of the encrypted phones was in Mississauga and never connected with Vito Buffone. Nonetheless, evidence was given that a call took place with a phone later found in Vito's office. There was no evidence to determine conclusively that the Mississauga phone was the phone that placed the call into question. It was likely that the police relied on the phone found in Vito's desk as the suspicious object since the police could not complete a chain of custody showing who held the phone free of tampering up to the trial date.

Notably, no recordings of Buffone using a PGP phone were presented at trial. His only recorded interaction with the device was to ask technicians if it could be repaired. The phone ultimately had no business value, and Buffone abandoned plans to resell such devices.

These three explanations that suggest a miscarriage of justice—Stereotypical Thinking, Misinformation, and International Pressure—form a quiet cascade of acts of darkness: not overt misconduct, but systemic neglect, assumption, and bureaucratic carelessness.

Trial Tactics

It may be that the trial format itself contributed to the flawed outcome. Vito Buffone and Jeffrey Kompon were tried together before a judge and jury, likely the result of one co-accused requesting a jury, which then bound both. This strategic choice may have been ill-considered, given the complexities of the case and the risks of jury misperception.

The trial carried on over 50 days. The evidence was often dull, boring, and repetitive. The Crown took 40 days to present its case. At one point, a juror sent a note to the court saying, "Ya, this reality show is boring and has gone on far too long. I want to go home now." This message attacked the Crown and accused the defence counsel of trial delay. It included technical information about where and when covert surveillance was installed and monitored.

Nonetheless, it was also evident that police were able to prove drugs had been imported. The large quantity of drugs found in Ed Oliver's office was indicative of some form of organized importation scheme. Furthermore, many of the co-accused pleaded guilty rather than go to trial. The only two who went to trial were Vito Buffone and Jeffrey Kompon.

The defence theory—if clearly articulated by counsel—was straightforward: Vito and Jeffrey had no involvement in the drug importation scheme, even if they knew or worked with those who pleaded guilty. Their lawyers, choosing a jury trial, faced the challenge of ensuring the jury understood this distinction. It wasn't enough to prove drugs had been smuggled into Canada; the Crown had to prove that Vito and Jeffrey were directly responsible or conspired with others to commit the act. Given the complexity of the case, there was a real risk that jurors might assume guilt by association—reasoning that because drugs were imported and the accused were connected to those who admitted guilt, they must be equally culpable.

Prosecutors often tell jurors that a trial is like assembling a jigsaw puzzle, where each witness contributes a piece of the

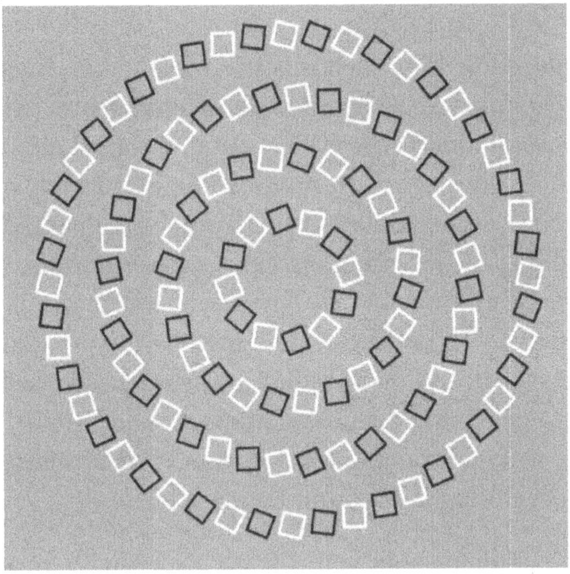

These circles are difficult to assess as intertwined or concentric.

picture. But that analogy can mislead. Not every piece needs to fit perfectly, and not every memory is reliable. We tend to believe memory functions like a video recording, but it doesn't. Memory can be distorted, reshaped by time, emotion, or suggestion.

In a long trial where evidence unfolds gradually, jurors may misinterpret what they hear—just as we can be fooled by an optical illusion. We rarely consider that aural illusions exist too. Yet, science confirms that the mind can be misled by sound just as easily as by sight. Complex and fragmentary testimony can create false auditory linkages, leading jurors to believe they heard a coherent pattern where none existed.

Looking at the image above, one can see a grouping of intertwined circles when, in fact, the circles are separate and concentric. The same mistakes can happen in jury trials, especially where our social norms are to abhor criminal organizations and cocaine trafficking. Hearing the evidence with the pressures to adhere to our social norms creates an inadvertent situation where a jury can confuse what it hears and wrongly conclude something that doesn't exist[9]. Vito Buffone and Jeffrey Kompon were arrested and charged with others who were, without doubt, involved in cocaine importation and trafficking. Just because Vito Buffone knew and even conversed with his co-accused does not mean he was involved in their wrongdoings. The trial transcripts suggest that the jury that convicted Vito Buffone may have been susceptible to this type of confusion. The evidence presented by the prosecution was long, involved, and tedious. But the blame need not be placed solely on delivering the prosecution's case.

A striking example was heard in Crown counsel Amber Paschuk's closing remarks on June 8, 2017:

> Mr. Buffone told you, I keep my business relationships separate. [...] And yet somehow all these people, all connected through Mr. Buffone, end up at the Nugent Road warehouse within days of each other. [...] I'd suggest to you that Mr. Buffone's testimony is not believable on this point because he did connect these people [...] in this very sophisticated enterprise.

Paschuk's argument encouraged the jury to see overlap as collusion. Yet, the overlap may have been circumstantial—business relationships running concentrically, not intertwined. the jury should have been explicitly directed to observe that the concentric circles of associations did not intertwine. Legitimate operations could be carried out at the same time as illegal operations.

9 Dr. Gustav Kuhn, Associate Professor of Psychology at the University of Plymouth has investigated what he called "auditory magic." A significant number of magic tricks rely on sleight of hand or misdirection that deceives the eye. Few magic tricks rely on other senses but Dr. Gustav has found that a few can involve auditory misperception. There can be auditory illusion just as we understand the existence of optical illusion. It is therefore important that defence counsel in jury trial ensure that a jury hears what is actually said is not misperceived into believing what the prosecution wants the jurors to hear.

When reviewing the trial transcripts, it is difficult to identify any clear articulation of a defence theory by counsel. In representing a client who maintained innocence, one might have expected the defence to concede that drug importation had occurred—and that trafficking was likely—but to assert firmly that the men on trial were not involved. Yet, in the cross-examination of the first police witness, a surprising amount of time was devoted to technical details—specifically, how swabs were taken from the floor and machinery to determine the presence of cocaine. This approach seemed less aimed at establishing innocence than at finding procedural gaps in the Crown's case. It did little to persuade the jury that the accused were being unfairly implicated due to their proximity to others who had confessed.

Moreover, the defence failed to confront a crucial point: how to guide the jury away from making false connections. The risk was that jurors might draw inferences from association alone, concluding—without proper evidentiary basis—that Vito Buffone and Jeffrey Kompon were part of a larger criminal organization. Defence counsel Anthony Bryant did note that no actual evidence of such linkages existed, but he focused more on the Crown's failure to meet its evidentiary burden than on dismantling the flawed logic that could lead to a wrongful conviction by implication.

In his closing on June 7, 2017, defence counsel Anthony Bryant told the jury:

> Not one of the hundred witnesses called by the Crown testifies that Mr. Buffone personally trafficked in cocaine or had someone do it for him, not one. Not one of the hundred witnesses called by the Crown testified that Mr. Buffone conspired with others to import cocaine, not a one. And, of course, it goes without saying that not one of them that were called by the Crown could testify that Mr. Buffone

> had committed any offence for the benefit of or at the direction of a criminal organization, not a one. And, of course, when you think about the evidence that you heard from all the Crown witnesses, it would be difficult to find among them, among those hundred who actually remembered what they testified to as opposed to simply regurgitating what they had written in their notebooks. And even when they were just regurgitating stuff from their notebooks, not one of them had an entry that suggested, even suggested, that Mr. Buffone possessed cocaine for the purpose of trafficking, that he trafficked in cocaine, or that he was conspiring with others to import and possess for the purposes. Nothing, witness after witness after witness.

Jury Missteps and Missed Opportunities

Perhaps a simple denial of involvement was all the defence could offer. The trial lasted nearly three months and included 107 witnesses. Such length likely led jurors to default to the assumption that charges meant guilt. One critical misstep may have been the choice to proceed with a jury rather than a judge-alone trial.

Impartiality is essential in jury trials. Prospective jurors are typically asked to declare any ties to individuals involved in the case, especially police officers expected to testify. Even perceived bias can compromise the fairness of a verdict. The Buffone/Kompon jury can also be criticized because, according to Kompon, one of the jurors was related by marriage to the Staff Sergeant who served as the project's media spokesperson, which led to the takedown and arrest of the various co-accused.

We haven't considered the theory that jurors in complex cases may be subject to confirmation bias.

Confirmation bias is the tendency to search for, interpret, focus on, and remember information in a way that confirms one's preconceptions. In today's politically polarized climate, confirmation bias often leads us to oversimplify the complex situations.

When the spectre of an international drug cartel is raised, is it not likely that a jury will interpret the evidence as confirmation that the accused were complicit in importing illegal drugs? While the academic literature has examined this risk, it has rarely—if ever—served as the basis for challenging how a jury may have erred in reaching an unjust verdict. To overturn a conviction on appeal, it must be shown that the jury received improper instructions that compromised their ability to decide the case rationally. Typically, this is done by scrutinizing the judge's formal instructions to the jury.

However, it may be time for appellate courts to consider the broader context—specifically, how evidence is introduced and framed throughout a trial. Does the process itself set a tone that risks reinforcing confirmation bias? At a minimum, the judge's charge to the jury should contain a more forceful directive than the standard instruction to consider only the evidence presented. It should caution against letting overarching narratives, such as those involving global crime networks, colour the interpretation of the facts.

By choosing a trial by jury, the accused forfeited a key safeguard: the right to scrutinize the reasoning behind a verdict. A judge sitting alone must provide written reasons for a conviction. A jury, on the other hand, simply returns a verdict—its reasoning forever sealed. Under Canadian law, jurors cannot be questioned about how they reached their decision. The only avenue for appeal lies in identifying flaws in the judge's instructions. But even when those instructions are technically sound, there is no way to know whether they were misunderstood or misapplied in the secrecy of the jury room.

The trial began on March 20, 2017. The prosecutor, Ruth McGuirl of the Public Prosecution Service, started with her address to the jury. Opening remarks are critical because they suggest the overall case the Crown intends to prove beyond a reasonable doubt. They can be compared to the picture on a box containing a jigsaw puzzle in that they outline where each piece of evidence may fit in the overall image of the case that the jury will consider.

McGuirl began by saying,

> Very simply, this is a case about a scheme to import cocaine into Canada concealed within granite boulders and the distribution of that cocaine across the province.

She went on to state that such a scheme required warehouses in which to store the boulders. She quickly added,

> You won't see or hear about either Mr. Buffone or Mr. Kompon carrying bags of drugs. It is the theory of the Crown that they were the more sophisticated members in the group.

With this statement to the jury, it should have been evident that the Crown had no direct evidence linking the two accused men on trial with the importation and sale of cocaine. The prosecution's case would be convincing the jury that evidence inferentially linking the accused to the scheme was the only reasonable conclusion the jury could draw.

It was never explained to the jury that the imported stone was of two types. Vito Buffone had imported 22 truckloads of quarry stone from Mexico. The documentation for these shipments was put into evidence at trial. Vito had a legitimate use for this material. When crushed, the rock was used in paving and manufacturing house siding products. It could also be shown that this type of stone was helpful for these purposes because it flaked easily. Once hit with a drill bit, it would pulverize instantaneously. That was the reason this type of rock was so beneficial for the construction usage Vito intended. It could not be severed to store drugs since the quarry stone would shatter immediately.

The granite rock that the Crown alleged was carrying the cocaine secreted within it came from Brazil. Bulhosen shipped those containers of granite. He used a false name and a sham corporation to import them. There is no evidence Vito had any connection with importing granite boulders. The evidence was clear that the rock shipments from Mexico were incapable of containing secret compartments for the storage of cocaine. An expert was prepared to testify that the Mexican stone couldn't conceal drugs—but the expert was never called.

Basic questions went unanswered. How was cocaine inserted into granite? Such concealment would require drilled cavities and some form of sealing—yet no photos, tools, or expert testimony were offered. If this process of hiding cocaine were used, indeed, the prosecution would have photographic evidence of rock fissures or expert testimony as to how the material could be inserted into cavities in the stones. No such proof was produced.

The bulk of the testimony offered was to create an inference to support the conclusion placed in the jurors' minds by the opening prosecution statement. Evidence that Vito was the man in charge was inferred by the fact that phones capable of carrying encrypted messages were in Vito's possession.

An intercept of Ed Oliver's phones and messages showed he occasionally had dealings with Vito, who was understood to head up the illegal operation. Yet, there was no telephone interception in which Vito's calls could directly point to his involvement. Evidence showed that a key opening the stash house door was found in Vito's desk drawer. Again, there was no evidence of Vito ever using the key, even though the premises were secretly monitored by video. More telling was that the key found did not fit.

When Crown counsel Amber Pashuk addressed the jury on June 9, 2017, she said she would tie together all the strands of evidence the jury had heard to show conclusively that Vito Buffone was engaged in a conspiracy to import and be a trafficker in cocaine. She asked the jury not to believe the denials they heard from Jeffrey Kompon and Vito Buffone but instead to use their common sense to conclude that Vito was a crucial player in the illegal operation.

Pashuk did an excellent job of showing that Ed Oliver and Vilalta-Castellanos were heavily involved. She proposed circumstantial evidence suggesting Vito's possible involvement, but neither she nor her prosecution colleagues produced conclusive evidence implicating actual involvement. Yet, it was enough for a jury to decide that the whole group of co-accused were complicit in illegal activity.

We can never know the jury's reasoning process, but still, a guilty verdict was returned against Vito Buffone.

The trial ended with an unusual and questionable move: the judge gave the jury a USB stick containing his bench notes for use during deliberation. While jurors are instructed to rely only on evidence presented in court, this device introduced the possibility of judicial interpretation influencing the outcome. No objection was raised at the time, but the presence of a so-called "thirteenth juror"—the judge, via his personal commentary—raises troubling questions about fairness.

The Family

Sometimes, our justice system makes mistakes. The adage attributed to the preeminent English jurist, William Blackstone, that it is "Better that ten guilty persons escape than one innocent suffer," fails to account for the many other victims of a wrongful conviction, most notably the family of the person imprisoned.

Spending time in prison is challenging for the person incarcerated. But it is arguably just as hard, if not more difficult, for family members on the outside. Vito Buffone's teenage son shared his thoughts and insights while preparation for writing this chapter was ongoing.

> [Dad's] incarceration has completely obliterated our lives, and we have been rebuilding the foundation of it ever since. We lost everything: good friends, family, and my childhood home. Hell, even our cat ran away after. But on a serious note, his incarceration affected me a lot when I was a young teen, a time when I needed him the most.
>
> Not having my father there has negatively affected us all, and I can see my younger sisters slowly turning sour because of it. They are just beginning high school, and on top of all the negative influences out there, it concerns me that they do not have a father at home to support them and be there for them in these times.
>
> I try my best to teach them effectively, but at the end of the day, there is only so much they will listen to coming from me; they need their father home. Many things have fallen apart dramatically since his incarceration, as you can probably imagine.
>
> My mother does tremendous work to keep a roof over our heads. Even with my assistance, she is overwhelmed with both duties as a mother, a father, and a main provider. My mother is in her late 40s and is aging quicker than she ever has due to the stress. She has stuck by his side through this whole thing without ever having a single doubt in her mind. No

> matter what happened, she was always there supporting our family and my father tooth and nail. She has been through a lot.
>
> My parents raised us accordingly. They taught us respect, honesty, and integrity. I do not want my sisters or anyone in my family ever to forget that. I do not want my mother to forget what it is like to be happy again. And most of all. I do not want my father to forget what his freedom is like; to be in a place like that is something I wouldn't wish on my worst enemy (if I had one). The sooner he gets home, the sooner our family can return to normal and be happy again. We need our father at home; all of us do. He deserves to be here.

Vito Buffone continued to enjoy the support of his family, who never lost faith in his innocence. Yet, he is rocked that the false allegations and criminal conviction have dealt a death blow to the business he worked hard to establish. He immensely regrets that his 150 employees lost their jobs.

For Jeffrey Kompon, the toll was more personal. His partner, Chandra Marie Furney—once his closest supporter—changed her mind. In 2022, she self-published a book, *Forever: A Love Story. A Raid. An Arrest. Heartache. A Small Town Scandal. And a Journey of Self-Discovery* where she described losing that love and becoming convinced that he had indeed been involved with the Sinaloa drug cartel of Mexico.

> When [Jeffrey] walked into my life, everything changed. We fell in love.

Financially, she shared in Jeffrey's success. He was a successful entrepreneur who owned several businesses and an award-winning restaurant in Welland. But the police raid on their home took its toll on Chandra Furney's mental health. She feels she developed post-traumatic stress disorder and depression. She admits seeing no sign that Kompon was involved in anything illegal. "It's like someone whose partner had an affair or a gambling problem. You don't know until you know," she declared. That said though, she turned against him.

For Jeffrey Kompon, having the person he cared for the most turn on him means that the loss of liberty must be secondary to his best friend's betrayal.

The Continuing Battle

With or without family support, Vito Buffone and Jeffrey Kompon have vowed to continue the fight for exoneration. They have committed themselves to right the wrong done to them and engaged legal counsel to investigate a system that got it wrong. Studies undertaken in the United States estimate that between 4–6 percent of people incarcerated are factually innocent. Factual innocence means not seeking release because errors were made in applying the law. It means that the facts of the case do not add up to guilt.

It would be easy to blame the wrongful conviction on the lawyers representing them. They could claim that injustice was caused by ineffective counsel. There were mistakes made by the lawyers and occasions where the lawyers should have put forward relevant observations made by their clients. But to obtain an exoneration, these men must show that the "facts" put forward by the Crown did not add up to proof beyond a reasonable doubt that they were part of the conspiracy to import cocaine. They must demonstrate factual innocence.

There is hope and, encouragingly, awareness is growing. Carleton University's Kelly Lauzon, a researcher and advocate, has dedicated her work to studying and exposing wrongful convictions. Through her podcast "Real Life Wrongs" she shares stories of injustice and calls for public accountability.

Public understanding that legal errors can be made is crucial in developing a system that will admit mistakes and seek to remedy them. But it takes the courageous drive of people like Vito Buffone and Jeffrey Kompon, who will not simply accept a fate imposed upon them. Will they eventually be exonerated? No one knows. But it surely will not be because they failed to battle the wrong done to them and their loved ones, whether or not their factual innocence is accepted.

What can the public do when such cases come to its attention? The most apparent remedy is to demand that our politicians stop making law enforcement an issue. The clarion cry at election time is to get tough on crime. This desensitizes the urge to ensure mistakes in the criminal justice system do not get made.

We must also stop placing blind trust in judges and juries. Mistakes happen. Recognizing that is not an attack on justice—it's a necessary safeguard for it.

Complacency is the enemy of progress. We must reject the belief that the system always works as it should. We need to appreciate that mistakes are made and can happen to anyone. Once we accept this, we can work to see change.

We must be reminded that the criminal justice system is a human experience and that errors can occur.

Fortunately, we live in an age of access. We don't have to take the justice system's word at face value. We can and should question what we're told. We should look at the facts logically and dispassionately and evaluate the evidence to see if it makes sense. We can inform ourselves about how things can and do go wrong in criminal cases.

Contrary to conventional wisdom, people falsely confess; people don't always remember what they saw accurately; police officers can succumb to tunnel vision; prosecutors can get overzealous; defence counsel can present inadequate representation. The system is imperfect, and we must educate ourselves on its shortcomings.

There is tremendous power when society comes together to champion a cause, and wrongful conviction cases are no different. Think of the results of the Guy Paul Morin and Rubin Hurricane Carter cases.[10] While one person may not be able to do everything, they can be the start of something great.

The "bystander effect" teaches that people often fail to act when others are present—everyone assumes someone else will step in. The same dynamic applies to wrongful convictions. Too many believe these cases happen to "other people" or that "someone else" will demand justice. But the responsibility is ours. It is our responsibility to take this problem seriously.

We have to remember: we are all potential jurors. We could have been the people judging Vito Buffone's and Jeffrey Kompon's trial. As possible jurors, we must be mindful of the presumption of innocence and the Crown's burden of proof. We cannot assume that they are guilty just because they are on trial for a crime. We must approach these cases with humility and curiosity and hold the Crown accountable. Our responsibility is to ensure that the Crown meets its burden and proves its case beyond a reasonable doubt.

We cannot accept that justice officials are doing a public service by arresting and convicting innocent people simply because they can check a few boxes and solve a complex case. By pursuing innocent individuals, justice officials undermine the fundamental principles of justice, which should strike us all as worrisome. We must stop commending officials on a job well done when questions about the case remain. We should only celebrate a job well done when we are sure, beyond a reasonable doubt, that the guilty party has been brought to justice.

10 Guy Paul Morin is a Canadian who was wrongly convicted in 1984 of the murder of nine-year-old Christine Jessop, who lived next door to him. DNA testing led to the overturning of the guilty verdict in 2020. Rubin "Hurricane" Carter was an American middleweight boxer wrongly convicted and imprisoned for murder. He had served almost twenty years in prison until released on a petition for habeas corpus. Carter moved to Toronto and was a leader in establishing the Association for the Defence of the Wrongly Convicted (AIDWC), now called Innocence Canada.

Once all judicial appeal avenues have been exhausted, a wrongly convicted person can ask the Minister of Justice to undertake a review. Parliament has now passed an amendment to the *Criminal Code* to establish a Miscarriage of Justice Review Commission, commonly called David and Joyce Milgaard's Law. This Commission could investigate cases where there are reasonable grounds to believe a miscarriage of justice has occurred—or where justice demands review. Presumably, the investigation would take place promptly, with constant feedback on progress delivered to the applicant in a less politically charged situation than may now exist.

The public must understand that our justice system can sometimes be in error. The Saskatchewan King's Bench put it this way:

> ...the public interest in these [wrongful] convictions, both before and after they were overturned, is indisputable and important to the functioning of the criminal justice system. Indeed, few criminal proceedings will engage the public interest more than someone alleging they have been wrongfully convicted. The public is entitled to know the workings of the criminal justice system, including allegations of its frailties and fallibilities. (*R v. Quewezance,* 2022).

On January 5, 2024, the New Brunswick Court of King's Bench exonerated Walter Gillespie and Robert Mailman of the murder charge for which they had been sentenced to life imprisonment in 1984 *(His Majesty the King v. Walter Francis Gillespie and Robert Elvany Mailman,* 2024). A ministerial review had concluded that a miscarriage of justice had taken place in their conviction. The men had adamantly denied involvement in the killing from the time of their arrest. In the words of the Chief Justice:

> Miscarriages of justice should never occur. Regrettably, they sometimes do, and the only reasonable response is to double down on our efforts to improve our justice system and guard against these anomalies, which is accomplished first by shining a light on the circumstances that lead to these devastating situations.

It is through that light, however faint, however hard-won, that acts of darkness are finally revealed. One day, perhaps soon, another judge may offer similar thanks to Vito Buffone and Jeffrey Kompon, not just for enduring the injustice, but for standing against it.

Postscript: I have been in weekly telephone conversations with Vito Buffone and Jeffrey Kompon and their family members. They have provided me with the trial transcripts which I read. I feel there has been a miscarriage of justice, so I referred their case to a law firm that specializes in overturning wrongful convictions. After reading this chapter in preliminary manuscript form, the firm agreed to take on a ministerial review.

—John L. Hill 2025

2

Ray Rueger

Twist of the Knife

If you search for truthfulness,
you might as well be blind.

—Billy Joel, "Honesty"

THE CORNERSTONE of judicial criminal process is a reliance on truth. A client is expected to be truthful with the lawyer; police are expected to be honest in passing along the results of investigations; defence and prosecution lawyers should be truthful in dealings with one another; and everyone should be sincere in giving evidence to the court. This is fine in theory, but does it work in practice?

There was a time, many years ago, when the prosecution was not obligated to disclose to the defence the evidence it intended to present in a criminal trial. Today, such disclosure is standard practice. In fact, concerns about inadequate disclosure frequently lead to trial delays, and in some cases, can result in a new trial if the accused is convicted.

My first murder trial took place before these disclosure rules were in place. As defence counsel, I was not entitled to review the case assembled by police or develop a defence strategy informed by the evidence likely to be presented to the jury.

Lawyers are bound by a code of ethics that includes the *proviso* that a lie cannot be advanced in court. The way around this problem is to avoid asking a client charged with an offence if they did the wrongful act. If a client has not admitted guilt, there is no ethical violation presenting facts that support innocence. A theory of the defence emerges based on what facts are supported and what spin could be placed on those facts to make an argument for acquittal or a reduced charge. It is up to a jury to discern the truth. Trials are conducted to obtain the truth.

I recall an evening in January 1982 when I was about to sit down to an evening meal. The Ontario Provincial Police (OPP), in London, Ontario, called requesting that I attend the detachment to see a man who wanted to retain me for a criminal defence. I did not recognize the client's name but agreed to drive to the police station immediately.

Upon arrival, I was escorted into an office where a uniformed officer sat behind a desk. Before allowing me to see my client, he said he wanted to review the facts as they were currently understood by police. His demeanour caught me off guard—calm, almost subdued. Speaking in hushed tones, he confided that the man I was about to meet had made several confessions to murder.

The officer began his narrative by telling me that less than a month before, on Christmas Eve, 1981, 33-year-old Marilyn Dorothy Arthur was finishing work as a secretary at the Oxford Book Shop in London, Ontario. She'd called her parents in St. Mary's, Ontario, to tell them that right after leaving work, she would go to her apartment, feed the bird, and arrive at her parents' home in time for a Christmas Eve with her family.

Later that night, police discovered a vehicle in a ditch along Highway 7, between London and Woodstock—a city east of London and near the residence of the Arthur family. Ms. Arthur's body was found in a snowbank near the car. Her neck had been slashed. Notably, there was no blood inside the vehicle, indicating that whatever had happened to her occurred outside the car. It was Christmas Eve. If the incident were classified as a homicide, it would have triggered extensive paperwork and additional investigative procedures—an unwelcome prospect during the holiday period. Shortly after the discovery, the event was officially recorded as a single-vehicle accident.

Things changed a few days after that. It was revealed that 31-year-old Raymond Bruce Rueger had been admitted to the hospital after attempting suicide. He had subsequently been interrogated by police and confessed to murdering a woman on the roadside. He did not know the slain woman.

After hearing the synopsis, I was taken to a private room to meet with the man who had asked for my assistance. He identified himself, asking to be called "Ray." He said he had asked the police to contact me. He remembered my name and that I was a lawyer. He had worked at my house as part of a crew I hired to re-shingle my roof the previous autumn. It would be my first murder case if the client retained me. I recall both the excitement of being asked to defend a client charged with the most severe offence in the *Criminal Code* and the horror of trying to process a horrendous story of extreme violence.

I repeated the summary of events that the OPP had recounted to me. Ray listened intently but explained that he was willing to accept the narrative. However, he could not help me further since he had few recollections of what had happened.

He continued to tell me that after leaving the roofing company, he had obtained work as a courier. It was the afternoon before Christmas, and there were few deliveries. Most of his fellow couriers decided to throw an impromptu party. Everyone drank heavily. The party continued until approximately six o'clock in the evening. Rueger was extremely drunk, had not done any Christmas shopping, and had no presents for his wife and kids when they woke up Christmas morning. He had gone to the Woolco and K-Mart department stores to buy presents, but they were closed. He was both angry and embarrassed that he would have to return home intoxicated and empty-handed.

He recalled seeing a dark-haired woman exiting a store and getting into her car. He followed her for 25 miles and eventually ran her off the road. She had been driving slowly on icy roads—too slowly for Ray's liking—and anger caused him to act irrationally. He rammed the back end of the woman's car, causing it to skid and veer off the highway. After her vehicle left the road, he had no further memory.

I was puzzled by Ray's recollections (or lack thereof). If the police officer had accurately recounted the fact that Ms. Arthur had told her parents that she would return to her apartment to feed the bird, then it would have been likely that Rueger would also have followed the woman to her house or apartment and sat idling his car until she returned and continued to follow her. Ray didn't know the woman or that she planned to continue her journey. Why would he wait in the parking lot expecting her to return?

If the "feed the bird" story was correct and if Rueger was responsible for the death, the persistence of his pursuit would provide the Crown Attorney with substantial evidence of planning and deliberation—enough to secure a first-degree murder conviction.

My options were limited: I could try to raise a reasonable doubt that even if Rueger had followed the woman and ran her car off the road as Rueger claimed, the murder could have been committed by an unknown third party, or if Rueger killed the woman, he might have done so because of alcohol or insanity. Without a functioning mind, he could not form the intent to kill necessary to sustain a first-degree conviction.

The object of a trial is to discover the truth. I had been taught in law school that a confession to a crime is difficult to dispute because a person is not expected to make a statement contrary to the person's interests. Yet, I also recalled learning that police were becoming very sophisticated in interrogations. They were now using what has become known as the "Reid

Technique." This method of obtaining a confession begins with police telling a suspect that police already know the accused was the perpetrator of the criminal act. All the while, the interrogation proceeds, and the police conduct their interview in a manner that is patient and never demeaning to the subject of the questioning. As it progresses, the interviewer offers psychological constructs as to why the accused would have done the crime. The perception is that the policeman is the accused's friend, especially when an accused person lacks counsel, which often results in the signing of a confession. The problem is that the confessions are frequently false.[1] The Reid Technique had not been subject to judicial scrutiny at that time.

Today, defence counsel can reasonably expect full access to the evidence before trial, allowing for thorough evaluation and preparation. However, in this case, preparation for the murder trial took place before the Supreme Court established the obligation for prosecutors to disclose all material intended for use in court.

The Middlesex County Crown Attorney was Michael Martin—a stocky, white-haired gentleman I had dealt with in previous cases. He called me into his office, told me he liked me, and, on that basis, was willing to share what the Crown intended to prove. I suspected his goal was to convince me that the evidence was so strong it would be in my client's best interest to consider a guilty plea. Among the few documents handed over were autopsy photographs—hard to ignore, and even harder to forget.

1 Judge Mike Dinkel of the Provincial Court of Alberta (Criminal Division) threw out the confession of a childcare worker accused of harming a child in her care. He wrote, "I denounce the use of this technique in the strongest terms possible and find that its use can lead to overwhelmingly oppressive situations that can render false confessions and cause innocent people to be wrongfully imprisoned." He deemed the accused's confession inadmissible and dismissed the charges against her. (*R. v. Chapple*, 2012).

I had never seen autopsy photos before, and the depiction of the wounds was most upsetting. I knew it was my responsibility not to look away but to inspect the photographs for anything I could use to formulate a defence. It was only after staring at the pictures for what seemed an eternity that I could focus on something that looked unusual. The autopsy photos showed that Ms. Arthur's throat had been slashed by probably by a buck knife (although the murder weapon was never found). I carefully inspected each photo and noticed a peculiarity: the slash mark seemed at an angle, with the end of the cut being lower on the victim's left side than on her right. If a right-handed individual slashed at the throat of a person facing him, the angle would be higher on the left side. My theory was that the slashing of the throat was done by a left-handed person since the tilt of the wound would be in the opposite direction if the victim and her assailant stood face-to-face opposite each other. I could easily prove my client was right-handed. Maybe a left-handed passerby had found Ms. Arthur in distress and inflicted the fatal wound.

The "left-handed theory" played on my mind. On a bright, sunny Saturday afternoon, I brought a watermelon from my kitchen to my backyard. My wife expected to spend a leisurely afternoon sitting in lawn chairs, soaking up the rays and munching on watermelon. Instead, using a butcher knife, I tried to replicate the angle of the slash mark. In doing so, I readily concluded that the wound provided evidence that it was made by the swing of a knife from the left hand of the killer. My wife was horrified. She left me alone, jumped in her car, and spent the day visiting her parents. I was on a mission to discover the truth.

I knew I could never find the left-handed person to present as an alternative suspect to secure an acquittal. Still, I could ask a pathologist on the Western University's Medical School faculty to conduct an experiment and testify as to its results. A report and later testimony at trial showed that a similar experiment conducted by medical experts at the university on a cadaver verified my conclusion that it was more likely than not that a left-handed individual caused the fatal wound on Ms. Arthur's neck. After all, I just need one juror to have reasonable doubt that Rueger was the killer to have him acquitted.

Additionally, the evidence showed that the OPP officer, discovering the Arthur vehicle in the ditch and the slain woman's body close by, returned to his detachment and wrote the situation up as a single-vehicle collision. There is too much paperwork for the beginning of a holiday! With no eyewitness or forensic evidence, would it be possible to secure an acquittal on my first murder trial?

If the third-party suspect defence failed, my next step was to gather evidence suggesting that Rueger was either too intoxicated or legally insane at the time—anything that might prevent a first-degree murder conviction. This approach would require expert testimony. I reached out to my network for recommendations on who to consult to explore the possibility of an insanity defence. One name consistently rose to the top: Toronto psychiatrist Dr. Jerry Cooper.

I arranged to meet Dr. Cooper at his home. In preparation, I had learned that Rueger's wife was willing to testify that, on more than one occasion, she had awakened to find her husband's hands around her throat. I wondered whether this could support an argument that Rueger suffered from a mental disorder—one severe enough to prevent him from understanding the nature and quality of his actions, or from knowing that they were wrong. This would be essential to establish an insanity defence.

Could Rueger have acted as an automaton—his body functioning without conscious control, devoid of criminal intent? Dr. Cooper was sceptical. He asked what other avenues

I was pursuing. I then outlined Rueger's history of excessive drinking. Dr. Cooper suggested that a defence based on intoxication might be more viable than one based on automatism.

However, I recalled a point made during my bar admission course by none other than Eddie Greenspan, the renowned criminal defence lawyer. In his lectures, Greenspan had cautioned that it was rare for intoxication to successfully negate specific intent—especially in serious charges such as murder.Dr. Cooper said, "Let's get Eddie on the line." I was astounded that Dr. Cooper was so familiar with the great criminal defence counsel and that he had Greenspan's home number ready.

Greenspan was most generous and helpful in analyzing my approach. He said I was on the right track with the various defences but should concentrate on proving drunkenness. Although I was hired as Legal Aid counsel, I felt obligated to offer compensation for the consultation. Greenspan rejected my offer even though I had taken up an hour of his time.

"You think I can win with the alcohol defence?" I asked.

"No. But send my firm the appeal," he added.

The trial started in a London, Ontario courtroom in September 1982 with Supreme Court Justice John Harty Osler presiding. The first item of business was to determine the admissibility of evidence in a pre-trial proceeding called a *voir dire*. The primary item for consideration was the supposed confession Rueger gave the police.

A polygraph expert was called who testified that even without subjecting Rueger to the polygraph, he discussed with the accused and recorded the admission that Rueger had indeed killed Ms. Arthur. During cross-examination, I had the witness confirm that the expert was inordinately friendly in dealing with his subject and, indeed, became so endearing toward him that Rueger volunteered the statement. I argued that this approach was the flip side of the same coin as torture.

While no confession extracted using torture could be accepted, confessions that are obtained by endearing the subject to the questioner should be similarly rejected. The Judge agreed and ruled that the confession proffered by Rueger would not come to the jury's attention.

Middlesex County Crown Attorney Michael Martin (later to become head Crown Attorney for the Province of Ontario) was the prosecuting lawyer at the trial. He decided to argue this case himself rather than appoint an associate to prosecute what he led me to believe to be a sure thing. He was known as an excellent litigator. He presented his case and was looking for a first-degree murder verdict.

As the trial progressed, I noticed one striking omission: the Crown never introduced any evidence of the alleged phone call between the deceased and her parents. Where was the so-called "feed the bird" message? Had Michael Martin simply forgotten to present crucial evidence—evidence that could undermine our position by suggesting Rueger wasn't too intoxicated to form the specific intent to kill? Then it dawned on me—perhaps the message never existed at all. Could Michael Martin be so lax as to forget to tender evidence showing Rueger was not so drunk as to be unable to form the specific intent to murder? Then, I realized there likely was no "feed the bird" message. Ms. Arthur had left the store and headed straight to her parents' home. The feed the bird story had been fabricated by police to induce a guilty plea.

The implications were dark and troubling. They raised a broader concern about how the justice system sometimes operates. Techniques like the Reid Method of interrogation don't just pressure suspects—they can also discourage defence counsel from pursuing a trial. In some cases, securing a conviction seems to take precedence over uncovering the truth.

The penalty for first-degree murder is set in stone (life imprisonment without eligibility for parole for 25 years). There is no point in trying to negotiate a lesser sentence. Could it be that the "feed the bird" story was made up to induce me into believing that a first-degree conviction was inevitable and that the only way I could serve my client would be to beg the Crown Attorney to accept a plea to a second-degree murder conviction and avoid a trial? Could it be that it was to the advantage of the police to allow a resolution by way of a lesser charge so that they would not have to admit ineptitude in not investigating the "single motor vehicle collision" as a murder investigation from the outset?

With the "confession" ruled inadmissible and no mention of the "feed the bird" call, I truly believed I had a shot of avoiding a first-degree conviction.

As in any trial, things went differently than I had hoped. I felt Rueger could be believed and would portray himself as a hard-working "regular Joe" who could be counted on to tell his story as he had recounted it to me. Instead, he admitted to returning home and gathering a few trinkets to be passed off as Christmas gifts. His wife testified that he sometimes grabbed her by the throat when her husband was asleep. I sensed the jury was not impressed.

At the trial's conclusion, the prosecution and defence made their closing arguments to the jury. Much would depend on the Judge's charge or instructions to the jury.

The judge outlined my "left-hand" theory and the supporting evidence, but there was little instruction on how the jury should regard that defence.

The judge gave much more careful attention to the evidence that would see a conviction for a lesser verdict than first-degree. The most crucial determination the jury would have to make would be whether there was planning and deliberation sufficient to justify a first-degree verdict. He summarized the Crown's position as follows:

> [There is] evidence of intention, and I think of deliberation, Mr. Martin would say. There is evidence from the accused himself on the stand, and in some of the statements, he recalls a good deal of what is said to have happened that night. There is evidence that he was sober enough to deliver presents, to carry on a conversation with his brother and sister-in-law, and to sew up purses for the kids. Hence, he didn't have enough to drink to cast doubt on his ability to plan and deliberate or on his intention to kill or cause bodily harm.

The trial judge went on to instruct the jury as to the defence position:

> Finally, Mr. Hill says on all the evidence, including his partial memory and his lapses, his continuing depression, and his acts such as placing his hands around his wife's throat, which, according to her and to him, he sometimes performed without being conscious of them, or without recalling them afterward. He says on all the evidence you cannot be satisfied that his acts were planned and deliberate or even that he had the necessary intent at all.

The jury retired to consider its verdict and returned in a few hours. They marched in single file from the deliberation room directly to their seats in the jury box. No juror looked my way or at my client, which I always regarded as a bad sign. An occasional glance or even a smile was indicative of a not-guilty finding. The jury was asked for its verdict, and the foreman announced that the jury had unanimously found the accused guilty of first-degree murder. Since the sentence was mandatory, there was no use holding sentencing over to another day. Life/25. Rueger would be sentenced to imprisonment for life without eligibility to see the Parole Board for at least 25 years.

In the days following, I had Rueger sign a prisoner appeal form challenging both the conviction and the sentence. As promised, I turned the case over to the Greenspan firm to argue the appeal. Greenspan assigned the case to his associate, Marc Rosenberg.

The conviction appeal came on for hearing in November 1984. Neither Michael Martin nor I attended. In a unanimous decision, the Ontario Court of Appeal held that:

> The trial judge erred in failing to instruct the jury concerning the relevance of intoxication on the issue of planning and deliberation by the principles enunciated by the Supreme Court of Canada.

Ordinarily, the Court reasoned, this would be sufficient to order a new trial. However, the Court decided the ends of justice were met by quashing the first-degree conviction and substituting a conviction for second-degree murder. The appropriate sentence would be left for another Court to decide.

In March 1985, the sentence appeal came on for hearing. This time, Michael Martin participated along with the Ministry of the Attorney General counsel, Doug Hunt, with Marc Rosenberg continuing to act for the appellant. The sentence was reduced to life imprisonment without eligibility for parole for 18 years.

In murder cases, the Correctional Service of Canada calculates sentences from the date that the convicted murderer went into custody. The Appeal Court decision would allow Rueger to apply for parole in 1999.

"The trial of an issue of fact is not a game; it is a search for the truth," wrote one Supreme Court Justice using the words commonly attributed to Edmund Burke. The concept of a trial as a truth-seeking mission is overplayed. Trials are adversarial. Perhaps a "truth-seeking" function is inconsistent with our process. The Crown seeks to answer the question of who the killer was, while the defence seeks to find if there was proof to the requisite level of certainty that identifies the accused with the deed. They are two different approaches.

Nonetheless, the judicial system relies on truth-telling. I will never know if the "feed the bird" statement was accurate or if it was a misdirection by a crafty police officer to induce counsel to strike a deal for a guilty plea. Maybe I should have followed through on my original hunch that Rueger acted as an automaton—he had no conscious realization of the evil act he was performing. But how could I get a psychiatrist to buy into that position? Expert psychiatric evidence was necessary for the defence to have a ghost of a chance at succeeding.

After Rueger was imprisoned, I lost contact. His wife came to my office with a letter. It was a different tone from the previous letters she had received. She allowed me to read the letter. Could it be possible that her husband had been raped in prison? That was what she inferred without it being spelled out in so many words. Would the Correctional Service allow such behaviour to happen?

I had to admit to the grieving wife that such a tragic event could occur, and it would be essential to continue her visits with him and reassure him of her love.

Ray Rueger would have been entitled to apply for parole in 1999. The prison had become his home, and no application for release was made. He was later transferred to minimum security Pittsburgh Institution east of Kingston. When he fell ill, he was taken to Kingston General Hospital, where he died on May 8, 2013. He was 63 years old.

I tried to find an explanation for why Ray Rueger never applied for parole. Having cascaded from maximum security penitentiary to a minimum-security institution, it would be expected that some applications for escorted or unescorted temporary absences would have gone before the Parole Board for decision. Completing temporary absences would ensure the inmate had the trust of correctional authorities. It would help a case on why day parole or full parole should be granted. Yet, my queries to the Correctional Service and the Parole Board of Canada showed that no application was ever made. Could this be because Rueger was so remorseful for his actions on that Christmas Eve long ago that he felt he deserved imprisonment until he died?

Then, my mind wandered back to an incident immediately after the trial judge handed down the sentence. After the court concluded, I visited Ray Rueger in the holding cells with a lump in my throat and a tear forming in my eye.

"I'm so sorry," I whispered to Rueger, sitting across from him in a booth with a thick glass barrier between us. Every lawyer tries to believe that doing their best will lead to the best outcome for the client. When there wasn't an acquittal or even a conviction on a lesser charge, I felt I had failed. Yet, Rueger was smiling.

I was surprised. My client, just convicted of the most serious offence in the Criminal Code and sentenced to the harshest penalty available, was trying to comfort me. I had never been entirely sure Rueger had given me a full and truthful account. And now, here he was—his expression calm, his posture relaxed—offering me reassurance, as though I were the one who needed saving.

How could someone who had just been found guilty of slitting an innocent woman's throat seem so compassionate? Can alcohol so profoundly distort a person's behaviour? How could someone capable of such apparent empathy commit such a terrible act?

"I'm so sorry," I said again, more quietly this time.

"You did a great job," Rueger replied. "And you know your left-handed theory? Well, I did it from behind."

As a young, idealistic lawyer, I had believed that trials were about finding the truth. That belief fell apart when I realized that the police story—"feed the bird"—wasn't true, and was used to lead me toward recommending a guilty plea. My client had let me believe it. Of course, my client allowed me to wallow in a lie as well through his stunning admission that he did it from behind.

His final words weren't just an admission. They were a twist of the knife—proof that in court, truth is not always what wins. Everyone has their version. Everyone has their motive and darkness isn't always what it seems. It wears many faces. Sometimes it smiles.

3

Matthew Michel, Johnny Stavrou, and Dennis Edgar

Torturous Treatment

Jails and prisons are designed to break human beings,
to convert the population into specimens in a zoo—
obedient to our keepers but dangerous to each other.

—Angela Davis

THE AMERICAN AUTHOR Isabel Wilkerson, in her book *Caste: The Origins of Our Discontents*, places the blame for much of the racism she endured growing up as a Black woman on having to exist in a society where there is an unchallenged expectation that one is, or is not, a member of a dominant race. One should be compliant with one's rank in society. She draws parallels between this system and the caste structure in India, noting that American racial laws even served as a model for Nazi Germany in establishing Aryan supremacy over those they deemed subordinate, such as Jews and homosexuals.

A Canadian reader of the treatise might tend to disregard Wilkerson's theory as inapplicable in our country. Should we? As a long-time practitioner of prison law, I spot many issues that Wilkerson had to deal with that apply to society's view of penitentiary inmates.

More than twenty years ago, changes were made to how youthful offenders are treated in Canada. The primary goal was to reintegrate these young people successfully into the community. A key to this reintegration process is ensuring that those detained are adequately treated while incarcerated.

A 2023 CBC story documented how a young Indigenous offender, Matthew Michel, begged staff at a Regina youth detention centre to kill him since he could no longer mentally deal with his head encased in a motorcycle helmet and his body bound by a device called the "Wrap." His torso, legs, and ankles were bound and connected to a shoulder harness that kept his body at a nearly 45 degree angle with his hands cuffed behind his back, locked to a carabiner—a type of shackle with a metal loop and a spring-loaded gate. The Wrap, used by jail staff to punish Matthew into compliance, is authorized for use in Saskatchewan, Manitoba, and New Brunswick. The day following the airing of the CBC report, this merciless way of treating youthful offenders made headlines as far away as Australia.

The program sparked a petition urging the federal and provincial governments to abolish the Wrap as being a torture device. The petition noted:

> The Wrap, which immobilizes a youth into forced compliance, threatens their physical and psychological well-being and growth. It is essential to acknowledge that youth in detention are already vulnerable, having experienced various abuses and traumas contributing to their custody and detention, particularly for Indigenous youth. Subjecting them to further harm through such a restrictive and punitive technique is unjust and counterproductive.

Jorge Barrera, the CBC reporter who first broke the story, interviewed Matthew Michel and reported on his troubled upbringing. Matthew grew up in Saskatoon without the stability of a secure home, enduring physical abuse during his childhood. By the age of 12, he had already entered youth detention. His grandmother stepped in to raise him, taking the place of his absent parents.

She herself had been a survivor of Canada's day school and residential school system—institutions designed to forcibly assimilate Indigenous children. Michel never pressed her for details about her experiences. She masked her pain with alcohol, though he remembered the tears she sometimes shed.

Matthew's own trauma deepened when he was subjected to the Wrap. His first encounter with it came at age 14, when he was bound in the device for over an hour.

Reflecting on the experience, Matthew told Barrera that the intense physical and emotional pain pushed him to the brink of suicidal thoughts. "The suffering was so overwhelming," he said, "it felt like...just end it already."

He spoke about the lasting impact it had on him, admitting that he harboured deep resentment toward the guards and officers involved. The trauma, he said, left him distrustful of anyone in a position of authority. "I can still taste the blood to this day," Michel said. "That's how I learned to cope with pain—to trick myself. I used to bite the inside of my cheek or my tongue just to get through it."

Barrera also interviewed Dr. Gabor Maté, a world-renowned therapist who has studied the effects of trauma on childhood development. Dr. Maté's assessment was:

> What they're doing by treating people this way is creating a future drug addict and a future criminal. You could not create a better school for future anti-social behaviour. Or for mental illness, for that matter.

Despite the publicity, the Government of Saskatchewan has yet to reveal if it will discontinue using the Wrap.

In April 2024, reality star Paris Hilton testified before a US state Senate committee investigating the mistreatment of youth in California's residential facilities. Hilton, who was sent to a treatment centre in Utah at the age of 17, described her experience as abuse masked as therapy.

A 2021 law barred state-licensed California facilities from sending young people out of state for treatment, but new legislation aimed at increasing transparency and oversight of juvenile care is currently under review. Speaking before the committee, Hilton stated:

> Today, I stand before you not just as Paris Hilton, but as an advocate and survivor of the troubled teen industry. When I tried to tell my parents about the abuse, staff would snatch the phone from my hands, cut off the call, and punish me with violent physical restraints or solitary confinement.

Anyone who has practiced prison law will understand that many of the prisoners being counselled can trace their aberrant behaviour to childhood abuse. This pattern of abuse became so constant in my prisoner interviews that I started to think that Children's Aid Societies were simply make-work projects for the Ministry of Correctional Services. *Why can't somebody do something about the abuse that goes on?* I asked myself.

Finally, something is being done. A Toronto law firm has filed a 65-page, 238-paragraph statement of claim in the Superior Court of Justice in Toronto on behalf of Jonathon "Johnny" Stavrou claiming damages against the Province of Ontario and several youth treatment centres and group homes where Johnny was allegedly mistreated and abused during his wardship. None of the allegations made in the claim have been proven in court.

According to the court-filed document, Johnny and his twin brother were taken into care when it was determined that the boys' biological parents were involved with substance abuse and could not care for their offspring. Johnny and his brother became Crown wards in 2002 when Johnny was six years old. He was never adopted and "aged out" of the system when he turned 18.

Things did not go well for Johnny during his 12 years as a Crown ward. Paragraph 6 of the Statement of Claim summarizes the abuse:

> Johnny has a traumatic history as a Crown ward. The state became his legal guardian and assumed the role and responsibilities as his sole parent. The Crown, the Society and other residential foster care/treatment providers failed to keep Johnny safe from harm, including sexual abuse, physical abuse (including the improper use of mechanical restraints), bullying/discrimination based on sexual orientation and solitary confinement. The defendants each blamed Johnny for the injustices and harms that he experienced in the child welfare system, rather than providing safe homes and care for him or advocating on his behalf when he reported the abuse that he suffered.

Johnny matured and identified himself as gay. In June 1999, while at one foster home, he was targeted for his sexual orientation by the foster parents and suffered physical and psychological abuse. When Johnny attempted to defend himself from the physical attack by a foster parent, he was blamed for the assault and sent to a youth detention centre where he was kept in solitary confinement, had mechanical restraints applied, and psychotropic drugs administered to "pacify and sedate him." When he was 13 years old, Johnny was once again sent to a youth detention centre for defensive behaviour.[1]

Johnny once again experienced the physical and psychological torment—more precisely termed torture—that this facility administered. He was released when it was realized he did not meet the statutory requirement for incarceration.

1 Paul Miller, co-managing partner of the Toronto law firm Howie, Sacks & Henry, filed the lawsuit against the Ontario government and the Children s Aid Society of Toronto in the Superior Court of Ontario in December 2023.

Johnny's placement in youth care facilities involved inappropriate sexual discussions by staff and physical restraints such that he could not visit a washroom in private. At one point in his wardship, he attempted suicide.

Fortunately, Johnny has not turned to illegal activity like many of his peers whom I have spoken with. Nonetheless, his childhood abuse has had a lasting effect on him. The Statement of Claim sums up the difficulties he has experienced upon becoming an adult.

> Despite being raised in the instability of Society care, Johnny is highly intelligent. He has a strong drive to work and learn. Despite his many accomplishments, including his paramedic training and attempts to work, he has routinely struggled to get along with co-workers at any job and has filed various human rights complaints and grievances as a way to assert and protect himself at school and in the workplace. This has often led to employment breakdown. Johnny has sought extensive psychotherapy for his mental injuries, including weekly psychology treatment, psychiatric treatment and assessment, and in-patient treatment at various times in his life. He takes anti-depressant and/or psychotropic medication to manage his mood and mental health.

Johnny is claiming $5 million in compensation for past and future damages, as well as any special damages the court may find appropriate. The magnitude of this claim reflects not only the harm suffered, but also the urgent need for systemic change. A financial award of this scale could serve as a powerful deterrent, compelling governments and their agencies to take meaningful action to protect vulnerable children in their care. It would be an investment in prevention—helping to ensure that the trauma experienced by children in state-run facilities does not manifest later in life as anti-social or destructive behaviour.[2]

Infliction of bodily pain, even death, was excusable in a caste system that sees the subordinate as sub-human. Nazi Germany transported Jews to concentration camps in cattle cars. Are we any better?

There is a well-documented over-representation of Indigenous and racialized groups in Canadian prisons. This reality reflects the persistence of a *de facto* caste system—one that systematically limits opportunities for certain communities to achieve their full potential. By denying access to education, employment, and health supports, society pushes marginalized individuals into cycles of poverty and desperation, conditions that can increase the likelihood of criminalized behaviour.

In 1997, the Canadian Parliament attempted to address this injustice through a significant reform to the *Criminal Code*. Section 718.2(e) called for restraint in the use of imprisonment, particularly when sentencing Indigenous offenders. The Supreme Court of Canada interpreted this provision in the landmark 1999 decision *R. v. Gladue*, recognizing the need to consider the unique circumstances of Indigenous Peoples within the justice system. While the decision affirmed that Section 718.2(e) applies specifically to Indigenous individuals, the Court also acknowledged that its principles could benefit a broader population caught in similar systemic cycles.

Despite this precedent, the implementation of what are now known as the *Gladue* principles has been uneven. Courts

2 A *Toronto Star* investigation from November 2024 revealed that children with complex health needs, under the protection of children's aid societies, are often housed in unlicensed settings—including hotels, motels, Airbnbs, and even office buildings—due to a lack of proper residential treatment options. Many of these children are placed in care not because they are unsafe at home, but because their families cannot access the medical or psychological supports they require.

in several provinces have been slow to adopt the approach, undermining the intent of the legislation and perpetuating the very inequalities it sought to redress. The result is yet another act of darkness—this time by omission—within a system that continues to fail those it was meant to protect.

There are two schools of thought when it comes to sentencing. One perspective is that we will only achieve a peaceful society if violent crimes are treated harshly. People of this mind look to the crime and not to the perpetrator. To people who accept this approach, the *Gladue* principles are simply Parliament's attempt to give a "get out of jail free" card to a particular discrete population. The second approach is to look at the person about to be sentenced and recognize the "why" of how that individual became involved in crime and the brutal treatment that individual may suffer while incarcerated, as well as the availability of treatment and rehabilitation.

The perception that some people are of lesser worth may be considered a relic of the American South, where race relations were akin to the apartheid practices of South Africa; those days must be over, we tell ourselves. Yet, an April 17, 2024, report in the *Miami Herald* dealt with a complaint filed on April 16 in the Southern District of Georgia.

The complaint includes a photo from jail surveillance footage showing the chain around a black inmate named Harris, who had his eyes closed and mouth open. A white correctional officer named Rentz is seen standing over him, holding the chain around his neck. The photo shows three other officers looking down at Harris.

The complaint alleges that as Rentz choked Harris, he was accused of saying: "Gonna put you back in the cotton field with the other boys," in an apparent reference to slavery. Meanwhile, three other white correctional officers watched and didn't try to stop or report the unlawful use of force, according to the complaint.

Such situations are not confined to the United States. Here in Canada, our own informal caste system shapes how we treat those deemed to be of lesser worth. A recent court case involving Collins Bay inmate Dennis Edgar illustrates this starkly. Edgar was granted an escorted pass to attend his mother's funeral, requiring a seven-hour transport by the Correctional Service of Canada (CSC) from Kingston, Ontario to Windsor. Dennis was transported in a van, seated just a foot off the floor, forcing his knees above the level of his hips and placing intense pressure on the lower part of his spine. His wrists and ankles were shackled, with no chain linking the two sets of cuffs, further restricting his movement. Despite repeatedly complaining to CSC officers about severe back pain during both the trip to and from Windsor, no steps were taken to ease his discomfort. The constant jolting of the journey either caused or worsened a spinal condition that ultimately required surgery.

The supposed reason for taking precautions with Dennis was that he was considered to be involved in the institutional drug trade. He has never been convicted of any crime or institutional offence involving contraband, even though he had spent days in total isolation in a dry cell suspected of importing fentanyl into the institution. In that situation, he was criminally charged but was found not guilty *(R. v. Edgar)*. Sometimes, demeaning humans requires only suspicion and not proof.

Transporting humans worse than animals indicates how dominant groups treat their subordinates in a caste system. The Correctional Investigator has criticized this form of transportation, but no action has been taken to move inmates more humanely.

Public attitudes were again tested when it became known that Paul Bernardo was to be moved from maximum security to medium security. The "get tough on crime" crowd could not be appeased. Conservative Leader Pierre Poilievre has said the inmate should "rot [in a maximum-security prison] until he leaves in a coffin." Even though the operating policy of the Correctional Service of Canada is that inmates go to prison "as punishment, not for punishment," widespread sympathy is to look upon prisoners as less than human, undeserving of rehabilitative programming, and being treated worse than animals.

Dennis Edgar's claim for damages against the Correctional Service of Canada for injuries sustained was eventually settled out of court. There is no indication that the Service has modified how it transports prisoners.

Isabel Wilkerson suggests that the rise in calls for extremism and displays of right-wing fanaticism are no different from the attitudes that prevailed in Nazi Germany. It is politically popular to embrace this form of rhetoric. According to Wilkerson, it's in America's DNA. Is it in ours as well?

These examples reveal how acts of darkness are not confined to the actions of individuals—they are also embedded in institutions that choose inaction over reform, and in ideologies that dehumanize under the guise of nationalism.

4

Bogiatzis, Christoldolou, Cusato, Churchill

Satan's Choice

It is not possible to found a lasting power upon injustice, perjury and treachery.

—Demosthenes

IT WAS a wiretap case. The Crown prosecutors knew that a box of tape recordings sitting beside the Crown Attorney's table in a Toronto Superior Courtroom would be enough to convict four men accused of a dozen weapons-related offences and conspiracy to traffic cocaine. Nothing else could be used to obtain a conviction without the tape recordings being admitted as evidence in the trial.

Athanasios Bogiatzis, Thomas Christodoulou, Paul Cusato, and Reginald Churchill, among others, were apprehended and charged as part of the Ontario-wide investigation, Project Dismantle. During this investigation, a significant number of weapons were confiscated, including semi-automatic pistols, sawed-off shotguns, and an Israeli military rifle. The wiretaps, a crucial piece of evidence, were instrumental in establishing a direct link between the defendants and the various firearms.

The legal challenges mounted by the defence were formidable. The Ontario Provincial Police, working in coordination with forces from Toronto, Hamilton, Kitchener, Sudbury, and Thunder Bay, had spent years investigating the Satan's Choice motorcycle gang, aiming to dismantle it through a sweeping operation that began with clubhouse raids and dozens of arrests in 1997. Over time, however, charges against all but four men—Bogiatzis, Christodoulou, Cusato, and Churchill—were dropped.

Lawyers for the remaining accused launched a series of strategic legal manoeuvres to obtain full disclosure, pressing especially for the identity of the police informer whose intelligence had led to the arrests. The police refused, citing the policy that protects informants from exposure. But the defence had a narrow but critical legal opening: if they could convince the courts that "Informant No. 1" acted as a police agent rather than a mere informer, then that person could be compelled to testify. Such testimony might discredit the intelligence that supported the use of wiretaps—evidence that could determine the men's fate. It was a long shot, but the stakes were high. If the wiretaps stood unchallenged, the four accused faced years behind bars.

The attempt to reclassify the informer as an agent delayed court proceedings for years while the challenges went through the Court of Appeal and eventually to the Supreme Court of Canada. The defence challenges were unsuccessful in the Court of Appeal, and the Supreme Court refused to grant leave and hear the case. The defence lawyers were growing pessimistic that their clients could be acquitted.

One of the accused, Domingos Manuel Moura, initially hired me. The charges against him were eventually stayed in the Superior Court. However, the lawyer for Christodoulou could not continue, and since I was familiar with the case, he asked me to represent his client. Thomas Christodoulou agreed, and I took over representing him.

The case moved forward to trial under Justice John Macdonald. Before it officially began, several important legal arguments—known as pre-trial motions—were brought before the judge. One of these centred on gaining access to evidence the prosecution had not yet shared. Lawyers call this process "disclosure," and when they formally ask the court to order it, it's known as a *Stinchcombe* application. In this instance, the motion became unnecessary—the prosecution handed over the requested material voluntarily. And with that new information in hand, the defence made two key discoveries.

First, they gained a clearer picture of how Detective John Cavanaugh had persuaded judges to approve the wiretaps. Cavanaugh, a twenty-eight-year veteran of the Ontario Provincial Police, was their top expert when it came to preparing wiretap applications—a role that gave him significant influence over how the case took shape from the beginning.

We learned that Detective Cavanaugh had destroyed the investigative file used to draft the affidavits he swore to obtain the authorizations. Based on this information, the appellant applied for a stay of proceedings using a Supreme Court precedent known as a Carosella application *(R. v. Carosella, 1997)*. The Carosella case could be used to argue that police destruction of evidence could be grounds for the stay of proceedings against the accused men.

We also discovered something significant: Informant No. 1 hadn't just been a tipster—he had acted as a police agent, directly involved in matters relevant to the case when it first came before a judge. This came to light in a newly released summary of his affidavits, parts of which had originally been edited—that is, blacked out—when shown to the defence.

This revelation undercut the Crown's earlier claim that the informant was protected and didn't have to testify. With this new understanding, defence lawyers launched a fresh bid to halt the proceedings—this time using a legal strategy known as a "Babes application," based on a 2000 ruling from the Ontario Court of Appeal *(R. v. Babes, 2000)*. Our argument was simple: the defence had the right to know the identity of Informant No. 1.

The argument on these two applications began near the end of August 2002. At that time, Justice Macdonald ruled that he would reserve judgment on each of them until the evidence had been heard on a third application, a Garofoli application, which is also based on a Supreme Court of Canada case *(R. v. Garolfoli, 1990)* that held that an information to obtain a search warrant (an ITO) was invalid if it was based on false information. After considerable deliberation, the defence counsel for the individuals charged—Delmar Doucette, Glenn Orr, Marie Abraham and me—decided we must try anything possible to exclude the wiretaps from the evidence. The applications were a last-ditch effort to save our clients from lengthy prison sentences, and there was no expectation that the results would be in our client's favour.

Again, the earlier challenge to the legitimacy of the ITO was brought to the Court of Appeal's attention *(R. v. Moura, 1998)* because "this Honourable Court was misled by false evidence in its original decision in this matter." However, the Court of Appeal believed the evidential basis was too weak to grant relief. Its concern was summed up in a crucial paragraph of the Court of Appeal judgment:

> On the assumption that there is jurisdiction to set aside a judgment based on perjured evidence, the Crown has submitted that the alleged fraud is not supported by the evidence; that is, it is not shown that Detective Cavanaugh intentionally misled the court. In this regard, it refers to an observation of Macdonald J. in his ruling on the Carosella and Babes motions.

The Court of Appeal, quoting Justice Macdonald's ruling on the Carosella and Babes motions, noted that Detective Cavanaugh had not been directly accused of lying during his testimony on the stay applications. As Macdonald pointed out, Cavanaugh was never questioned about the allegation, and therefore had no opportunity, under oath, to respond or be cross-examined on it. The Court of Appeal remitted the case to Justice Macdonald to determine whether Detective Cavanaugh had misled the court in authorizing the wiretaps.

Detective Cavanaugh was called to give evidence to test the defence assertion that the Court had been misled by a lie in the first of the five affidavits signed by Detective Cavanaugh and repeated in the subsequent four that allowed the collection of wiretaps to continue.

Under the relentless cross-examination by Glenn Orr, counsel for Bogiatzis, Cavanaugh was forced to admit to fabricating information in the first affidavit, a lie that he shamelessly repeated in every subsequent request for wiretap authorization.

On September 3, 2003, Justice Macdonald read out a two-hour judgment savaging the conduct of the 28-year OPP veteran.

"An oath to tell the truth was close to meaningless to Detective Cavanaugh," the judge explained as he ruled the wiretaps inadmissible because of the police misconduct. At the beginning of the trial, the judge had given every indication that he was about to get tough on these accused men, and defence counsel could foresee lengthy penitentiary terms imposed upon conviction. Yet, there was a greater demand than sending these accused off to prison. Exclusion of the wiretap evidence was necessary "to protect the integrity of the wiretap authorization process from such deliberate and serious abuse."

The box of tapes containing the wiretapped conversations that indeed would have convicted the four accused men remained sitting at the prosecutor's counsel table. Those recordings would never be played in court.

Bogiatzis, Christodoulou, Cusato, and Churchill, after enduring the weight of the charges for nearly six years, were finally freed from the courthouse. Their faces reflected a mix of relief and disbelief.

A costly and time-consuming police investigation aimed at dismantling an outlaw motorcycle gang was for naught. The only black mark resulting from the endeavour was against Detective Cavanaugh. Cavanaugh was charged for his role in swearing a false affidavit, but his criminal charge was later dismissed because of the delay in bringing his matter to trial within the prescribed time. His right to a speedy trial had been infringed.

This case could be viewed as a costly investigation gone off the rails—driven by one officer's willingness to lie in order to secure a conviction. Sadly, it echoed another major drug prosecution I was involved in back in 2001, where I served as defence counsel for a man named Paul Vidotto.

Vidotto, along with Kurt Ianuzzo, David Nobleman, and a fourth man, was accused of conspiring to traffic between 175 and 750 kilograms of cocaine. The arrests came in late 1997 after an extensive police operation known as Project Dado.

The group was charged with planning to import drugs from Costa Rica, smuggled inside the metal frames of dozens of office chairs. Only a few of the chairs were found to have traces of cocaine, and those were tied to the fourth accused—who eventually pleaded guilty and received a prison sentence. He had rented two storage lockers in Cobourg, Ontario, where the contraband was discovered.

Ianuzzo, Vidotto and Nobleman went to trial. A key prosecution witness was Toronto Detective David Caravella. Caravella had posed as a Columbian drug lord and set up two meetings with Ianuzzo and Nobleman. During these encounters, Caravella accused the two of stealing the cocaine supposedly embedded inside the chairs.

Caravella testified that the meetings were arranged because a confidential informant told him that Iannuzo and Nobleman were trying to sell 750 kilograms of cocaine with a street value of $30 million.

The defendants denied this accusation and told the court they had been threatened by the officer, who had waved his hands suggestive of pointing and shooting a gun. This was denied by Caravella, who claimed on the witness stand that he had never taken his hands out of his coat pockets.

Caravella's testimony was contradicted by police observation photos that showed Detective Caravella was being less than truthful. Ontario Superior Court Justice Wailan Low complimented the detective as "creative" and "courageous" and having an "agile mind." Still, she concluded, "As a witness, he was less than truthful on some material points." The judge dismissed the charges against the accused because the key witness "bent the truth" while testifying.

Reporting on the 2001 acquittal, *National Post* journalist Shannon Kari noted that Detective Caravella wasn't the only officer who failed in his duty to tell the truth. In his August 22 article, Kari pointed out that ten former Toronto drug squad officers were facing criminal charges at the time. The fallout was severe: over the previous two years, the Federal Department of Justice had dropped or delayed 115 drug cases due to the scandal. In response, Toronto Police Chief Julian Fantino brought in a senior RCMP officer to investigate widespread allegations of perjury within the drug squad.

Our system of justice demands truthfulness in giving evidence. Examples of police lying on the stand not only jeopardize the successful prosecution of drug cases but also diminish the public confidence in the administration of justice.

The collapse of both Project Dismantle and Project Dado underscores a troubling pattern: when those sworn to uphold the law resort to deception, the integrity of the justice system is profoundly compromised. The officers' decisions to fabricate or distort evidence weren't just individual failings—they were acts that undermined years of investigation, drained public resources, and risked convicting individuals without fair process. The courtroom victories for the defence weren't celebrations of innocence but reminders of the high cost of misconduct in the pursuit of conviction.

In the context of acts of darkness, these cases reveal a deeper kind of transgression—where power, unchecked by accountability, turns justice into a performance rather than a principle. The darkness here is not only found in the crimes under investigation, but in the quiet, calculated decisions to bend the truth for perceived ends. These stories challenge us to consider what real justice requires: not just the punishment of the guilty, but the unwavering commitment to truth, even when it is inconvenient.

5

Jason Cofell

Stark Acts of Vigilante Justice

Beware that,
when fighting monsters,
you yourself do not become a monster.

—Barry Eisler, *The Night Trade*

When we think of drugs and the law, our minds often turn to traffickers and users. Rarely do we associate violent crimes with those who claim to be preventing the spread of illicit narcotics. Yet, in the shadows of that moral high ground lies the story of Jason Cofell—a man who committed unspeakable acts in the name of stopping drug trafficking. His crimes raise an unsettling question: What happens when the fight against darkness becomes a path into it?

By the early 1990s, Canada's drug problem had seeped beyond the borders of its cities. Small towns and rural communities—once seen as wholesome and untouched—were not immune. What would later be called "the opioid crisis" had already begun to unravel quietly across these landscapes. By far the most common street opioid in the 1990s was heroin. It was usually injected, but it could also be snorted or smoked. It could also be mixed with cocaine and injected. The drug was often referred to by slang like smack, H, or horse. It was addictive and expensive. Its users were not confined to big cities. It was everywhere.

Everybody knew it existed, but it was a dirty little secret that seldom made the news. In small centres, drug busts happened, but few were willing to discuss it in the media. It might spoil the locals' reputation for their quiet, rustic surroundings. Yet, when they gathered at coffee shops or bumped into one another on the street, the discussion often turned to the syringes found in an alleyway or to homeless youth disturbing local businesses. Beneath it all, the persistent pulse of addiction—the hunt for the next heroin fix—pushed quietly through the community.

In the 1990s, community newspapers gave no indication of a looming crisis—there was little to no public discussion of what would later become a significant social problem. Fast forward to 2019, when a CBC report shed light on the scale of substance use in the region over the previous decade. The report, authored by Teresa Bendo, Director of Public Health, confirmed what many had suspected but few had spoken aloud: between 2000 and 2020, hospital visits for opioid poisoning among Chatham-Kent, Ontario residents had risen by 225 percent, and hospitalizations by 45 percent. These figures point to the early undercurrents of an opioid crisis that had gone largely unrecognized during the time period covered in this story—except by an underground group of young men whose actions, sadly, resulted in three homicides that greatly shocked the rural area. Indeed, the murders shocked the whole of Canada.

If the police couldn't eliminate the drug problem, could ordinary citizens succeed where authorities had failed? In the Ontario town of Chatham, a covert group stepped in—not as vigilantes, they insisted, but as public servants. Among the earliest of these anti-drug efforts was a group called the Orion Foundation, founded by Jason Shawn Cofell.

Cofell, then a high school student, claimed the inspiration struck during a trip to Toronto in the late 1980s. While visiting the city with his parents for a horse show, he somehow found himself alone in a bar—despite being underage—where he met a man who said he was a drug enforcement officer. What followed was, by Cofell's own account, extraordinary.

He said he witnessed the man being shot, presumably by opioid traffickers, though the injuries weren't fatal. Cofell claimed he transported the wounded man to a warehouse to help him, and the next day, met with him again. The officer, he said, urged him to return to Chatham and form a group to combat the local heroin drug trade.

Inspired by this experience, Jason Cofell founded the Orion Foundation. Though he had no background in mythology, he saw himself as a modern-day disciple of the Furies—the Roman goddesses of vengeance. He embraced the mission with near-religious zeal, determined to correct what he saw as society's failings. This would seem to mark the beginning of Jason Cofell's radicalization. He felt he was doing as instructed by a police officer and was intent on cleaning up the drug trade he perceived was harming his community. It also allowed him to be seen as a leader.

Maybe he or a group led by him could do what the police could not do. They could rid the country of drug dealers who were such a curse on his community. To achieve his goal, he would need followers, and he would need guns. He knew by the action taken against the drug enforcement officer that he could not do this alone. He would need loyal followers.

Cofell returned home and did as he was instructed. He wrote up a Charter containing rules to be obeyed and recruited other grade 11 and 12 students. They formed a paramilitary-style militia group to train the members in procedures and tactics. The target of their aggression was drug traffickers. Once started, the group set out to purchase guns from the United States. The local war on drugs had begun.

Recruitment came easily. Cofell attended a high school that hosted a military reserve group, and he joined the reservists, believing the experience would benefit his covert involvement with the Orion Foundation. While serving in the Essex Kent Scottish Militia Regiment, he became acquainted with military codes of conduct. Although he adapted readily to the discipline expected in paramilitary operations, he received consistently poor evaluations regarding his performance, deportment, and dress.

The Essex Kent Scottish Militia, which included several of Jason Cofell's classmates, offered him a sense of structure that had been largely absent in his upbringing. He lived with his parents and a younger brother, but the household seemed unaware of the depth of conflict and alienation he experienced as he transitioned from boyhood to adulthood. His parents remained oblivious to signs of trouble: a noticeable decline in academic performance, influenced in part by his growing obsession with "Dungeons & Dragons"; a steadily expanding cache of firearms; and an intense fascination with military drills and tactics. Cofell often boasted that he was the highest-ranking officer in the Orion Foundation for nearly three years—without ever disclosing that he had founded the organization himself. His frequent target shooting drew no concern.

His school attendance was minimal, and his marks declined significantly. By September 1991, he considered dropping out of school. He could get gainful employment in the military reserve as a machine gunner. Although he wanted to be a soldier, his main ambition was to stamp out drugs.

Today, Canadians are familiar with alt-right groups such as the Proud Boys. This exclusively male North American far-right neo-fascist organization promotes and engages in political violence in the United States, such as the January 6, 2021 Capitol insurrection. In the late eighties and early nineties, Canadians had no such frame of reference. The public could appreciate street gangs, but young men, especially those connected to Canada's armed forces, were respected even if some members fervently wanted to rid the streets of drug users and sellers by brutal means.

In the fall of 1991, Alfred and Virginia Critchley moved from Newfoundland to Chatham, Ontario. Virginia Critchley had a son, Richard Pangburn. Richard lived in Chatham with his wife Constance, who was usually called Connie, and their children, Julie and Jasen. Alfred and Virginia were in their seventies and had minor health issues. Living with the Pangburns would provide them some security in their elder years.

The Critchleys hoped the move would offer a better opportunity to build a relationship with their grandchildren—an incentive that led them to take up residence with the Pangburns. One of the first things they observed about their grandson, Jasen Pangburn, was his deep involvement in extracurricular activities, which often kept him preoccupied. While attending Chatham Kent Secondary School, Pangburn developed an interest in the local militia, encouraged by several friends already involved.

He formally enlisted on March 28, 1989. Soon after, Pangburn obtained a Firearms Acquisition Certificate, which allowed him to legally purchase a number of firearms and ammunition. He regularly invited fellow militia members to join him for target practice in a wooded area near the Thames River, just east of the family home. Within the household, Jasen was known to proudly display his growing collection of firearms—stored in his upstairs bedroom—to his male peers. Among the weapons, he showed particular pride in an AK-47, a gas-operated assault rifle that symbolized, for him, a kind of authority and identity.

Jasen Pangburn and Jason Cofell met through their association in the Essex Kent Scottish Militia Regiment. Jasen Pangburn shared Jason Cofell's interest in firearms but disliked what he saw as Jason Cofell's illegal means of acquiring them. Jason Cofell was envious of Jasen Pangburn's AK-47.

In late 1990, Chatham Police Service received information from a "reliable source" that Jason Cofell was dealing with stolen guns. Detective Fred Lachine of the Chatham Police Service followed up on the tip by interviewing Jason Cofell. During the interview, he inadvertently let it slip that the informant had the first name "Jasen." Cofell immediately assumed the snitch was Jasen Pangburn. After that, the two never really got along. The relationship further cooled when Cofell overheard Pangburn discussing how reports can be made to Crime Stoppers. To Jason Cofell, this was all the proof he needed that Jasen Pangburn was the rat. Cofell vowed to other friends that Pangburn was going to get it.

To Jason Cofell, his desire to rid the countryside of drug dealers ranked first on his objectives. One disloyal member of his militia should not spoil his attainment of his goal. Action needed to be taken to ensure drug trafficking was forbidden, even if it meant breaking other laws. Jason Cofell was on the hunt to rid himself of the irritant known as Jasen Pangburn.

By the end of September 1991, Jasen Pangburn was running low on cash and decided to sell some of his firearm collection. Jasen took some of his collection to the armouries, announcing his intention to part with some of his collection. Cofell saw the guns and wanted them badly.

Shortly after, a man, now believed to be Jason Cofell, partially dressed in camouflage clothing, stopped by the Pangburn residence. He was met at the door by Constance Pangburn, Jasen's mother. The man introduced himself as "Jason." He asked to see "Private Pangburn." The mother directed Jason to the backyard where Jasen Pangburn was helping his father.

There was a conversation, but the content was never revealed. Jasen Pangburn told his mother that he did not like the visitor and that the guy was crazy.

On October 6, 1991, Jarrod Zimmer and another friend were with Jason Cofell, returning from Toronto. Cofell pulled his truck into the Pangburn driveway. Jason Cofell pulled a handgun from the glove compartment of his truck and put it in his jacket pocket. He approached the house and then went to the backyard. Cofell returned almost immediately. He told his buddies that there were too many people around and that he would have to "do him some other time."

One week later, Cofell met with Zimmer and three others. This time, Cofell is more explicit about wanting revenge. A discussion ensued on the best way to kill Pangburn. Cofell suggested it could be done in a gangland style by entering the house and slaughtering all the occupants.

Everything came to a head on October 18, 1991. Constance Pangburn left home for work at 7:45 a.m. while her husband Richard was away on business. Jasen Pangburn was off to school at Chatham Kent Secondary School while his grandparent, Alfred Critchley, was recovering from surgery at home with his wife, Virginia Critchley.

Jason Cofell attended Pines Secondary School but left at two in the afternoon. Jasen Pangburn left school at about a quarter past three that afternoon, along with a boy we'll call Daniel C. Daniel. Daniel C. wore a Pittsburgh Penguins hockey shirt, an unusual sight in a town where almost everyone cheered for the Toronto Maple Leafs or the Detroit Red Wings.

Daniel C. and Cofell met up at a variety store. Cofell said he intended to sell a shotgun and invited Daniel to accompany him, although he did not specify where they were headed. The two ended up at the Pangburn residence sometime between four and four-thirty. Jasen Pangburn was led to Cofell's truck and was shown the shotgun Cofell said he wanted to sell. Cofell also displayed a .22 calibre handgun capable of firing nine shots. The three young men seemed fascinated by that weapon and proceeded to the wooded area to take some practice shots. A neighbour spotted the three, including the one with the unusual hockey sweater, headed into the bush around four-thirty.

Daniel took the fully loaded pistol and fired three rounds into a tree. He handed it to Pangburn, who did the same. When the gun returned to Cofell, he fired two shots—then turned and aimed the final round at Pangburn's chest.

Pangburn, wounded, tried to flee. He ran a short distance before Cofell struck him in the head with the butt of the pistol, dropping him. Cofell and Daniel dragged him into a heavily wooded area. "Why did you shoot me?" Pangburn asked. Cofell replied, "Because you pissed me off," then kicked him repeatedly in the chest and smashed an empty wine bottle over his head. Finally, he crushed Pangburn's skull with a large rock. Cofell left the body covered with dirt and leaves, warning Daniel to stay silent and obedient—or his family would be next.

But killing Pangburn was only a means to Cofell's true goal: acquiring Pangburn's guns. He had justified the violence as part of a mission to fight heroin trafficking—a claim that made the brutality all the more disturbing. Back at the truck, Cofell handed Daniel a knife and ordered him to conceal it up his sleeve, ready to use when called. They knocked on the door of the Pangburn residence. Mr. Critchley answered. Told that Pangburn's grandfather was expecting him home soon, the men were invited inside. They waited for over fifteen minutes—until the grandfather went to the bathroom.

It was when the two men were alone with Virginia Critchley that Cofell issued his order to stab the grandmother. "Remember what I told you. You don't do this; you're dead."

Daniel C. inflicted three shallow wounds on the older woman. Those stab wounds, it was later determined, would not be life-threatening. Cofell grabbed the knife and thrust it deeply into Mrs. Critchley's throat and neck area. She dropped to the floor. Mr. Critchley was coming out of the bathroom when he was stabbed three times in the chest by Cofell. He fell backward and, in doing so, disconnected the bathroom clock. It read 5:12 p.m.

With no witnesses, the men took Jasen Pangburn's gun collection from upstairs. For good measure, they also stole Mr. Critchley's wallet, money, and identification.

They spotted a woman on a bicycle when they departed the Pangburn residence. It was Jasen's mother returning home from work. Had she spotted Cofell's truck? The men considered returning to the crime scene and giving Constance Pangburn the same treatment. Fortunately for her, a police cruiser was parked on the side of the road near the Pangburn home. Cofell and Daniel C. could not take the chance.

Jason Cofell did not seem troubled by the killings. After the murders, Cofell spoke with his friend Mark Foster. Foster recalled Cofell telling him that when Pangburn agreed to go to the ravine to shoot the pistol, Cofell reacted, "Good. He's taking us to a place where I can kill him silently." Cofell claimed to be fighting heroin crime—but his actions were nothing short of calculated executions.

When Connie Pangburn arrived home from work, she discovered the Critchleys in pools of blood and immediately summoned the police. Virginia Critchley was still alive and trying to speak. When asked who had harmed her, her dying words were to raise two fingers and whisper, "Boys."

Inside the house, police noted that Jasen's guns were missing—and so was he. The immediate suspicion was that Jasen had killed his grandparents, stolen their weaponry, and fled the scene.

Police continued the search outside with the help of a canine unit. Neighbours were questioned. From the responses, it was learned that three young men had been seen crossing the road to enter a nearby ravine at about 4:30 p.m. It was also reported that a uniquely coloured truck had been parked in the driveway.

Later in the evening, the police dog led its handler to the location of Jasen Pangburn's remains. Jasen's parents were distraught about the loss of their son and the Critchleys. The entire community could not recall such violence. A triple homicide had everyone on edge.

In trying to follow up on the leads provided, Connie Pangburn recalled that the man dressed in military garb, who was asking for Private Pangburn days before, had driven up in the uniquely coloured truck. Further tips led police to question Daniel C. about his ownership of a Pittsburgh hockey sweater. Although he denied it or claimed it was lost, his story was unconvincing.

A few days after the killings, Jason Cofell reported a break-in and stolen weapons at his parents' home in Paincourt, a small village near Chatham. The timing—two thefts of gun collections within days—raised suspicion. Police attended the Cofell residence, but something felt off. Ontario Provincial Police (OPP) Constable Philip Wong was assigned to investigate. Jason and his father met him at the door, and Jason handed over a list of allegedly stolen items: several firearms, some jewellery, and coins.

But the details didn't add up. There were no signs of forced entry. A key had been left in the door, and valuables like the stereo, television, and jewellery in the parents' bedroom were untouched. Despite limited evidence, police arrested Jason Cofell and two youths. But to make the charges stick, they would need more.

Police received permission from Jason's parents to search the property. The Cofells lived on a farm, and the expectation of the police that anything would be found seemed miniscule. Yet, upon searching the barn, police found a treasure trove of stolen goods. Not only did they find Jason Cofell's reportedly lost collection, but they also found the guns that had been taken from Jasen Pangburn's bedroom. The stash included

Alfred Critchley's wallet and ID. OPP Constable Glen Hall found the guns, knives, and more than 630 rounds of ammunition. Most importantly, they found the nine-shot pistol used in Jasen Pangburn's murder.

Jason Cofell, was charged on November 1, 1991, with three counts of first-degree murder in the deaths of a fellow militia member and the slain man's grandparents. The charges were laid just two weeks after the killings occurred.

Cofell "was an average 18-year-old," according to his militia commanding officer. "He's a typical citizen, and there's nothing in his file to indicate otherwise," said Lt.-Col. Hardy Wheeler of the Essex and Kent Scottish Militia when asked about Cofell, one of 180 young men under his command.

Provincial police investigators told the media that another arrest in the murders was expected soon but refused to give details. Subsequently, Daniel C., then 15 years old, was arrested and charged under the Young Offender's Act with the second-degree murder of Virginia Critchley. He made a full confession and received a maximum sentence of three years. Another 15-year-old who had helped dispose of the guns was also charged as an accessory after the fact and received a two-year suspended sentence.

The police interviewed Cofell. In the interrogation, Cofell detailed how he had killed Jasen Pangburn by chasing him as he ran, hitting him over the head with the butt of a gun. He also told police about stabbing Alfred Critchley, watching him fall, and hitting his head on the bathroom sink. He described Virginia Critchley lying on her back, bleeding, and uttering the words, "I'm okay. I'm okay."

Cofell told Virginia that he understood and that she "would be [okay]" as he slit her throat. The interviewing police officer was shocked by the forthright admission. "Why would you kill two innocent old people?" he asked. Jason Cofell's response was, "Nobody's innocent."

Jason Cofell hired David Jacklin, a well-regarded criminal defence lawyer. The trial proceeded in November 1992.

Before the trial, Jacklin arranged for Jason Cofell to undergo a psychiatric fitness assessment to ensure he was capable of standing trial. The evaluation was conducted by psychiatrist Dr. Balbhadar Sood, who concluded that Cofell was fit. However, Dr. Sood's report noted that Cofell operated within a distorted internal world shaped by "grandiose, paranoid, and persecuting ideas." These delusions allowed Cofell to justify any actions he deemed necessary to eliminate individuals or institutions he believed were obstructing or violating his self-assigned mission. Dr. Sood suggested that this mindset may have stemmed from an insidious form of mental illness that had been gradually developing since Cofell's adolescence.

Several reports at the Mental Health Centre commented on Cofell's superior intelligence levels and ability to maintain good interactions with co-patients. But when it came to discussing the murders, he presented as exhibiting some form of amnesia and blamed his co-accused, Daniel.

Another psychiatrist, Dr. Angus McDonald, diagnosed Cofell with a mixed personality disorder, marked predominantly by antisocial and narcissistic traits, with additional obsessive features. In his assessment, Cofell was "strikingly devoid of ordinary moral sensibilities"—a chilling clinical observation that underscored the darkness of his psychological disturbance. Yet, despite these troubling characteristics, expert psychiatric opinion could not establish that Cofell suffered from a mental disorder severe enough to meet the legal threshold for not criminally responsible (NCR)—that is, a disease of the mind rendering him incapable of understanding the nature of his actions or knowing they were wrong.

With no basis for an NCR defence, David Jacklin, Cofell's lawyer, focused instead on mitigating the outcome of a mandatory first-degree murder conviction. His primary goal became securing a fair trial and minimizing the impact of local publicity that could bias jurors. He successfully petitioned for a change of venue, moving the trial from Chatham to Goderich, a town approximately 140 kilometres to the north.

The evidence against Jason Cofell was substantial. At the outset, he pleaded not guilty to three counts of first-degree murder, but guilty to the lesser included offence of second-degree murder. Defence counsel David Jacklin had assessed the situation and concluded that Cofell's only chance of avoiding the mandatory sentence for first-degree murder—life imprisonment without parole eligibility for twenty-five years—was to admit to the killings and argue for a reduced period of parole ineligibility. However, Crown Attorney Paul Bailey rejected the plea, and the trial proceeded on all three first-degree murder charges.

The case was heard before Justice James Donnelly of the Ontario Court (General Division) [now the Ontario Superior Court of Justice] and a jury in the first week of November 1992. In his opening statement, Bailey told the jury that in October 1991, 77-year-old Alfred Critchley, his 73-year-old wife Virginia, and their 19-year-old grandson Jasen Pangburn were brutally murdered. He stated that Jason Cofell "participated directly in every one of these murders," motivated by the belief that Pangburn had "ratted on him" to police about his suspected involvement in trafficking stolen firearms.

The Crown Attorney further illustrated the dark and deliberate manner in which Cofell acted. He told the jury that they would hear how Cofell had attended the Pangburn home in Chatham in September 1991 with a loaded .22-calibre revolver but refrained from using it because "there were too many people around."

The Crown was then obligated to prove its allegations by presenting evidence through exhibits and oral testimony. As the trial continued, more than one hundred exhibits were entered, essentially the findings of incriminatory material obtained in search of the Cofell barn. The most damaging was the production of Alfred Critchley's wallet and Jasen Pangburn's silver ring.

As the trial progressed, jurors heard the testimony of Constance Pangburn, the dead boy's mother. She recalled how she returned home from her job at a Chatham daycare centre. She found it strange that the house's entrance door was open, although it was usually kept locked. When she entered, she saw Virginia Critchley lying on the kitchen floor in a "huge pool of blood." Her eyes were still open, and she had "a wound in the throat that pulsated open and shut, but there was no blood coming out." Constance grabbed the phone but found it did not work. She leaned over Virginia and asked, "Who did this?" She repeated what she had told police: Critchley raised two fingers. Pangburn asked if it was men who did this. The dying woman was able to utter the word "Boys."

Constance then found a severely injured Alfred Critchley in the bathroom. Even in the horror of the situation, Constance recalled seeing a police car parked a block and a half away. She left the house on her bicycle to seek the police officer's assistance. Constance and the officer returned to the home, and a police radio call summoned emergency crews to attend. Virginia died in the ambulance on the way to the hospital, and her husband died on the operating table shortly after that.

Even more dreadful for Constance was the news she received the following day. She and her husband believed that their son Jasen was away on a weekend camping trip. The young man's parents were told of his death as well.

The jurors heard from Dr. Marvin Oxley concerning the autopsy performed on Virginia Critchley. Eleven wounds on her arms, hands, and fingers were regarded as defensive wounds, five cuts to the right side of her neck, and two cuts that severed her jugular vein caused her to bleed to death.

OPP Constable Philip Wong was called to describe the investigation after a break-in was reported at the Cofell home. He told of going to the basement accompanied by Jason Cofell's father. Jason seemed calm and asked if there was any way he could help in the investigation.

Sixteen-year-old Jarrod Zimmer told the jury of the visit to the Pangburn home in September. "We thought he was going to kill Jasen Pangburn," Jarrod said, recalling how Cofell had removed a handgun from the glove compartment of his truck and walked alone up the Pangburn driveway. Cofell briefly rejoined Zimmer and his friend and put the gun back in the glove compartment. Zimmer testified, "he said there were too many people back there.... We'll have to come back and do it later."

Eighteen-year-old Steven O'Rourke told the jury about a conversation with Cofell hours after the killings. "He said he had rolled a person by the name of Jasen Pangburn," and explained that to "roll" he understood to mean "to kill someone." He also described the details that Cofell recounted about the murders. The court also heard from another eighteen-year-old, Mark Foster, who detailed Cofell's admissions to him about killing Jasen Pangburn and Jasen's grandparents.

When the calling of Crown evidence concluded, the Crown Attorney forced home his contention that the murders were premeditated. "These plans were foolish; they were brutal, they were senseless, but they were planned," Paul Baily argued.

The defence tried to raise doubt about planning and deliberation. It was noted that he wrote detailed plans for almost every other aspect of Cofell's undertakings. Cofell had considered breaking into a London, Ontario, gun shop to steal weapons. He wrote out a detailed plan for that endeavour. But nothing was written down about the Critchley and Pangburn killings. Although Jacklin admitted the crimes were "horrific," the evidence, he argued, did not show premeditation.

After a two-week trial, Justice Donnelly delivered his charge to the six-man, six-woman jury. The jury deliberated and returned its verdict: "Guilty" to each of the three first-degree murder charges Cofell faced. The sentence was mandatory. Jason Cofell was sentenced to life imprisonment without eligibility for parole for twenty-five years on each of the three counts, with all sentences to run concurrently. The nineteen-year-old would be either in prison or subject to state control even if paroled for the rest of his natural life.

The criminal trial had focused squarely on the murders themselves. The defence relied heavily on psychiatric evaluations in hopes of securing a verdict of not criminally responsible. When that avenue failed, the strategy shifted to damage control—seeking a second-degree murder conviction in order to argue for a reduced period of parole ineligibility, shorter than the mandatory twenty-five years attached to first-degree murder.

What was striking, however, was the absence of any real exploration into why Cofell committed the crimes. The defence never attempted to frame his actions within the context of his self-styled crusade against heroin trafficking—a justification he had voiced in earlier conversations. That twisted rationale, as disturbing as it was, never made it into the courtroom in any meaningful way. The trial confined itself to the more conventional questions of who, when, and where—leaving the why largely unexamined.

At the time of sentencing, section 745 of Canada's *Criminal Code* allowed inmates to apply to have a jury reconsider parole eligibility after serving fifteen years of the life sentence. The press called this the 'faint hope' clause. Before a case would go before a jury for reconsideration, it was necessary to have "judicial screening." In essence, the Chief Justice of the Province would assign the task of evaluating the case by a judge to determine if the case had sufficient merit to warrant a review by a jury. Cofell asked me to make the application. My job was to point out that Cofell had gained the maximum benefit from imprisonment and that we should look to the future rather than retrying past crimes.

Madam Justice Lynda C. Templeton was assigned the file and thoroughly reviewed how well Cofell had adapted to penitentiary life. After his initial placement and classification in a penitentiary, he was "pen placed" in maximum-security Millhaven Institution. He was assessed as rigid in his outlook and was seemingly unaffected upon receiving word of his parents' separation. In July 1993, he was segregated when prison staff concluded he would be unsafe in the general population. A month later, he was transferred to Kingston Penitentiary (KP).

At KP, he enrolled in schooling. He was considered gifted intellectually and demonstrated skills in graphics and drafting. He showed no signs of mental illness, although he was still seen as stubborn, prone to misinterpret the behaviour of others, and inclined to displace blame and criticism. He remained very much a loner. Staff regarded him as soft-spoken, articulate, and realistic about his situation. His overall risk was calculated as low.

He had come to grips with his involvement with the Orion Foundation. He now understood that his beliefs and thinking were radical and extreme during his offences. He admitted that the Orion group obsession was based on fantasy and immaturity, fostered by revolutionary right-wing military propaganda and his fascination with guns. Still, Cofell found difficulty in accepting any personal weakness. He had an intense desire to be regarded as correct and a winner.

He was successful in obtaining a transfer to medium-security Warkworth Institution and upgraded his education.

While all reports showed, as Justice Templeton put it, "little doubt that Mr. Cofell's conduct and character development while incarcerated over the last sixteen years reflect a changing mental and emotional attitude, maturity and a profound and remarkable development of intellect and self-awareness," Justice Templeton could not overlook the pain that Victim Impact Statements had demonstrated. There would be no mitigation of this negative aspect since Cofell has not shown remorse nor anguish that the murders had caused the surviving family members. As such, Cofell's "faint hope" of lowering the parole ineligibility period was dashed. He would have to wait the entire twenty-five years before becoming eligible for parole.

In 2016, Jason Cofell applied for and was granted day parole. He was permitted to reside in a halfway house under strict conditions imposed by the Parole Board of Canada. These included no direct or indirect contact with members of the victims' families, no association with individuals involved in criminal activity or those with a criminal record, and no association with anyone believed to be a member of the Canadian Armed Forces. His parole status was reviewed every six months, and over time, his privileges expanded to allow him five nights per week away from the halfway house.

On January 14, 2020, at the age of 46, Cofell was granted full parole. He informed the Board that he intended to continue operating his leather business, live in an apartment with a roommate, and maintain supportive family relationships. He reflected on his time in prison, stating that the most difficult lesson he had learned was that taking the law into his own hands to combat drug trafficking was a mistake. Although he had believed he was addressing a societal problem, the consequences were ultimately devastating—not only for his victims, but for himself.

Cofell will be under state oversight for the rest of his natural life and must regularly submit to interviews with a parole officer. Cofell has not breached his parole and has successfully reintegrated into the community. There is a stark irony in his trajectory: once a young man who sought to impose vigilante justice in the name of stopping heroin trafficking, Cofell now lives under the enduring and exacting supervision of the very system he once tried to circumvent.

6

Mary Dawson

Dubious Tenure at Kingston Penitentiary

As Warden Lawes once said of convicts,
no man can be called a failure until he has
tried something he really likes and fails at it.

—Sydney J. Harris

THE CITY OF KINGSTON, ONTARIO was poised to celebrate the 150th anniversary of its most infamous institution—Kingston Penitentiary, known informally as KP. The maximum security prison had been constructed in 1833 and 1834 to be the Provincial Penitentiary of the Province of Upper Canada and had been the most significant public building in Upper Canada. Throughout its history, its senior administrators had all been men. Not one of the previous 22 wardens had been female. It was seen as a mark of progress that, for the first time, a woman would be in control. Or would she?

The year was 1984 when Mary Dawson officially became the warden at KP, the first female warden in its history. She had grown up on an Ontario farm and dreamed of becoming a concert pianist. But she married a man who worked for the Correctional Service of Canada (CSC) at Walkworth Medium-Security Institution and, in 1967, 24-year-old Mary was hired at Walkworth as a secretary. Three years later, her duties were expanded when she filled in for an ailing deputy warden in charge of organization and administration, and by

1975, she was in charge of the personnel department, the training programs, and the administrative support services for the prison. By the end of 1975, she had acquired the title of Assistant Warden at Walkworth and by 1980 she became Warden; the first female warden of a male prison in Canada. She was Warden at Walkworth for four years before taking on the role of Warden at KP.

Mary Dawson had not had an easy time when she was warden at Warkworth Institution. Her tenure had been marked by a series of escapes that infuriated residents living near the medium-security prison in rural Ontario. One of the most disturbing incidents involved a 20-year-old inmate named Leslie Beke. Convicted at age 14 for the brutal killing of a London-area farmer, Beke was working on an outside cleanup crew when he slipped away from his guards. Later that day, he forced a 35-year-old Toronto woman—who had been visiting her weekend cottage near the prison—to drive him to Ottawa. The woman was released unharmed at 3 a.m., shaken but alive, and drove herself home. The local community, outraged and fearful, quickly organized a petition aimed at Dawson and their Member of Parliament, George Hees, demanding tighter security.

In total, eight escapes occurred under Dawson's watch—a fact that cemented her controversial reputation in the area. But it was not just the escapes that troubled people. It was the sense that, behind the wire, the rules bent strangely for certain men.

Public outrage peaked after an incident in September 1980 that left even seasoned observers of the prison system stunned. Peter Demeter—a former Toronto real estate developer serving a life sentence for hiring a hitman to murder his wife—was permitted to leave Warkworth Institution. His destination? A poolside cocktail party at the Cobourg home of a penitentiary employee. Demeter did not go alone.

Another inmate, 51-year-old Sydney Rosen, a convicted fraudster and stock promoter, accompanied him, escorted by a female prison clerk. Rosen was a Toronto stock promoter and moneylender. His convictions included conspiracy to defraud $1.8 million in mining stock and perjury.

The *Globe and Mail* report of the incident, published September 18, 1980, is remarkable in the response of prison officials who failed to consider the optics. Demeter, already notorious, had survived a slashing attack while at the maximum-security Millhaven Institution before being transferred to the relative comfort of Warkworth. Now, he was drinking rum and cokes by the pool, while the public—especially victims' families—were left to wonder how justice operated behind the walls.

When Dawson was asked why Demeter and Rosen had been allowed to attend the party, she offered only that they had consumed alcohol but were "not badly under the influence." It was a statement that missed the point entirely.

To the public, the darkness was not just in the crimes that had brought men like Demeter and Rosen to prison—but in the quiet, insidious permissions granted within the system. There was a growing suspicion that for some inmates, prison could be porous, privileges elastic, and punishment negotiable—especially if you knew the right people or navigated the right bureaucracies.

Mary Dawson told The *Globe and Mail* that when Demeter and Rosen were returned to the institution, "I would not consider they were badly under the influence, but they consumed alcohol." The question of why they were allowed to attend the party went unanswered.

That is when the Correctional Service of Canada (CSC) did as was expected and promoted Mary Dawson to Warden of Kingston Penitentiary.

She had just settled into her role as Warden at KP when a letter arrived. It came from the inmates' committee secretary, Sonni McLaren. In stark, incendiary prose, the letter reawakened the dark horror of the 1971 riot:

> If things don't get changed around here, instead of having a 150th birthday with candles on the cake… you will instead be faced with a large bonfire in the centre of this complex and bright lights around the world telling the public of the unnecessary bloodbath.

A few days later in February 1985, Phil Whaley, the guards' union president also delivered a letter. His letter warned Dawson that she might reasonably expect a riot because the guards disliked that she was kowtowing to inmate demands. He wrote:

> It is time you gave firm, clear, and concise directions to start to take control back of this prison before problems get out of hand.

Phil Whaley had been a guard at KP for over 15 years and had been on the job for two years already when, in 1971 the notorious Kingston Penitentiary riot had erupted. He had seen first-hand the havoc a riot could wreak. He ascertained that Mary Dawson's inability to soothe distrust between inmates and guards could become a repetition of the 1971 conflict ... or worse.

Lessons not learned

What had caused the 1971 situation to erupt and how the problem was resolved is worthy of examination. The Kingston Penitentiary riot that began on April 14 had been brewing long before any violence erupted. Among the frustrations inmates were experiencing were overcrowding in the facility, harsh punishments that inflamed resentments, and mental torture brought about by solitary confinement.

The 1971 Kingston Penitentiary riot, incidentally followed six months later by a prisoner uprising at Attica in New York State, convinced administrators that safety valves must be put in place to ensure the brutality of prison riots would not reoccur. One of the measures put in place in 1973, following the Kingston riot, was the creation of the Office of the Correctional Investigator (OCI).

Although the Office of the Correctional Investigator (OCI) was to provide independent oversight of both individual and systemic issues within Canadian prisons, its legislative framework limited its authority from the outset. Reports from the Correctional Investigator were delivered directly to the Minister responsible for corrections, rather than being tabled in Parliament. Moreover, internal administrative reviews of inmate complaints were often conducted by the very staff whose behaviour had prompted those complaints, a structure that typically produced only minor corrective adjustments.

One of the enduring lessons from the 1971 Kingston Penitentiary uprising was the urgent need for independent oversight and greater transparency in how prison policies were created and enforced. At the time, inmates were also gripped by rumours about a new, even harsher form of prison control said to be planned for Millhaven Institution, a new maximum-security penitentiary then under construction just a few miles west of Kingston.

By early 1985, shortly after Warden Mary Dawson's arrival, OCI had been in operation for over a decade but many prisoners at Kingston Penitentiary remained deeply sceptical of OCI's effectiveness in addressing their grievances. Rather than place their trust in official complaint mechanisms, many turned instead to Claire Culhane—a relentless prison justice advocate from British Columbia who spent her pension income travelling across Canada, visiting prisons, listening to inmates, and amplifying their voices beyond prison walls.

Claire Culhane began receiving letters from KP inmates who were worried that changes were in sight that could impact the prison population. In early January 1985, one of the letters Culhane received and copied to me was from a prisoner concerned with the prospect that the prison could devolve into a split population that could reduce yard time and cell placement between those deemed protective custody inmates and those designated to serve their sentences in general population. The prisoner wrote to Culhane that his fellow inmates were concerned things could get ugly if a split population was implemented and that most of the men had signed a petition against the move, but that it didn't mean much. He further advised that the 414 prisoners housed at Kingston Penitentiary were nearing the breaking point. He described how one correctional officer had been pelted with raw eggs and tomatoes while doing his rounds. Prisoners were also upset by the lack of work and restricted social programs. The possibility that increasing the prison population by another hundred inmates, who would not be conditioned to be housed with known police informers and sexual offenders, was driving the frustration level to the breaking point.

Another prisoner, Chuck Armstrong, wrote to both Clair Culhane and Mary Dawson at about this same time. Armstrong objected to windows being bricked over and said that reducing air and light in certain cell block areas was unnecessary. Government cutbacks forced a reduction in things considered essential by inmates. Visiting areas were cramped, and inmates did not have a hot water tap in their cells for washing and housekeeping. Those inmates who could afford a television set could only access those channels that could be picked up on rabbit-ear aerials. Armstrong pointed out that limited financial resources were being spent on frills rather than on what he considered to be severe deficiencies in prison infrastructure. He pointed out that instead of improving prison conditions, the administration constructed a fountain in honour of the prison's 1985 sesquicentennial.

Anger mounted, and prisoners staged a week-long work strike that ended on March 5, 1985. During the week, $17,000 in damage was done to Canada's oldest prison. "Things are going to be heavy," a guard told a prisoner's wife. And things did get heavy.

The 1985 hostage taking

On March 14, four women nurses and a guard were taken hostage by three prisoners in the prison hospital. At 9:30 pm, one nurse was released unharmed after six hours of negotiations. The release was made when the woman was traded for coffee and food for the captors. Relatives of the other hostages were notified but were not offered much information. Staff Sergeant Bernard Jamieson of the Kingston Police told The *Globe and Mail* that negotiations would continue throughout the night. However, prison officials offered little insight into the situation. It was noted that the area where hostages were held had access to radio and television. Correctional Service Canada (CSC) feared that media reports might jeopardize negotiations. Once again, lack of transparency seemed to be the go-to position of the Correctional Service.

Mary Dawson had been presented with a list of prisoner demands when the work stoppage had occurred, and she could not say if the hostage-takings were connected with prisoner discontent. Nothing was resolved, although she met with the five-person inmate committee concerning the demands. Once the hostage-taking occurred, her response showed little sympathy for inmate dissatisfaction. She vowed to be "as tough as the situation demands." Accordingly, she had all inmates confined to their cells with no release until negotiations with the hostage takers ended. The definition of "tough" had already been spelled out the previous July when guards shot a prisoner who had taken a shop instructor hostage.

The hostage-taking did not last long. The four remaining hostages were released after an eighteen-hour ordeal. Prison negotiator Ross Toller held a press conference to explain how the release came about. Toller said,

> The inmates were moving the hostages back and forth [between separate hospital areas] all the time. While the inmates were talking to me, the hostages took the opportunity to move into a separate room. Removing themselves enabled the rescue team to enter.

The hostage-takers surrendered without incident and turned over the homemade knives or "shivs" that they armed themselves with.

Correctional Service of Canada spokesperson Dennis Curtis was pleased to announce that the three hostage-takers, Harold David Cameron, 33, David Wayne Chute, 27, and Ernest Scott, 46, were now in solitary confinement. Curtis did not reveal the names of the hostages. Toller noted that aside from the provision of coffee, food, and cigarettes that led to the early release of one hostage, no formal demands were made. Throughout the negotiation process, the hostages seemed calm and approachable. It was unknown how much of the situation was known in the rest of the institution, although it was admitted that inmates with radios or televisions would no doubt know of the problem.

Punishing the three inmates responsible for the hostage-taking did nothing to alleviate the general prisoner discontent. The hostage-takers were not representative of the inmate population. Their inmate committee, had warned that a "bloodbath" would result unless prison conditions like overcrowding, cold food, and lack of exercise time improved. The treatment of the three did nothing to enhance the reputation of

Warden Mary Dawson with the guard's union, which had been critical of her performance.

Mary Dawson's press conference following the capture of the three hostage-takers did nothing to satisfy the guards' union leaders. Dawson announced an internal inquiry to understand how three prisoners could take control of five staff members. Dawson told reporters that there was no reason to believe the hostage-taking was in any way connected to the inmate discontent that had caused the earlier work stoppage. She offered no insight as to whether her order to lock down the institution and not permit inmate visits effectively dissuaded further violence or if it increased inmate rage against the system. She understood that the atmosphere in the prison had been relatively calm recently and dismissed any motivation the hostage-takers had as symptomatic of inmate unrest. "If publicity is what they wanted, that's what they got," Dawson remarked. Other than eventually prosecuting those involved with taking five captives, there was no announcement as to how the prison aimed to ensure that inmate dissatisfaction would not lead to future and perhaps fatal incidents.

Apropos to Dawson's level of authority, a report from the Solicitor-General's office released in November 1984 had stated,

> Wardens and superintendents [have] little actual authority and no perceived authority to manage their institutions. Institutional authority has been usurped by regional and national functional managers.

Indeed, centralization of authority was cited as a means of controlling inmates. Arthur Trono, the Deputy Commissioner of the Ontario Region of the Correctional Service of Canada, to whom Mary Dawson reported, had said, "We have Commissioner's Directives a foot high. [Wardens] dot the i's and cross the t's for you. There is no room to do anything." Without perceived authority, the fear is that inmates would try whatever they could get away with. A former KP Warden, Andrew Graham, commented that it was essential that a Warden appear to be in command even if they lack the power to make crucial decisions.

When Mary Dawson was appointed warden in Kingston, she was immediately confronted with hostility from inmates and guards alike. Inmate Donald Germaine, high from sniffing glue, acted out by holding shears to a guard's throat and was shot and killed by a fellow guard. Inmate hostility against the guards simmered in the belief that the resolution of Germaine's threat could have been accomplished less violently. The overall inmate hostility continued with the work stoppage and the destruction of property that entailed, as well as the hostage-taking incident. Barry Thorne, a Queen's University Professor and a Citizen's Advisory Committee member, declared, "It's wartime in Kingston Penitentiary right now. Anything can happen."

The guards' union also pressed Mary Dawson to exert authority to control the situation. Graham Stewart of Kingston's John Howard Society commented on the difficult position in which Mary Dawson had been placed, saying,

> She has to break all the ground and meet all the expectations. She's much more public than any other warden in the area and more prone to testing. She has to keep proving herself. I think there's a lot of pressure on her to be tougher than a man.

Creation of H Block

Subsequent to the hostage taking at KP, Mary Dawson took action to soothe distrust between inmates and guards. To her thinking, the best way to deal with the inmate troublemakers and alleviate staff disgruntlement would be to have the most troublesome inmates put into segregation. These inmate leaders could not be sent to solitary confinement without judicial process or transferred to other institutions without substantial reason so her solution was to create a particular cell block where the rabble-rousers could be contained separately from the rest of the population. In essence, Mary Dawson made what we would call a structured intervention unit today. It would be less severe than solitary confinement but be a means to control perceived troublemakers.

The problem was that nothing in the legislation governing prison operations or the Commissioner's Directives would designate who would be kept under these conditions or for how long. Who gets placed there? What sanctions are appropriate—curtailing yard availability, visitation rights, access to media? All these things could be determined later. If the lid was to be kept on this powder keg, the leaders needed to be rounded up and placed in a designated prison section while the cell block was reconstructed around them to fit the peculiar need of their segregation.

One inmate leader confined to H Block was a 27-year-old French Canadian, Howard Massicotte, serving a seven-year sentence for bank- and jewellery-store robberies. I was newly hired at the time by the Queen's University Law School faculty to teach and supervise second- and third-year law students as Director of the Correctional Law Project, a clinical offering at the law school.

My first encounter with Massicotte did not go well. Before the construction of H Block was underway, Massicotte wanted legal intervention to ascertain that either the rifle or, more likely, the ammunition used to shoot Donald Germaine was illegal. Donald Germaine was one of Massicotte's fellow inmates who, high from sniffing glue, had acted out and was killed by a guard. It was not a case I was willing to take on, given that the caseload in which the law students were involved would be better suited to their learning the ins and outs of prison law. However, Massicotte was a self-styled lawyer who used the inmate grievance system to right perceived wrongs for himself and other inmates. He was highly regarded and looked up to by his fellow cons.

Through professional visits, I learned of Massicotte's struggles in determining his legal rights in a newly invented system of segregation and the troubles inmates were having with noise, fumes, and disruptions necessarily involved in constructing the new unit.

I met Warden Dawson at her office across the street from Kingston Penitentiary. This massive limestone building now houses the Canadian Penitentiary Museum.

I entered the building and turned to my left upon entering. Her office was large and well-furnished, with landscapes and seascapes on every wall. She sat at her massive desk with her back to a window, with the penitentiary visible across the street. I sat on an oversized, comfortable chair the Warden had the inmates reupholster for her use when she first took the job. I had hoped to have a meaningful discussion of the inmate complaints and ascertain the Warden's position, but the meeting was short-lived. She went immediately to the bottom line. She stated, "You are no longer allowed to conduct interviews or visits inside Kingston Penitentiary."

Without access to my inmate clients, I could see little hope of helping them obtain a peaceful resolution of their complaints. I was restricted to receiving letters from inmates as my only means of learning what caused their discontent.

Massicotte, whose motto was "The pen is mightier than the sword," was not disheartened. He sent me a moving letter documenting his concerns and what it would take to resolve the inmates' concerns before they reached a breaking point. The letter was so powerful that I mailed a copy to then Solicitor-General Perrin Beatty, requesting a meeting to discuss the matter. An editorial in the *Globe and Mail* pleaded for someone to do something to avert a disaster.

Much to my surprise, I received a call from the Minister's office agreeing to a meeting and setting a schedule for it.

By December 1985, I found out that others were also concerned with the new segregation unit that had been built. My predecessor at the Correctional Law Project and now a practicing Kingston lawyer, Fergus O'Connor, told the *Kingston Whig-Standard*,

> I fear that by creating such a segregation area, the perception of the inmates will be that it is merely an administrative attempt to stifle the most vocal of the inmates. The special handling unit concept at Millhaven Institution didn't reduce violence in any way. The violence continued to escalate. I believe what has always been needed is a vent for the frustrations that build up. That would include more communication between prisoners and staff and between prisoners and the outside world. There is a risk in allowing more freedom, but, in the long term, making things too secure and oppressive will increase the problems. History has proved that.

O'Connor concluded by suggesting that putting inmates into a segregated area with fewer opportunities for meaningful programs would aggravate violence and guards and wardens did not allow inmates to work their way back into the general population, the proposed system could be worse than solitary confinement.

Even with the construction of a new segregated area underway, prison staff still showed signs of discontent. In early December 1985, sixty of about three hundred guards at the prison signed a petition calling for Dawson's removal as Warden. Union President Bernie Evans quickly noted that the petition was started anonymously without union backing. The union confiscated it without being presented. But tearing up the petition did nothing to quell unrest amongst the guards. There was resentment that while they were facing growing inmate unrest, the Warden was absent from the institution. Not only was her office located in a building distant from the penitentiary, but she was busying herself with concerns away from Kingston. For three months in the fall of 1985, Dawson served on a Solicitor-General task force in Ottawa. On her return, she once again departed to tour the Pacific Region. One of her speeches in Vancouver raised eyebrows when she commented that if Canada were to reintroduce the death penalty, the population of KP would be reduced by 25 to 30 percent.

The Ministerial meeting

A meeting had been arranged for me to bring the inmates' concerns to a conference with Solicitor General Perrin Beatty in Ottawa on January 17, 1986. When I entered the meeting room, several upper-echelon CSC personnel were seated across a table and facing me, including the Commissioner of Corrections, Rheal LeBlanc. Shortly after I arrived and was sitting, Minister Perrin Beatty, entered the room. He was wearing a shirt and tie but no jacket. His shirt sleeves were rolled up, indicating he meant business. He took the central seat beside LeBlanc and got straight to the point.

"What do you want done to resolve the situation at KP?" the Minister asked.

"First, I want to be readmitted to speak to clients. Warden Dawson has barred me from entering," I responded.

Beatty looked to his right at LeBlanc and said, "That won't be a problem. Will it?" The Commissioner looked sheepish and immediately responded, "No."

With one problem resolved, the Minister asked me to list other items of concern the inmates had expressed. Everyone at the table was making notes as they set out a litany of inmate demands, including more favourable visiting conditions for family, friends, and lawyers, cable TV outlets installed in the cells, and the most significant demand of all, hot water taps in every cell.

The meeting terminated without a response to the inmates' demands. I was told that the Ministry would study the population's needs and that I would be asked to return to Ottawa in about six weeks to learn of the decision. However, I was warned that all items are off the table if there is any uprising or bloodshed.

I returned to Kingston and conveyed the warning to Massicotte, hoping the inmates could be enticed to remain calm. Because I could now freely enter without restriction, I could deliver the news face-to-face. Massicotte promised he would ensure inmate hostility would be kept in check. Indeed, that is what happened. The inmates settled down ultimately, and no signs of unrest would jeopardize the negotiations. I was worried the night before the date six weeks later when I was to return for the follow-up meeting with the Minister. What if the Minister rejected the demands? Would this give rise to the riotous bloodbath and dark horror of 1971 that we were desperate to avoid?

The next day, I sat at the meeting prepared for the worst. The Minister took his seat and announced that the inmate demands had been studied, and a decision had been made: All inmate demands would be accepted.

On February 27, 1986, Regional Deputy Commissioner Art Trono announced $1.6 million for a new visitor and correspondence unit, $975,000 for hot water in individual cells, and $40,000 for cable TV links. To address guard concerns, a $975,000 emergency locking system would also be installed.

A week later, Finance Minister Michel Wilson delivered a budget that clamped down on government spending. The Correctional Service budget was cut by almost 15 million dollars, a two percent reduction from the previous year. However, the government's commitment to KP upgrades continued, allowing inmates to enjoy increased recreational space and improved kitchen services. In addition to the new remote locking system, it was announced that additional guards would be hired. An increase in the security level envisioned for H Block troublemakers was not approved.

The spending and construction certainly relieved tension. When Kingston Penitentiary closed on September 30, 2013, the possibility of a riot had never again surfaced.

A fragile order

The darkness that lingered over Kingston Penitentiary during Mary Dawson's time as warden was never simply about the crimes committed by its inmates. It ran deeper than violence, beyond the desperate acts of hostage-takers or the tragic death of Donald Germaine in the prison yard.

Time and again, the most disturbing acts were not the dramatic ones splashed across headlines, but those buried in routine decisions and systemic patterns: the creation of H Block without policy or oversight; the blocking of legal advocates from clients; the culture of silence that met inmate complaints with stone walls and bureaucratic evasion. Each was, in its own way, an act of darkness—small, administrative, often invisible, yet corrosive to the fragile order inside the walls.

And yet, it was not violence or repression that ultimately restored a measure of calm to Kingston Penitentiary. It was the restoration of voice. The willingness, however belated, of the system to listen. Hot water taps in cells, improved visiting areas, cable television, and the symbolic return of inmate access to their legal counsel were not just concessions to comfort. They were recognitions, however reluctant, that human dignity remains one of the most powerful tools against chaos.

As for Mary Dawson, the Correctional Service of Canada (CSC) did as was expected and promoted Mary Dawson to a newly created position at Ontario Regional Headquarters.

7

David Miclash

Con Code and Tyranny of Silence

A penal system must be conceived as a mechanism...
to administer illegalities differentially,
not to eliminate them.

—Michel Foucault

Being called a "tattle tale" is one of the most vicious insults that could be levelled against a youngster in a playground. Yet, the prescription of being an informant has become a widespread cultural taboo. University of Toronto's Julius Haag has written about "anti-snitching codes" that are widespread amongst Black youths in disadvantaged communities.[1] He points out that except for cases involving severe harm, most young people are reluctant to report crimes to the police or cooperate in police investigations. He posits that public perceptions of policing have become a barrier to effective crime prevention. His conclusion was that there exists an almost overwhelming dissonance between what police are expected to do and what is being done. He writes:

> Given the importance of crime reporting and witness cooperation in detecting and solving crimes, the pervasive nature of anti-snitching codes should represent a central concern for the police. Without the

1 *Canadian Journal of Criminology and Criminal Justice*, 2022 64, 3, (July / juillet), 71-91.

> willing cooperation of young people in the most affected communities, the Police have little hope of detecting, let alone preventing, many serious crimes.

It has been said that our prisons are a microcosm of society. Given this, snitching would be intolerable within the unique prison society. Prisoners call snitches "rats." Snitching constitutes a breach of the unwritten governance expectations in the prison population. That standard of conduct is called the "con code."

However, unlike the greater society where policing discourages silence from those affected by crime, the attitude in prisons from an administrative perspective is that the con code of not ratting can assist prison administrators in keeping inmates relatively safe. Some inmates require personal details to be kept secret, and prison administrators want to avoid any disruption that exposure of confidential information may cause.

An example is the upset caused in 1999 when a computer at Kingston Penitentiary containing sensitive information was inadvertently turned over to inmates. That computer had particulars that might ordinarily be kept secret in a prison. This information included the crime for which a prisoner was serving a sentence; whether an inmate was a sexual offender, if a prisoner cooperated with police or prison officials, whether the inmate's life had been threatened and by whom, and even, perhaps, if the prison roster designates the offender under an alias due to widespread trial publicity.

The information breach at the now-closed Kingston Penitentiary was treated as extremely serious. Ever-present on the minds of prison authorities was the 1971 Kingston penitentiary riot when sexual predators were rounded up and maimed by a population that dehumanizes pedophiles and sex offenders. Many inmates have been the victims of sexual and physical abuse and lack tolerance for such offenders.

Another class of inmates occupy the lowest rung of the prison hierarchy: informants. These are the so-called "rats", prisoners who provide information to police or prison staff, often leading to another inmate's placement in segregation or transfer to a higher-security facility. In the closed world of prison, this is seen as the ultimate betrayal, an act of darkness committed not against the system, but against one's own.

The unwritten but ironclad "con code" leaves no room for doubt: You don't rat. The penalty is swift and brutal, anything from a savage beating to a violent death.

But silence brings its own peril. In places where secrecy reigns, rumour rushes in to fill the void. And in prisons where trust between guards and inmates has all but vanished, rumour often carries more weight than fact. The violence Kingston Penitentiary narrowly avoided in 1999 erupted two years later at Atlantic Institution in Renous, New Brunswick.

An internal Correctional Service of Canada (CSC) investigation found that prison management had failed to quash a wildfire of rumours, specifically, that the Warden planned to release high-risk offenders into the general population. With no real communication between the keepers and the kept—only suspicion, silence, and shadow—the result was inevitable. Four riots tore through the prison, fuelled not just by anger, but by fear of the unknown.

As the situation at the Renous facility worsened, there was a hardening of attitude rather than a conciliatory approach. Prison staff relied on video surveillance to monitor inmate activity rather than directly associating with the inmate population, which could have permitted "positive staff-inmate relationships," the report found. But maintaining secrecy led to the turmoil that authorities sought to avoid.

The spark that ignited hostilities between guards and

prisoners was as symbolic as it was reckless. During a routine cell search, a correctional officer deliberately burned Sweetgrass—a plant held sacred by many First Nations Peoples. Officers later justified their actions by claiming that Sweetgrass was being used to conceal syringes for intravenous drug use. But the damage was done. Making matters worse, the same search disrespected an Eagle Feather: another sacred object imbued with deep spiritual significance.

What followed was inevitable: prisoners erected barricades, set fires, and smashed furniture. The situation spiralled into a series of riots. Correctional staff were ill-prepared and poorly trained to handle the crisis.

Yet, secrecy itself often operates as an essential—if dangerous—tool of prison administration. In the outside world, police failure to control crime can carry political consequences. "Get Tough on Crime" slogans become easy bait for politicians eager to appear strong while feeding the public a false sense of safety. Inside prison walls, staff function as police, enforcing control over an unpredictable population. Infractions and rule-breaking demand swift discipline to maintain order. But what happens when the public glimpses the truth: that prisons, far from being places of sterile control, are often hotbeds of illicit activity, violence, and cultural disrespect?

For prison officials, the answer has long been to keep the curtain firmly closed. Secrecy isn't just strategy, it's survival. The less the public knows, the safer the illusion of control remains. But when this institutional silence collides with the "con code"—the prisoners' own refusal to "rat"—it breeds a dangerous vacuum. And in that vacuum, dark acts fester on both sides of the divide.

There has been no #MeToo movement in Canadian prisons. In outside society, we appreciate people coming forward and reporting sexual abuse so that the physical and psychological harm that such behaviour causes can be addressed and hopefully curtailed. However, sexual assault in prisons remains a deep, dark secret. Victims are prevented from reporting their assailants because of the con code, and prison administrators are unwilling to confess that they cannot maintain control. The systemic silence perpetuates a cycle of abuse that remains shrouded in secrecy, with little hope for reform unless these barriers are confronted. Secrecy and the con code team up so that the scandal of sexual abuse in our prisons remains undisclosed.

A report published back in 2002 by *The Record* in Kitchener, Ontario, pointed out statistics on Ontario provincial jails that were obtained under the *Freedom of Information and Protection of Privacy Act* (FOIP). The facts disclosed inmate assaults. Guelph Correctional Centre reported 203 cases of inmate-on-inmate assaults between 1999 and 2000. The Metro Toronto West Detention Centre in Mississauga recorded 364 assaults. In the whole of Ontario, there were 4,428 inmate assaults in the 2000-01 fiscal year—a forty percent increase from those reported a decade earlier.

Of course, these statistics do not specify what sort of assaults they were. The numbers could include unwanted touching, such as being pushed, and more serious, violent assaults, such as rape. Since our jails do not report these assaults and inmates are loathe to refer attacks to the police or lay private information to bring the matters to court, the public remains blind to the dangerous situations ongoing in our lockups.

A more recent indication of the scale and persistence of this problem appears in the *Office of the Correctional Investigator Annual Report,* written by Dr. Ivan Zinger. That report offers a stark portrait of sexual victimization existing largely in the "shadows" of Canada's federal penitentiaries—hidden from view, rarely acknowledged, and too often accepted as an inevitable consequence of incarceration.

According to Zinger, the CSC has never conducted research studies on sexual abuse in its facilities, nor does it have clear policies to guide staff on how to prevent or respond to it. Inmate victims, the report noted, are often reluctant to report abuse—whether the perpetrator is another prisoner or a staff member—because doing so risks retaliation, disbelief, ridicule, or even punishment. Inmates indicated they don't feel comfortable reporting and that it would require a basic level of trust between inmates and staff that simply does not exist. The report states:

> They face the risk of not being believed, being ridiculed or even punished for reporting coerced sex. Inmates indicated that they do not feel comfortable reporting and that this would require a basic level of trust between inmates and staff that simply does not exist.

The lack of trust underscores the importance of developing more comprehensive training programs for prison staff, focusing on building rapport and understanding with inmates. Such initiatives could potentially bridge the gap between inmates and staff, fostering a safer and more transparent environment where abuses are reported and addressed.

In a study sponsored by Health Canada by Dr. Frederick Matthews,[2] the author says that there is a disparity in the way we think about abuse when it is done to males. Yet, the ill effects of violence and sexual abuse are just as horrendous for men and boys as they are for women and girls.

Shortly after the Zinger report was released, the then-Minister of Public Safety in charge of Canada's Corrections, Bill Blair, spoke at a press conference. He proclaimed that offenders should be able to serve out their sentences with dignity and without fear. Said Blair,

2 *The Invisible Boy: Revisioning the Victimization of Male Children and Teens*, National Clearinghouse on Family Violence, Ottawa, 1996.

> A zero-tolerance approach to sexual coercion and violence is fundamental to CSC's operations to protect the physical and mental health and overall safety of those who live and work within federal correctional institutions.

He promised that a research study would be conducted on detecting, preventing, and responding to sexual coercion and violence in prisons. However, the promised reforms have yet to materialize in any meaningful way, leaving victims without the support they desperately need. Yet, years later, the secrecy and the con code avoid an open and rational discussion aimed at ending the brutal use of violence and sexual intimidation.

Martin Luther King Jr. said, "The ultimate tragedy is not the oppression and cruelty by the bad people but the silence over that by the good people." In a prison setting, the silence of the victims of oppression by their fellow prisoners because of the con code is reinforced by the secrecy of the prison system itself, which will not admit that wrongdoing exists. It is seldom that these twin forces of oppression are exposed.

Therefore, it is rare that we can glimpse the inner workings of a prison, but *Miclash v Canada 2003* gives us a direct example. On March 2, 2000, two fellow inmates assaulted David Miclash in his cell. Miclash was serving a five-year sentence in a medium-security penitentiary, Joyceville Institution.

Miclash was returning to his cell to be present for the count that was to take place at four-thirty in the afternoon. Upon arriving at his cell, Miclash observed that his cell had been entered by a person or person unknown, and his medications were missing. It was just too much to endure. This was the third time his medication and stamps had been stolen. Although the meds could be replaced, it was a hassle to do so. More concerning was the loss of his stamps. Inmates are paid such a small amount that the cost of a stamp represents a significant expense. He'd had enough. This time, he wanted to find out who was stealing from him.

Miclash initially chose to handle the theft through informal channels, consistent with the unwritten rules of inmate culture. He approached Boston, the inmate committee representative, and explained that his missing property was the work of a "box thief." If the committee could see to it that his belongings were returned, Miclash told him, he would consider the matter settled. In Miclash's view, this approach did not violate the con code. After all, stealing from other inmates was despised behaviour within the general population. Resolving the matter internally, without involving penitentiary staff, was both acceptable and expected.

But the inmate committee reported back that they were unable to identify who had entered Miclash's cell and taken his things. For Miclash, that answer was not good enough. Determined to escalate the matter, he went to the security office vestibule to file an official complaint. When Boston saw him there, the message was clear. Miclash didn't need words to understand that Boston disapproved. The look on Boston's face said it all. Miclash had broken ranks by taking the problem to staff.

The guard's office, or the "bubble" as inmates call it, was staffed by a relatively new correctional officer named Vankoughnett. She had been working at the Joyceville prison for only a month. Before that, she had been a guard at maximum-security Millhaven Institution, where interactions between staff and inmates were rare.

Miclash showed Vankoughnett an empty blister pack and complained that his cell should have been double-locked when he was absent so that a cell thief would have been unable to enter his "house." Miclash said he was frustrated with his treatment and asked to be considered for a transfer elsewhere. Vankoughnett appeared sympathetic. She noted the reported break-in in her log and advised that a report would be made to the nursing staff so that replacement meds would be available.

Boston entered the bubble as the complaint was being recorded. He was not happy. Vankoughnett ordered Miclash back to his cell, saying arrangements would be made to replace the pills quickly. Miclash complied by returning to his cell. Boston knew Miclash's visit to the bubble and confronted Vankoughnett to advise the officer that other inmates on the range wanted Miclash to move.

Shortly after, Boston and another inmate known only as "Johnny" entered Miclash's cell. Johnny grabbed Miclash's arms to prevent him from defending himself, while Boston punched Miclash with considerable force in the cheek. The first punch was followed by a second and a third. By this time, Miclash was in extreme pain and almost unconscious. Blood was streaming from his nose and oozing from his mouth.

One of the punches was near his ear. This left a ringing sensation that added to his discomfort. Once the beating had been administered, Boston and the man known only as Johnny left the cell. Miclash then realized it was likely Boston who was the cell thief. Going to staff with the complaint was considered a breach of the con code. But if indeed Boston had been the perpetrator, he had much to lose since nobody in the prison had any regard for a box thief.

Miclash was given medical treatment for his injuries and was placed in voluntary segregation until he was transferred to Mountain Institution, another medium-security penitentiary in Agassiz, British Columbia. Besides a broken jaw, Miclash suffered tinnitus and problems with his equilibrium. Eventually, he made a full recovery.

The pain and suffering inflicted upon Miclash inspired him to try something new. Miclash hired me to assist him in seeking a judicial remedy. The Statement of Claim in the lawsuit criticized the Correctional Service for breaching the duty to keep him safe while in state custody. Case law developed at that time recognized the obligation to keep inmates safe. However, the prison service always defended claims because it should not have had to compensate when it could not have known that an attack would be made.

One of the methods the Correctional Service used to determine if there was hostility between inmates relied on inmates themselves to declare incompatibility. In this case, Miclash had no prior dealings with Boston and was unaware of incompatibility.

The defence of lack of knowledge that harm would occur to Miclash was at the heart of the prison's defence to the civil action. However, in deciding if liability for harm existed, the presiding judge, Prothonotary (principal court clerk) Rosa Aronovitch, addressed the defences in allowing Miclash's action in the Federal Court of Canada. She wrote:

> I take the point that the consequences of breaches of the "con code" may not be fixed and invariable; that situations may be resolved or diffused through the intervention of staff, and finally that there has to be some reliance on the judgment of front-line officers in assessing the degree of risk to a particular inmate at a given time. That said, while these events transpired in a relatively short time frame, and the absence of factors like inmate incompatibility, I find that the harm to Mr. Miclash in the circumstances was not unpredictable, to the contrary.

In the circumstances, the court held that although the correctional officer was capable, her lack of experience blinded her to a much too ready acceptance that Boston, whom the court suggested "was the perpetrator and likely cell thief," was a danger to Miclash. The court ordered the award of $12,000 in damages to compensate inmate Miclash for his injuries.

The amount of money awarded is minor compared to the case's significance. It was because the Miclash case was one of the first to undermine the reliance that the Correctional Service is not immune from risk because of the degree of silence required by the "con code" and from its reluctance to admit error.

A press report in the *Kingston Whig-Standard* on February 3, 2003, summarized the judgment. The report read,

> The judgment means that prison authorities must analyze all information relating to the safety of inmates, including unwritten but well-known codes of conduct....The judgment could lead to a flood of inmates seeking redress for attacks that they argue Corrections should have foreseen.

Although the case has been cited in other judgments, it has not led to the flood of litigation the Kingston reporter predicted. Instead, the silence of both the inmates and their keepers, the silence of both the oppressors and the oppressed, continues. Theft, violence, and sexual abuse continues unabated. It won't go away just because we don't admit it happens.

8

Michael McGray

Serial Killer in Plain View

I'm a lean dog, a keen dog, a wild dog and lone;
I'm a rough dog, a tough dog, hunting on my own;
I'm a bad dog, a mad dog, teasing silly sheep;
I love to sit and bay the moon to keep fat souls from sleep.

—Irene Rutherford McLeod

IN LATE 2016, longtime Moncton, New Brunswick, SPCA employee Claude Paquet lost his job and was convicted of willfully causing unnecessary pain, suffering, and injury to an animal. A vicious dog brought into the shelter had bitten Paquet. When the dog attacked, Paquet kicked the dog. He was charged with animal cruelty. Pacquet was represented in court by Moncton lawyer Myer Rabin.

"The dog grabbed Mr. Paquet's arm, and he just lost it," Rabin told the court during sentencing. The defence counsel argued there was no intention of cruelty; it was a reflex action. He hoped the judge hearing the case would impose a discharge rather than accept the Crown's position that the 31-year animal shelter employee should be placed on probation for injuring the black Labrador mix scheduled to be euthanized.

Judge Troy Sweet was unimpressed. "You're very lucky the Crown wasn't looking for jail time because I would have given you 15 days for what you did to that poor dog," said the judge, glaring at Paquet. He added that the SPCA is supposed to be the place where animals find refuge and protection, not more abuse.

Myer Rabin, defence counsel, had faced a far more disturbing vicious dog case six years earlier. The family of Jeremy Phillips retained him to bring suit against the Correctional Service of Canada (CSC)—a case steeped in tragedy.

Thirty-three-year-old Jeremy Phillips had been in good spirits in the weeks leading up to his anticipated release from Mountain Institution in Agassiz, British Columbia, in November 2010. He was nearing the four-year mark of a six-year sentence for aggravated assault, a sentence imposed after an altercation in his Moncton apartment. Statutory release was just weeks away. Phillips had plans. He intended to return to Moncton to care for his mother, who had suffered devastating injuries in a fire and was grieving the recent death of her husband from cancer. But Phillips never made it home.

His killer was his cellmate, 47-year-old Michael Wayne McGray, a man whose acts of darkness were neither hidden nor subtle. In a 2000 CBC News interview, McGray openly embraced his violence. "It's like a craving or hunger," he said. "It's something I have to do… It gets to a point where I can't control it anymore."The CBC News interview was a precursor to this tragedy. On being convicted for an earlier murder, McGray commented,

> Just because I'm locked in prison doesn't mean the killing's going to stop. I mean, I'm almost on the verge right now where I'm going to commit another one. I'm very, very close, and it's almost inevitable that it's going to happen again. I can't control it.

McGray had been convicted of six murders but was proud that his body count numbered sixteen.

As a former Correctional Investigator said, one goes to prison as punishment, not for punishment. To paraphrase what Judge Sweet, the judge in the animal cruelty case, would later say, "[Prison] is supposed to be a place where [prisoners] find refuge and protection, not more abuse." The Phillips family decided to sue for compensation for Jeremy's loss. The family retained Myer Rabin to process their claim.

Bringing a lawsuit against McGray would be pointless. He wouldn't be eligible for parole until he was 72 and still highly likely ever to see release. He had no assets. After all, you can't get blood from a stone. The deep pockets rested with CSC. Rabin would have to prove that CSC expected that violence would ensue and let it happen. Rabin had scant knowledge of how the prison system operated. He asked me to join him as co-counsel in his lawsuit. I agreed.

Michael Wayne McGray

Like many inmates in federal penitentiaries, McGray did not have a fairy-tale upbringing. He suffered from sexual abuse and was beaten by his father as a small child.

Even before McGray amassed a series of murder convictions, he had built up a sizeable criminal record. His first conviction was on December 21, 1982 in Yarmouth, Nova Scotia for dangerous use of a firearm. He was sentenced to five months imprisonment. In the next ten years, he ran up a string of convictions for theft, forgery, assault, and mischief. The record is strewn with convictions for parole violations and misconduct while supervised. All convictions were in the maritime provinces except for a sentence registered in Provincial court in Brighton, Ontario, where fifteen months was added to his sentence for theft over $1,000 and assaulting a peace officer. He was serving time at Ontario's Warkworth Institution.

During a 1991 three-day pass from La Macaza, a medium-security prison in Quebec, for the Easter long weekend, McGray went to Montreal and killed Robert Assalay and Gaetan Ethier. He had met up with 59-year-old Assalay in a

Montreal gay bar, returned to Assalay's home, and slew him with a knife. The next day, he met 45-year-old Ethier in another gay bar. Upon returning to Ethier's home, McGray smashed a beer bottle over Ethier's head and stabbed him. Police did not suspect his involvement, and he returned to serve his prison sentence without suspicion of having committed homicides.

When McGray was paroled in 1993, he returned to Halifax and hooked up with a girlfriend named Tammy. The two drifted across Canada and into the United States for the next four years, returning to Halifax occasionally. Tammy became pregnant and in February 1995, gave birth to a baby boy. The child died from medical complications three days after being born.

McGray and his girlfriend held down jobs in North Dartmouth. Tammy worked as a maid at a hotel, and Michael worked as a landscaper at a seniors complex. They were renting an apartment on Brule Street in North Dartmouth. McGray became a heavy drinker.

The Halifax authorities received numerous reports of missing persons. They had been warned that Michael McGray had moved to the area. Even though Halifax police maintained a log of missing persons, McGray's name was never attached to any disappearances, although he was considered a suspect responsible for missing persons.

He had no contact with police until June 10, 1995, when police attended the Brule Street residence where McGray slit his wrists in a suicide attempt. In a note he left, Tammy blamed his depression for losing the child. Tammy had discarded the note but told police her memory of the contents:

> It said something like I…It's not your fault…It's my fault…blame myself for my son's death…fer [sic]… stuff I've done in my past…and this how [sic] God's paying me back…

By 1998, Michael and Tammy were living in Moncton, New Brunswick. It was there that Tammy met Joan Hicks, a 48-year-old homeless mother who had travelled from Newfoundland to New Brunswick with her eleven-year-old daughter, Nina. Joan's goal was unusual—she hoped to marry a prisoner she had been corresponding with by letter.

On March 1, 1998, police were called and advised that Michael McGray had slashed Joan and Nina's necks. McGray was arrested and admitted to killing Joan but denied killing the daughter. The admission that he killed Nina did not come out until 2001 when he said his denial was on account of not wanting to be branded as a child killer in prison.

For killing Joan and Nina, McGray was sent to the maximum-security Renous Institution in New Brunswick. He spent years in solitary confinement. He had been in solitary since 1998 and concluded that the only opportunity to achieve release into the general population would be to confide in the prison psychiatrist.

In the 2003 letter to the psychiatrist, McGray divulged that he had experienced hearing voices and screams that were getting closer, right outside the window of his cell, and the voices "can bore right into my head." He also admitted to seeing phantoms. It had him worried. He wrote,

> I am really scared of what I am going to see…I am afraid that I am going to see something truly horrifying, and every day, I feel it's coming closer to revealing itself.

Some would see this letter as a ploy to obtain sympathy and perhaps a release from solitary confinement to a psychiatric hospital. The concept that solitary confinement is torture and can have lasting and permanent effects on those subjected to it was little understood. It was not until the work of such people as Dr. Stuart Grassian of Harvard University, who studied the dehumanizing effects of this abusive treatment, that correctional authorities and the courts were made aware of the damage that it inflicted.

It is not as though McGray deserves sympathy. He was himself motivated by dehumanizing attitudes. The letter sent in 2003 to the institutional psychiatrist talked of his killing "suitable victims." These included marginalized victims already looked down upon by polite society: sex workers, gay men, and prisoners.

The intensity of McGray's inner turmoil is caught in one passage from his letter:

> Doctor, it's not that I have an anger problem. I'm sure I do, but I have to hurt people to survive. It's like food or air. I need it so badly. Sometimes, I feel the only reason to go on living is so that I can kill an inmate someday and have that release again.

McGray took great pains to assure the psychiatrist that any future victim would not be a guard. The "suitable victim" would most assuredly be a fellow penitentiary inmate. He addressed this succinctly:

> I do have a hunger and urges, but I have always been able to control them until I found a suitable victim. An inmate may be a suitable victim, but a guard is definitely not!

By the time he was transferred from Renous Institution to maximum-security Kent Institution in British Columbia, he had been convicted of six first-degree murders, including the stabbing death of Elizabeth Gale Tucker, a New Brunswick teenager, and Saint John resident Mark Gibbons. The CSC should have been well aware of his past and the letter written to the psychiatrist at Renous as an indication of his future.

The Phillips Murder

Even with this substantial body of information on file, the case managers at Renous looked kindly on McGray. No doubt, their satisfaction with this inmate was due to his willingness to consult with staff about the wrongdoings of his peers. It is a mortal sin in the penitentiary to "rat" on one's fellow cons, but McGray enjoyed the favours that breaking the con code bestowed upon him.

A proper reward the CSC managers allowed was a transfer to a medium-security Mountain Institution. The facts surrounding Jeremy Phillips' death are concisely set out from the presiding coroner's summary published following the October 2012 inquest:

> At 0958 on November 22, 2010, a call for assistance was made to the on-duty Correctional Officer from cell A1 at Mountain Institution in Agassiz, B.C. Two Correctional Officers (CX1 Janzen and CX2 Woods) responded to the cell. They found inmate Mr. Wayne McGray standing at the cell door, requesting that they check on the wellness of Mr. Jeremy Michael Phillips. Mr. McGray claimed that Mr. Phillips had not responded to his earlier attempts to wake him. The officers testified that they entered his cell, attempted to wake Mr. Phillips, and noted that he was 'cold to the touch and stiff upon turning him'.
>
> The officers immediately summoned medical assistance. Nurse Bonita Hess was working in the adjacent living unit and responded within seconds. Nurse Hess testified that she checked for a pulse, but there was none. She testified that *rigour mortis* and *livor mortis* were present and that Mr. Phillips had been 'dead for a while.' Other medical personnel, including an on-site physician, responded to assist, but Mr. Phillips was deceased.

Shortly after Mr. Phillips was found, Mr. McGray admitted to correctional staff that he was responsible for the death. He subsequently made the same admission to the police. The jury viewed a warned video statement that was taken by police on the evening of November 22, 2010, wherein Mr. McGray described the sequence of events that led to Mr. Phillips' death. Mr. McGray alleged that both he and Mr. Phillips jointly hatched a plan to fake a hostage-taking scenario. The intended outcome was that Mr. McGray would be moved back to Kent Penitentiary and Mr. Phillips would get time off at the infirmary or possibly early release.

The findings of the coroner suggest that the murder of Jeremy Phillips was a scam gone wrong. It is not for a coroner's inquest to assign blame or wrongdoing. However, the coroner's jury viewed the videotape of McGray's statement to police, which would cause jurors to suspect the killing was not as genteel as the recorded summary suggests. That recorded interview contains McGray saying the following:

> You fuck with me; somebody will fucking pay. They always fucking pay. I'm a sociopath. I'm a serial killer. I shouldn't be here [at Mountain Institution]. I shouldn't be in medium. I'm not a medium inmate. I've never been. I didn't have any problem with Jeremy. I didn't know the guy. It is what it is. It's just another sentence to me.

The suggestion that Phillips and McGray hatched a scheme to stage a hostage-taking for mutual benefit overlooks the fact that Phillips objected to being "double-bunked" with McGray and had requested that McGray be moved. Is it likely that Phillips could have refused to go along with McGray when McGray dreamed up the hostage-taking plot? Could it be that McGray's instincts to kill another vulnerable person had taken over?

The Civil Suit

Mayer Rabin commenced a civil suit on behalf of the Phillips family, seeking $11 million in damages for the wrongful death of Jeremy Phillips. He asked me to act as co-counsel in the action—a case that would expose not only McGray's monstrous violence but the institutional blindness that allowed it to unfold.

Several Mountain Institution inmates were prepared to testify that Jeremy Phillips was a well-liked individual, terrified of McGray, and desperate to be moved out of their shared cell. His requests were met with indifference. He was told to "just suck it up."

McGray himself had also asked for a cell change. At Kent Institution, he had enjoyed the isolation of a single cell—a privilege befitting his notoriety and danger. Being placed in a two-to-one cell situation was, in his eyes, a humiliation. For a man like McGray, it was a provocation.

His correctional records painted a chilling portrait: a history of brutal violence and a stated desire to kill again, particularly if his victim was another inmate.

These were not hidden impulses. They were documented, known, and ignored. Acts of darkness are sometimes committed in full view, aided by silence, indifference, or misjudgment.

Nothing in McGray's record suggested rehabilitation. His only currency with Kent staff was cooperation, a shallow indicator of compliance, never of safety. There was no reasonable basis, no logical rationale, for moving him out of maximum-security Kent Institution. But move him they did, and Jeremy Phillips paid for that decision with his life.

The lockdown at Mountain Institution confined inmates to their locked cells throughout the evening in which Phillips had been killed until the following day, when the body had been discovered. Cells are supposed to be checked regularly throughout the day and night to ensure they are occupied by living, breathing bodies. Why had Phillips' death taken so long to discover? The Department of Justice lawyers had no logical explanation for the missteps taken by Correctional Service Canada staff.

The case was settled by mediation before going to trial. The Phillips family accepted the sizeable settlement and signed a nondisclosure agreement. The public was barred from hearing the amount the Correctional Service had to pay. CSC has never admitted liability, and requests by news outlets as to what has been done to ensure that dealings with dangerous inmates such as McGray never happen again.

The Aftermath

Who should answer when mistakes are made? Should the Minister responsible for overseeing the Correctional Service of Canada be held to account if errors are made? Should the Minister be advised of high-profile prison transfers? Should the Minister have the right to intervene to block transfers approved by officials in his department?

Such questions arose again in 2023 when departmental officials approved the transfer of serial killer Paul Bernardo from maximum-security Millhaven Institution to medium-security La Macaza Institution in Quebec. The sudden and unexpected transfer set off a firestorm of criticism, most notably from the lawyer who had represented the families of Bernardo's victims.

Despite my involvement in criticizing CSC for the horrendous outcome of the McGray transfer, I could not join the uproar the Bernardo transfer was causing.

The situations between McGray and Bernardo were very different. Bernardo had not killed another person again as an inmate and has never voiced any intentions of doing so. The transfer from an institution where he was receiving little by way of rehabilitative programming to an institution that offered specific treatment was logical.

Of course, as with McGray, mistakes can be made. Upon being criticized, it was reasonable for the Minister to request the CSC review how decisions in the Bernardo case were made and, if made contrary to common sense, re-evaluate the transfer. It would be seriously wrong for a Minister to overrule his departmental officials and put in place a directive that might be more politically popular.

There was an outpouring of emotion that people like Paul Bernardo should be locked away forever in maximum-security institutions. That dehumanizing attitude reflects the same consideration McGray gave to his victims. Suppose a penitentiary inmate remains dangerous even after exposure to rehabilitative programming. In that case, it is appropriate to detain that person in custody at the required security level for as long as necessary.

Mistakes have been and will continue to be made. They should be reviewed, and an admission of their making and what corrective actions will be implemented. It is crucial to recognize that the correctional system's ability to learn from these errors and improve should be considered a positive aspect of our justice system. A willingness to reassess and correct mistakes shows a commitment to fairness and justice, which is essential in a democratic society.

Furthermore, treating inmates with dignity, even those convicted of heinous crimes, reflects our society's values and our belief in the potential for rehabilitation. This approach not only upholds human rights but also increases the chances of successful reintegration into society for those who one day may be released. The worst possible outcome is to assume the offender is less than human and act with a vengeance on that account—the treating of inmates as "vicious dogs" rather than as human beings demeaning us all. If the SPCA is a place where vicious animals are supposed to find refuge and protection and not more abuse, as Judge Sweet stated, shouldn't the same be said of Canada's prisons?

9

Brian Donald Hickey

Losing Control

Prisons do not disappear problems;
they disappear human beings.

—Angela Davis

Brian Donald Hickey has also been likened to a vicious dog. Was it anger towards his stepfather that caused Brian Hickey to lash out? Was it the emotional scarring after he was raped at age 12? He grew up in Toronto's poverty-stricken Regent Park neighbourhood, built in the late 1940s as a public housing project. He relocated to Vancouver, British Columbia. It can be said that Brian Hickey's adolescence was not typical of young men growing up in any city in Canada. He left home and was spotted hanging out in gay bars when he was 15 years old. What could go wrong?

Police had recorded complaints from five men who were violently robbed after taking home a young man they had met in a gay bar. But by mid-May 1995, the situation became much more severe. A hotel executive from the resort town of Whistler was found dead in his 15-floor West End, Vancouver apartment. Someone had beaten 40-year-old John Morgentale, struck him on the head with a cylindrical object, and asphyxiated him. Morgentale and his pick-up had left a bar on May 20.

The Fairway Hotel in Whistler, where Morgentale worked, had recently been recently sold, but Morgentale stayed to assist in transitioning to the new owner. He finished work on Friday, May 19, and told fellow employees he was heading to his apartment in Vancouver. He expected to return to work the following Tuesday. His body was found on May 26.

The police issued a warning that the murder began similar to robberies that had been reported earlier. The victim would meet someone in a bar, return to an apartment, and then be beaten and robbed.

The number of robberies could have been higher than the police were even aware of. Pick-up robberies in the gay community are not commonly reported. Many victims are just too embarrassed to admit what had transpired.

But a murder in the community caused widespread concern. After about a week of investigating the killing, police urged bar patrons to be much more careful. The person who killed John Morgentale should be considered desperate and dangerous. A Canada-wide arrest warrant was issued for 28-year-old Brian Donald Hickey on the charge of second-degree murder.

A volunteer group called Q Street Patrol, with the support of Vancouver police, handed out pamphlets with Hickey's photo. People who may have seen the good-looking blond man, 183 centimetres tall (about 6 feet), weighing 68 kilograms (150 lbs.), and who may be sporting a scruffy beard or mustache, were urged to call the police immediately.

Then, there were reports of people who had suspected they'd had prior dealings with Hickey. Kerry Owens, a 28-year-old Vancouver car rental agency manager, spoke with the *Vancouver Sun*. "He's a psych," Owens said after having been bound and gagged at knifepoint. "I was a basket case afterwards," he recalled having spent months in psychotherapy. "It was more psychological than anything else, but he was full of hate, absolutely full of hate. He's very violent." A darker human being is not likely to be found.

The Q Street Patrol printed three thousand leaflets as "Wanted" posters, urging anyone spotting Hickey to come forward. The media also posted Hickey's picture.

Then, on June 3, 1995, police had the break they wanted. Hickey was spotted by a vendor at Vancouver's nude beach (Wreck Beach). The man was somewhat different from the photos that had been distributed because Hickey had dyed his hair black.

Within minutes after the reported sighting, police dispatched officers and search dogs. Hickey surrendered himself without incident in bushes near Trail Five. Hickey was transported to the Vancouver police station, where fingerprints confirmed his identity. He was scheduled to appear in provincial court the following day.

After news of the arrest spread, the gay community was ecstatic. Many wanted to change the word "Wanted" on the posters to "Captured." People gathered in the streets, celebrating until three o'clock in the morning.

Punishment

On April 18, 1996, Vancouver's *The Province* newspaper bore the headline: "'Predatory' killing of gay man nets life." British Columbia Supreme Court Justice Pamela Kirkpatrick sentenced Hickey to life imprisonment without eligibility for parole for fifteen years. The prosecutor, Kerr Clark, had urged the judge to impose a sentence beyond the minimum for second-degree murder.

Instead of limiting parole eligibility to ten years, Clark impressed upon the judge that the circumstances warranted an increase. The circumstances of the killing were horrendous. Morgentale had been beaten, hogtied, and stuffed into an old steamer trunk, where he suffocated. His apartment was ransacked, and his credit cards were stolen. Police traced the use of the cards to prove Hickey had used them to make purchases and withdraw from bank machines. Hickey's previous record included over thirty convictions for theft, robbery, and assault. Hickey had shown no remorse in court.

The court was made aware that Hickey had been the victim of a sexual assault and had, as a teenager, hung out in gay bars. It did not look to why Hickey may have been so angry as to carry out a severe escalation of his anti-social behaviour. The community, particularly the gay community, sought vengeance. Since a life sentence was mandatory, the only way to appease this vengeance was to increase the years of parole ineligibility. That is precisely what Justice Kirkpatrick did.

In hindsight, we can see a young man who had been sexually abused taking out his anger by victimizing gay men. He failed to show remorse because he saw himself more as a victim than an oppressor. Going to prison increased his rage. However, for the Correctional Service (CSC), the only way to tame a vicious dog is to beat it more.

His first penitentiary placement was at Matsqui Institution in British Columbia in June 1996. About two years later, in 1998, he was transferred to Kent Institution, also in British Columbia. On May 27, 1999, Hickey was notified that he was to be involuntarily transferred from the maximum-security Kent Institution to the Special Handling Unit (SHU) in Quebec. On September 1, 1999, the Acting Assistant Deputy Commissioner of the Pacific Region upheld the decision to transfer after Hickey had sought to use the internal dispute mechanism to challenge the decision. Hickey understood that moving to the SHU would mean physical removal from any contacts he had made in British Columbia and mental restraint since the SHU required extensive time in solitary confinement. The aim of taming the whipped dog resulted in more aggressive whipping.

Before the transfer occurred, Hickey had a lawyer apply for *habeas corpus* to quash the decision of the CSC and order that he not be transferred out of the Pacific Region without leave of the Court. That application was dismissed. The Supreme Court of British Columbia found that it did not have jurisdiction to order a federal board to cancel the transfer.[1]

Undeterred, Hickey appealed that decision to the British Columbia Court of Appeal. A written ruling was handed down on January 16, 2003 (*Hickey v. Kent Institution*, 2003). Hickey achieved a partial victory. The appeal delayed his transfer for years. The Court of Appeal found that Madam Justice Loo, who had ruled on the original application, had erred in law when she concluded that the Supreme Court of British Columbia lacked jurisdiction to hear the habeas corpus claim. But that was only half the battle. The Court of Appeal noted that Hickey had failed to provide evidence showing he had pursued other available remedies, such as using the inmate grievance procedure or filing a judicial review in Federal Court. While the appeal court accepted it had jurisdiction to consider the matter, it exercised its discretion to dismiss the appeal.

Ultimately, the transfer proceeded. Hickey was moved to the Special Handling Unit (SHU), Canada's highest-security federal facility. His stay there ended in May 2000, when he was transferred to Ontario's maximum-security Millhaven Institution. That placement proved short-lived. Whether due to the nature of his offence or institutional considerations, Hickey was voluntarily moved just a few months later, in August, to Kingston Penitentiary, a facility known for its protective custody population.

His journey through Canada's prison system continued. In May 2001, Hickey was transferred once again, this time to Warkworth Institution, a medium-security prison.

1 *Hickey v. Director,* Kent Institution, unreported, Oral reasons of Madam Justice Loo dated November 12, 1999.

Diagnosis

Hickey was in ill health when he first arrived at a federal penitentiary. When he was first placed at Matsqui Institution, he was diagnosed as having been infected with the human immunodeficiency virus (HIV). At the time, he was under the care of contract physician Dr. E. Dick.

Dr. Dick referred Hickey for care and treatment by an HIV specialist, Dr. J. Montaner, the Director of the AIDS Research Program and Infectious Disease Clinic affiliated with St. Paul's Hospital in Vancouver, BC. Dr. Montaner met with Hickey twice: once in October and again in November 1996. Dr. Montaner recommended a course of antiviral medications to treat HIV. One of the drugs recommended was a medication called d4T or Stavudine. The prescribed dosage was a 40 mg tablet to be taken twice daily. Dr. Dick accepted the recommendation. However, Dr. Dick incorrectly noted the amount of medication, causing the penitentiary to administer twice what Dr. Montaner had advised. The error was found in February 1997. Employees of the Health Care Unit at the prison administered the dosage.

After the drug was taken, Hickey developed severe pain, he described it as an intense burning sensation in his feet. The pain at times was intolerable and resulted in hypersensitivity, making it unbearable to wear shoes, socks, or be under bedclothes. The situation was diagnosed as peripheral neuropathy. The neuropathy spread not only to his lower legs but also to his hands.

Although it was admitted that Hickey had been given an incorrect dosage of d4T, who was to blame for the resulting neuropathy? Medical experts agree that d4T can cause neuropathy even in recommended doses. HIV can cause neuropathy. The doubling of the recommended dosage could exacerbate the development of neuropathy. Should the CSC be liable for the inmate's pain and suffering given that penitentiary employees had provided the incorrect dosage?

Progress notes maintained by Health Care revealed Hickey had been given d4T and two other HIV medications starting on November 19, 1996. The d4T provided was 40 mg. four times per day. Dr. Dick was alerted that Hickey was complaining of pain, and a month later, on December 18, 1996, discussed the use of morphine for pain control, even though the AIDS specialist, Dr. Montaner, had not made any recommendation for pain relief.

Hickey reported his pain to the British Columbia Persons with AIDS Society, who wrote to Dr. Dick about the complaints of severe discomfort. By January 17, 1997, Hickey had had enough. He returned all his prescribed medications to the prison Health Care unit.

Dr. Montaner reviewed the situation. He believed the d4T caused neuropathy and found the error. His recommended amount bore the notation "bid," meaning twice a day, while the nursing notes recorded "qid," meaning four times daily.

Hickey launched a lawsuit claiming damages for the pain he experienced due to the recording error (*Hickey v. Canada*, 2007). In arguing the case, I tried to stress that it was prison employees who incorrectly interpreted the expert doctor's instructions and continued the medications even after complaints of adverse reactions were made.

In what has been called a "controversial case,"[2] a Federal Court judge dismissed the suit. The case held that the doctors were independent contractors, and the prison administration was not liable for their errors.

Even though the legislation establishing Canada's prisons states that prisoners are entitled to the same rights as all Canadians, they cannot enjoy those rights that are necessarily limited because of a prisoner's incarceration. The authors of the academic article point out:

2 Adelina Iftene, L. Hanson & A. Manson, *Tort Claims and Canadian Prisoners*, (2014) 39:2 Queen's L.J. at p. 669.

> As long as medical staff is working for the correctional system, even as contractor or subcontractor, there is no legal reason not to apply principles of vicarious liability. This point is reinforced by the fact that prisoners cannot freely contract with the health professionals of their choice and are completely dependent on the decisions made by CSC in that regard.

One senses that competent medical care can be deprived of prisoners because they are lesser human beings. The heart of the case was trying to have the courts blur the distinction between victim and offender. Had the case been decided in Hickey's favour, it would have led to a greater need to address the root causes of violent behaviour and the impact of past trauma on criminal actions. It could have led to a greater focus on mental health and support systems within the correctional system.

Hickey must have felt that he was no more than a dog in a cage being treated, but without recourse to direct what treatment should be administered.

When an adolescent is sexually abused and feels life is out of control, are we looking out for society's best interest in maintaining a sense that the individual remains without any control over that person's life? Or are we saying that the best way to demand obedience from a whipped dog is to continue the beatings?

10

Buxbaum, Greenspan, and Martin

Pharoahs

'My name is Ozymandias, King of Kings:
Look on my works, ye Mighty, and despair!'
No thing beside remains. Round the decay
Of that colossal wreck, boundless and bare
The lone and level sands stretch far away.

—Percy Bysshe Shelley

ONE NEED NOT have been to Egypt or viewed the pyramids to be familiar with their mythology. About four thousand years ago, the ruling pharaohs built the structures with the expectation of becoming gods in the next world and filling them with the luxuries considered necessary in the afterlife. The number of pharaohs was few. However, the construction required thousands of people to build these giant monuments.

Buxbaum, Greenspan, and Martin can be considered Canadian pharoahs, but they were not megalomaniacs thinking of themselves as gods, nor did they exploit their fellow man. Each of them in their own way used their impressive talents for the greater good of their fellow citizens and in so doing erected monuments that proclaim their compassion and desire for a greater good.

In that business world, Helmuth Buxbaum (he preferred to spell his given name Helmut) was a pharaoh. He had developed a chain of ten nursing homes in and around the London, Ontario region. He could watch his business from his home in Komoka, a short distance from London. He derived great satisfaction from the industry, but most of all, he revelled in the money his companies earned. He had grown rich and enjoyed the fact that he was regarded in the community as a multi-millionaire.

Helmut's wife, Hanna, was more of a "people-person." Hanna was the daughter of a German-speaking Polish family. She had brought several relatives out to live in Canada from behind the Iron Curtain before the fall of the Soviet Union. She retained a trace of a German accent when speaking, although she chose to communicate in English to please her husband.

Helmut, the son of Austrian parents, had lost his accent from his upbringing in East Prussia. He was careful not to display any accent for fear that it could damage his chances of becoming even more successful in English-speaking Ontario.

Hanna's dedication to family and her efforts to support and bring relatives to Canada demonstrated her compassion and commitment to helping others, reflecting values contrasting with Helmut's business-focused approach. Her actions contributed to a more robust, supportive family network and enriched their community.

Both Hanna and Helmut were devout Baptists. Hanna had even wanted Helmut to consider becoming a missionary. Still, Helmut quashed that idea by saying the greater good could be done by his becoming even wealthier and donating funds to charitable causes. Helmut always focused on the bottom line.

It was July 5, 1984. Helmut drove home along the main expressway from Toronto's Pearson International Airport, Highway 401, to their Komoka home. Hanna and Helmut were returning from a visit with Helmut's older brother, Isbrandt, who lived in Abbotsford, British Columbia. Isbrandt confessed to Helmut during their meeting that he feared losing his business and hoped Helmut would lend him sufficient funds to keep the cab company operational. Helmut declined.

He expressed his fear that Isbrandt would squander the cash. It would be throwing good money after bad. Forget family ties. This was a business decision.

Helmut had become rich by making the right choices based on logic, not emotion. He would help out in one respect, however. It was agreed that Isbrandt's 14-year-old son, Roy, would return to Ontario with the Buxbaums for the summer. The family would spend a weekend relaxing at the cottage near Huntsville, which an employee from a nursing home readied as they drove from the airport.

Next, Roy would be hired as summer help as a groundskeeper at the Buxbaum properties. He might even gain some insight into how successful businesses are run.

As the Oldsmobile station wagon, carrying Helmut and Hanna in the front seat and Roy in the back, took the newly installed Highway 402 to Komoka and veered off to access a county road to Komoka, there appeared to be a car stopped on the shoulder with a man crouched down behind its bumper.

Helmut suggested to Hanna that the vehicle ahead appeared to be in trouble. They should stop to see if the stranded driver needed assistance. But Hanna was tired from the flight and the drive home. She urged her husband to drive by, but Helmut pulled behind the vehicle.

It all happened very fast. Before anyone could assess the situation, the right rear passenger door was pulled open. A big man wearing a baseball cap and face obscured by being covered with a nylon stocking yelled at Roy, "Get your fuckin' head down and keep it down." Roy saw a revolver pointed at him.

Almost immediately, the front passenger door was opened by a second man. The revolver was now pressed against Hanna's temple. Grabbing Hanna's hair, he shouted, "I want your fuckin' money and jewels." When Hanna turned to see how her husband was reacting, she was amazed to find he had exited the vehicle. He was not fighting in any way to assist his wife. Roy remained in the car, obeying the order to keep his head down.

Hanna was led to a ditch at the side of the road. Three shots rang out. The first .32 calibre bullet entered Hanna's skull through her temple. A second bullet grazed her upper left arm. The third bullet missed her completely. She fell silently to the grassy embankment.

The two men grabbed Hanna's purse and drove away in a blue car with obscured licence plates. Helmut ran to the back seat and urged Roy to look up and remember details of what he had seen. Helmut believed the boy's statement would be helpful in the future when police would ask questions.

Canadian pharaohs include more than wealthy business tycoons. They can also be found in academia, sports, entertainment, and the service sector. These are the people who become superstars in their chosen professions. One of the most notable Canadian lawyers of all time was a short, chain-smoking criminal defence lawyer named Eddie Greenspan.

I first encountered Edward L. Greenspan while preparing for my bar admission course examinations. I was placed in a section where Greenspan was the advisor/tutor in the criminal law section. In other courses, such as property, family law, or civil procedure, section leaders of prominent and experienced lawyers were ready to assist future bar members. Nonetheless, many soon-to-be lawyers skipped the sessions. Yet, Greenspan's section was different. No one missed a class. Students would show up early, and when the session began, Greenspan would keep his audience enraptured by tales from his well-publicized case files. When one cigarette was finished, Greenspan would toss the butt to the tile floor of the Osgoode Hall lecture room, grind it out with his shoe and then light up another.

When the time came for the tutorial to end, students would often call out, "More!" I had not been very interested in a criminal law career until that series of seminars. After Eddie

Greenspan's talks, that branch of law became my passion.

Eddie Greenspan, as he was known, grew up in Niagara Falls, Ontario. He decided he wanted to be a lawyer at the age of 13 following his father's death. Becoming a lawyer would be an accomplishment that would make his father proud. His dad operated a scrap yard to pay for the family's upbringing in less-than-luxurious surroundings. Many of his father's family had met untimely deaths in Nazi concentration camps. But the father was an inspiration to the son. He had completed one year of law school before being forced to move back home to support the family business. Eddie saw his task as completing what his father never had the chance to do.

"My dad wanted to be a criminal lawyer," he told the *St. Catharines Standard* in a 2013 interview. "I wanted to live out his dream because he never got to, and I felt somewhat responsible." Greenspan earned a Bachelor of Arts from the University of Toronto in 1965 and graduated from law school in 1968. He was called to the Bar in Ontario in 1970.

Eddie Greenspan developed a media following from the time he was junior lawyer in the trial of Peter Demeter. Demeter was an incredibly wealthy real estate developer. On July 18, 1973, Peter Demeter's 33-year-old wife, Christine, was attacked and bludgeoned to death in the garage of the upscale residence she shared with Peter in Mississauga, just to the west of Toronto. Christine's skull had been crushed by over a dozen blows to her head. Brain tissue was sprayed into the floor and walls of the garage. Peter Demeter was arrested and charged with having his wife executed by a hitman. News reports at the time often referred to the fact that Peter Demeter was born in Hungary.

Peter and Christine had married in 1967, but even with the birth of a daughter, the marriage had become unhappy. There was a hint that Christine may have been plotting Peter's death, since both the husband and the wife had taken out a million-dollar life insurance policy should one of them die. The marriage was plagued with infidelity. Peter, then 39, had been consorting with a 29-year-old Austrian mistress.

Police arrested Peter for arranging a "hit" that took his wife's life while their three-year-old daughter was inside the house watching television. Canadian authorities never arrested the person who did the killing. The suspect died a few years later in Hungary before he could be extradited to Canada.

The trial venue was changed to London, Ontario, due to the publicity the case attracted in Toronto. After an eleven-week trial, one of Canada's longest trials, Demeter was found guilty by a jury in a London, Ontario courtroom. Demeter was sentenced to life imprisonment. The evidential issues regarding the admissibility of a statement that would have led to an acquittal, if believed, were argued ultimately in the Supreme Court of Canada by Greenspan but were dismissed (*Demeter v. R.* 1978). He was released to a halfway house in 1983 and later charged with other crimes. He has always maintained his innocence.

Although the lead counsel, Joseph Pomerant, would later be publicly disgraced and disbarred on allegations he misappropriated half a million dollars in client funds, Eddie Greenspan's career blossomed. He hosted a popular television show on CBC, and wrote a book intending to provide insight into true Canadian crime stories rather than having to depend on American cases.

Helmut Buxbaum was charged with orchestrating the death of his wife, Hanna Buxbaum. Like Demeter, he hired Eddie Greenspan. The brutal killing of Hanna, a well-liked mother of six, enraged London residents. The preliminary hearing of Buxbaum and co-accused Terry Armes began on January 10, 1985, and ran for 18 days, but was adjourned at Greenspan's request to resume in April of that year. The court set aside another month to determine if there was sufficient evidence to send the men to trial. Three London residents had earlier pleaded guilty to being accessories and conspiring in the murder. Thirty-one-year-old Gary Foshay, widely believed to be the shooter, had already been committed to stand trial in the fall.

Even though a preliminary hearing is meant to test the sufficiency of the evidence, and the accused parties rarely take the stand, the case was so high profile that over 70 people lined up for over an hour to gain entrance to the courtroom where the narrative would unfold. Provincial Court Judge Alan Baker was told that there would be a change in security arrangements. Two Ontario Provincial Police officers who were supposed to be excluded as possible witnesses would act as security during the proceedings.

Crown Attorney Michael Martin made the announcement. Martin, then 58, had been a prosecutor in London for 20 years. He was considered a formidable opponent for any defence counsel. He regularly refused negotiations for "plea deals" unless the plea would be guilty.

Martin was another "larger-than-life" figure in the justice system. He had come to London in 1963 after leaving private practice after seven years. Because of his white hair, he was sometimes referred to as the "White Knight." I suspect the nickname was not so much for the colour of his locks but his passion for seeing the guilty convicted.

His passion was fully displayed during his jury summation in the Ray Rueger murder trial I had defended a few years before. During his address to the jurors, he wanted to dramatize the brutality that, according to him, my client had exerted on the victim when her throat was slit. He removed his barrister's robe and laid it on the floor as though it was a body and then, pretending to hold a knife, reached over the make-believe corpse and slashed where the neck would be. One press report stated that Martin used the victim's blood-stained clothing in this dramatization. That was not the case. Nonetheless, the shock value of the demonstration helped ensure conviction. Martin was unrepentant when faced with professional and media criticism of his tactic. He told the press that it was necessary to use extreme tactics to ensure justice was done. "But we are not doormats for the defence," he added.

Martin used his exceptional cross-examination skills to demolish the affidavits sworn in support of Buxbaum at the bail hearing held before Justice Anthony Maloney. The judge said those affidavits made Buxbaum appear to be "a living saint." However, Martin's cross-examination painted a different picture. Martin wanted the court to see Buxbaum as the prosecution saw him. Rather than saintly qualities, Martin focused on Buxbaum's secret life as a drug addict and an adulterer. These were both qualities Martin found personally offensive.

When Buxbaum's son, Paul, was put on the stand to testify for his father, and after hearing Martin's demolition of the accused's character, Justice Maloney posed a question from the bench to the young man. He said,

> I read that affidavit and thought, my gosh, there could be no finer man in all of Canada. Is that what your father is, or do you agree that the picture today is somewhat different than your affidavit?

Not wanting to betray his father, Paul looked down at his feet and sheepishly replied. "Yes."

In their first matchup, Martin had scored a victory. Buxbaum was denied bail.

Eddie Greenspan was 17 years younger than Michael Martin when the trial began. There was also a difference in style. Martin was deadly serious in his aim of having the matter proceed to trial. On the other hand, Greenspan was quick-witted and never hesitated to display his sense of humour when the occasion was right. Since Martin was in a salaried position, money did not concern him. Nonetheless, as Greenspan pointed out, the state had more resources to spend trying to convict Buxbaum than even his millionaire client could muster. It was leaked that Greenspan had asked for and received a $1 million retainer from Buxbaum. There was a provision for a $250,000 bonus should Buxbaum be acquitted. That astounded even senior practitioners of the Ontario Bar.

It also allowed reporters to compare Buxbaum and Greenspan's earlier client, Demeter. Both were wealthy businesspeople with an Eastern European background and were suspected of carrying on illicit affairs.

Greenspan sloughed off the comparison. Greenspan told a reporter the cases were dissimilar: Demeter had a net worth of $400,000, but Buxbaum was worth about $28 million. Buxbaum must have been impressed. Greenspan and his articling student worked tirelessly before the preliminary hearing and late in the night while the hearing was in progress to ensure their readiness as each prosecution witness took the stand.

The preliminary hearing went differently than Greenspan had planned. Terry Armes, a co-accused who had been present at the shooting, refused to make a deal for a lesser penalty. However, other co-accused defendants, Allen, Barrett and Hicks, worked out a plea deal through their lawyers. The preliminary hearing was adjourned so the mechanics of the arrangement could be worked out. Greenspan had not been kept in the loop by the lawyers representing the co-accused that a deal was in the works. Only when the adjournment was called did Greenspan realize the case had taken an unexpected twist.

"What does this mean, Eddie?" Buxbaum asked.

The reply was direct: "It means Helmut, you're fucked."

The plea deal was finalized with the prosecution agreeing

to accept guilty pleas from Barrett and Allen to charges of conspiracy to commit murder, while Hicks pleaded guilty to being an accessory after the fact. All other criminal charges were dropped. As part of the agreement, all three agreed to testify against Buxbaum and Armes.

Although prison time was inevitable, the deal offered them a critical advantage. Even if their testimony would brand them as "rats" within the prison system, a fixed sentence with the possibility of early parole was far preferable to risking a conviction for first-degree murder, a charge carrying a mandatory life sentence with no chance of parole for twenty-five years.

The plea deals were accepted by Justice Horace Krever in the Supreme Court of Ontario—now called the Superior Court of Justice—in London on December 18, 1984. Greenspan sought to intervene and successfully argued that fairness to his client required a publication ban on the names and charges so that Buxbaum's trial could proceed without the shame that he had been involved in a conspiracy to murder. Barrett was sentenced to ten years; Allen received an eight-year sentence; and Hicks received a sentence of fifteen months as an accessory after the fact of murder.

When the preliminary hearing ended, the provincial court judge ruled that there was sufficient evidence for the matter to go to trial.

When the trial began on October 15, 1985, the location of the proceedings had been changed from London to St. Catharines. The reason for the change of venue was that fewer people were expected to have followed the extensive publicity generated in London and Toronto. Moving the trial by two hundred kilometres to a city in the Niagara peninsula allowed the selection of a less-biased jury. It was also a shorter drive for Greenspan to attend court from his home in Toronto. It also meant that Buxbaum would be moved from London and held in the detention centre in Thorold.

Martin focused on the background of the killing rather than the factual scenario of the event. Martin's concept of justice made him understand that a conviction would be more straightforward if the prosecution's theory were to paint a picture that stressed the moral turpitude of the accused.

Martin's opening address to the 10-man, two-woman jury summarized the evidence he wanted the jurors to accept. He started by alleging that Buxbaum had grown disinterested in a loveless marriage and wanted out. He stated that Buxbaum had become addicted to cocaine and fulfilled his sexual fantasies using sex workers. Eventually, he approached his pusher, Rob "Squirrel" Barrett, and placed a twenty-five-thousand-dollar contract with Barrett to end Hanna's life. He said he would prove that Barrett received thirteen thousand dollars at the London airport the day after the killing. The gunman had received five thousand, Armes was paid thirty-five hundred, Allen one thousand, Hicks five hundred and Barrett getting three thousand. Martin believed that the drama of the plan ning and deliberation involved in a contract hit would enrage a jury similar to his re-enactment of the killing that had shocked a jury in the Rueger murder trial.

Perhaps the most forceful evidence came from Terry Armes, who had pleaded guilty to second-degree murder and was sentenced to life imprisonment without parole eligibility for ten years. Armes claimed he was excluded from a plea deal offered by the prosecution because he couldn't give evidence damning enough to get a short-fixed term of imprisonment, unlike the others. He claimed no intention to be part of a murder plot and that he had an alcohol use disorder. He was in the wrong place at the wrong time. "I wasn't guilty of murder in my heart. I didn't want that woman dead. I got to do a fucking life sentence because I'm a drunk." The trial judge, John O'Driscoll, warned him of using foul language, but the jury was given the impression that this was indeed a planned and intentional hit. It might have been worse, Armes suggested. At one point during the stop, Tom, the nephew, disobeyed instructions and looked up. Armes ensured he forced the boy to bury his head once again. Armes expected the gunman would have also shot Tom if the gunman had seen him watching.

After calling 60 witnesses for the prosecution, Greenspan started delivery of an opening address that went on for over an hour. In that speech, Greenspan admitted that his client's sexual relationship with his wife was unsatisfactory. After suffering a stroke in 1982, Buxbaum became impotent and sought out other women. Although he had used cocaine before the stroke, Barrett had upped the ante by introducing Buxbaum to the practice of injecting the substance. There was money paid. The reason, however, was not to finance the killing of Hanna. Still, instead, it was to set up a "wholesale" supply chain for the importation of cocaine from Florida into London and to ensure an easy source of high-grade cocaine for Buxbaum's use. There was a transfer of funds the day after the murder. But that money was given because Buxbaum feared that his wife's killers would turn on him if he discontinued cooperation. The strategy was to persuade a jury that Buxbaum was a naïve, flawed businessman but not evil and sinister.

However, not everything went as expected for Greenspan. While giving his summation to the jury, an earthquake measuring five points on the Richter scale forced a break in proceedings. When court resumed, Greenspan continued his address by saying, "And for my next trick, I'm going to part the waters of Lake Ontario."

As the *Toronto Star* reported, the testimony at the 75-day trial painted "an indelible picture of an apparent God-fearing middle-aged man who was a pillar of the community by day but who turned into a cocaine-snorting consort of London prostitutes by night."

For the jury, it might have been easier to part the waters of the Great Lakes than to summon sympathy for the man sitting before them. Their verdict came swiftly: guilty of first-degree murder. Under the *Criminal Code*, the sentence was mandatory—life imprisonment without eligibility for parole for twenty-five years. This was a final reckoning for Helmut Buxbaum, a man whose acts of darkness had stood in stark contrast to his polished public image.

Not long after his conviction, Buxbaum wrote a letter to his lawyer, Eddie Greenspan, offering an oddly gracious reflection on his defence.

> The defence did far better beyond expectation, and the time spent in the courtroom was one of the highest levels of professionalism and competence, even though we lost. Your greatful [sic] client and friend, Helmut.

It did not take long before Buxbaum's money obsession returned. Even though taken to commence his sentence at maximum-security Millhaven Institution, Helmut Buxbaum objected to the million dollars and more Greenspan had charged him. He hired counsel to have the fee "taxed," a procedure requiring a lawyer to justify the charges before a judicial officer. He also hired another highly reputed lawyer, Clayton Ruby, to appeal the conviction and sentence. The grounds for appeal would focus on the failure of his trial counsel to mount an insanity defence.

While at Millhaven, it was announced that he wanted to remarry. He had met a divorcée through correspondence while awaiting trial, and now that he was a widower, he decided to take a new bride. He announced his intention to wed a 33-year-mother of two teenage sons, Liza Dikih of London. However, being a federal inmate, he needed Warden's permission to marry. The provincial attorney general must agree that the wedding would not present a problem by making the new spouse's testimony inadmissible if she were called upon to testify against him in a retrial or pending criminal charge. The *Toronto Star* cited a "prison worker" as confirming that the marriage took place in mid-February 1989, with the honeymoon taking place in a trailer provided for conjugal visits on condition that Buxbaum sticks his head out the window at noon, 4 p.m., and 11 p.m. so inmate counts could be conducted.

Helmut Buxbaum had a relatively short stay at Millhaven Institution. He reported to prison staff that he had been attacked in the prison gymnasium in 1986. The CSC must protect the inmates in its custody. In January 1987, it was announced that Buxbaum had been moved to maximum-security Kingston Penitentiary. KP, as it was known, was a protective custody institution. There were no reasons for the transfer, and CSC did not admit any laxity in providing safety for the inmate while he was at Millhaven. Prison spokesperson Dennis Curtis told the *Kingston Whig-Standard*:

> It was just that he had been identified as a high-profile inmate who qualified for protective custody, and it was decided to move him. There has been nothing that happened recently to cause the move.

Upon arrival at the penitentiary, I suspect that Buxbaum carried an aura of grandiosity that he had become accustomed to as a multi-millionaire in London, Ontario business circles. Shortly after he arrived at KP, he contacted my office, demanding to see me the day he made the call. I was teaching prison law at Queen's University and decided to add him to the list of prisoners to be seen later in the week. My assistant cautioned me, "No. He wants to see you today." I rearranged my schedule and booked an appointment for a professional visit later in the day.

When I arrived at Kingston Penitentiary, my first meeting with Helmut Buxbaum ended up rocky. He started by giving directions as to the work he needed to be done. I cut him off short. "Mr. Buxbaum," I said, "that might be how you talked with your staff in London. But you are here now. If we are to get along, I want to be treated much more respectfully." I doubt anyone had confronted him in that way before. He immediately changed his attitude. We ended up having a productive meeting. After that, he was always polite and friendly with me.

I have heard other inmates say that he also positively changed his interactions with them. He started to cooperate with other inmates, sometimes to his detriment. He spent seven months in solitary confinement, accused of trying to assist another prisoner to escape from KP. He began to sign his letters with an additional notation, "Imprisoned but free." It seemed as though money no longer mattered to him. He settled civil suits from his family, including a payout of almost half a million dollars to his nephew Tom. He divorced Liza but paid support for her boys. He lost his appeal based on insanity and came to grips with the notion that he would likely spend the rest of his life in prison. It was as though he realized that although he professed a devout faith in Christianity, he was idolizing a golden calf. After several years in maximum security, he was eventually transferred to medium-security Warkworth Institution.

The three individuals discussed in this chapter, Buxbaum, Greenspan, and Martin, are, in my estimation, Canadian pharaohs. What is the difference between a Canadian pharaoh and the term we understand from ancient Egypt? Pharaohs stood apart from the masses and used the masses to enhance their grandeur as they prepared to become gods. On the other hand, Canadian pharaohs used their fame and prestige for the greater good of the masses.

Michael Edward Martin served in the Royal Canadian Navy during the Second World War before earning his law degree at the University of Manitoba. He moved his practice from Manitoba to St. Catharines and then to London, Ontario where he was named as the Crown Attorney and later became Regional Crown Attorney for Southwestern Ontario. In 1986, he was made Director of Crown Attorneys for the Ministry of the Attorney General. In 1988, he was appointed as a Judge of the Ontario Court.

As a lawyer, prosecutor and judge, he was always considered tough but fair. His drive to ensure justice guided every ambition. I remember walking a short distance down a Toronto sidewalk with him as he beamed about his new role as Director of Crown Attorneys—finally able to extend and reinforce his passion for justice across the province.

Michael Martin, QC, passed away on January 13, 2019, one month before his ninety-third birthday. Many colleagues who saw Mike as a role model, mentor and comrade attended his Funeral Mass six days later in Niagara-on-the-Lake.

Despite the notoriously high legal fees charged to wealthy clients, Edward L. Greenspan generously shared his expertise for the greater good. He, too, acted as a role model, mentor, and friend to many of us in the legal profession. But he wanted the public to understand and appreciate Canadian criminal law. He told the *Vancouver Sun* in 1987 that he wrote his book, *The Case for the Defence* because there was an absence of discussion of Canadian criminal cases in Canadian literature. Canadians were forced to extrapolate how our justice system works from books written by American luminaries such as Melvin Belli, F. Lee Bailey, and Louis Nizer.

"There had been nothing written about the Canadian system, examining it through the use of cases," he said while cautioning that Canadians might be horrified that even a multi-millionaire has little chance when the deck is so heavily stacked against him. Greenspan was not urging that Buxbaum had been wrongly convicted. He used the case as an example of how the average citizen is disadvantaged by the scarce resources available when making a defence. Although the essence of the system cannot be changed, he urged state funding for a "vigorously independent defence system and to build up a legal aid plan so that it works properly."

He used his fame, along with CBC producer George Jonas, to write his book and get his message across through television. If a lawyer could change public attitudes, it would not be in the courts or academia; it would be by urging radio and television viewers to understand how the criminal justice system operates. He fulfilled this passion by hosting a series called *The Scales of Justice* that aired from 1982 to 1994.

Greenspan was alert to advocating for political issues impacting the criminal justice system. For example, he was an unrepentant opponent of the return of the death penalty. His opposition shone brightest when confronting Bill Domm, the leading proponent of the restoration of the death penalty.

Domm had been elected as a Conservative Member of Parliament for Peterborough, Ontario. He was known to rebuke the metric system and favoured bringing back the noose. Greenspan seemed incredulous that when Brian Mulroney's Progressive Conservatives defeated the Pierre Trudeau Liberals, then led by John Turner, in the 1984 general election, Domm would go through in attempts to reinstate capital punishment. The two had faced off several times, but one of the most publicized debates occurred in Toronto in April 1987.

The event was booked as "Greenspan v. Domm," and it drew a large crowd. Greenspan was sceptical that the House of Commons would even consider reconsidering restoration. He told the *Ottawa Citizen*,

> I never really believed it would happen. But when I realized it was coming, I went for a very, very long walk and decided I had to do something. I had to know that if this vote goes through and we vote to restore capital punishment, that at least I'd done everything I possibly could.

But it was Eddie Greenspan's experience that dictated his opposition:

> The temper of the judge, the skill of defence counsel, the emotional climate, whether you're up against a tough prosecutor—all of these factors are so arbitrary that it's like a freakish lottery as to who will live and who will die.

This uncertainty became the source of Greenspan's condemnation of giving judges the power of life and death.

> Make no mistake about it. If you bring back the death penalty, there's no way you're only going to kill a Clifford Olson. Someday, you're going to kill a Donald Marshall.

Even though public opinion leaned heavily toward bringing back capital punishment, Greenspan's country-wide tours denouncing the practice could be considered instrumental in a 1987 free vote in the House of Commons to continue the abolition. "It's over now," Greenspan proclaimed. "If it couldn't be returned with the largest Conservative majority in history, it won't ever be."

Edward Greenspan died peacefully in his sleep on December 24, 2014, in Phoenix, Arizona, at age 70. Toronto Mayor John Tory eulogized him as "a tireless champion for human rights." Supreme Court Justice Michael Moldaver said, "He stood out because the law was more than a business to him; it formed part of his very being."

It was in his recognition that one's being is more than the business one carries on, which is why the definition of Helmut Buxbaum can also be included in a list of Canadian pharaohs.

The change in demeanour that Buxbaum exhibited once he gave up on the preoccupation of being a multimillionaire allowed Helmut Buxbaum to use his notoriety for the greater good. He spent his final years of imprisonment as a jailhouse advocate preoccupied with treating older inmates.

In 1999, at age sixty, Buxbaum chaired a group of 85 inmates aged over 50 and held a one-day workshop on how society should come to grips with problems facing not only the elderly prison population but the cost taxpayers are forced to pay. At that time, it was estimated that some fifteen hundred geriatric and terminally ill inmates were in Canadian prisons, each costing the system at least sixty thousand a year. Their ages ranged from 50 to 92, representing a growing proportion of the prison population. Yet, most rehabilitative programming overlooked the older population. Crime was considered a young man's disease, with the only cure being birthdays.

However, the public's "get tough on crime" sentiments meant an increasing prison population spending a longer time behind bars. Treatment of diseases such as cancer and Alzheimer's were ratcheting up costs.

Buxbaum became a leader in advancing the cause of older inmates. He proposed an Older Offenders Act to deal with aging inmates just as the *Young Offenders Act* carved out special treatment for youthful offenders. He suggested an accelerated release program for first-time offenders over 50. In return, those released would be required to contribute to society by performing community service. He argued:

> No one should have to spend their last years in prison. By personally confronting our offence, analyzing the circumstances that led to it and vowing never to commit any offence again, senior inmates can undemonize themselves.

The well-being of older inmates became his passion. He also continued his Bible studies and never gave up his religious beliefs. Helmut Buxbaum died on November 1, 2007, at the age of 67. He had been transferred to the Kingston Penitentiary Regional Hospital for unspecified health concerns.

The causes he stood for have never been addressed, but his proposals for more humane treatment of aging offenders will become more pressing as time passes. My first meeting with Helmut Buxbaum was contentious, but I could see a much more understanding and compassionate side to this man over the years. Indeed, he continued to send me a Christmas card every year until his death.

11

Edwin Alonzo Boyd and Gilbert Galvan

Bandits

No man knows how bad he is till he has
tried very hard to be good.

—C.S. Lewis

A THEORETICAL MODEL established by Mancur Lloyd Olson, Jr. suggested that in days gone by, merchants carrying their wares would be randomly picked upon by roving gangs of bandits in a society without controls. A trip into town could wipe out one's supply of merchandise, rendering the merchant penniless. To prevent this, citizens banded together and gave a monopoly to the stationary bandit, who could relieve them of oppression. This bandit would be paid by annual dues, which we call taxes. The stationary bandit's job, the government, was to keep regular folks safe and prosperous.

In modern societies, groups of roving bandits have yet to be eliminated. If Olson's theory is accurate, governments should have stopped this group long ago. The truth is that these roving thieves continued to exist and became the subject of admiration and folklore in many cases. For example, look at Bonnie and Clyde.

The fascination with outlaw figures often reflects a complex relationship with societal norms and the idea of rebellion against perceived injustices. These characters can become symbols of resistance or agents of change, even when their methods are criminal. Their stories often highlight broader themes of defiance and adventure that resonate with the imagination. Perhaps these outlaws enjoy the fame.

When done correctly, nobody gets hurt. This is the story of two thieves who operated years apart. They never hurt anyone, but both relished the attention they received. Bank robberies are the stuff of legend. Unlike crimes of violence such as murder, the perpetrators are often considered folk heroes. Especially in sleepy little towns, the story of a local bank heist lives on for years.

Such was the case on March 27, 1951. The Canadian Bank of Commerce[1] in the Ontario village of Colborne was robbed. The robbers were none other than some of the men who comprised the infamous Boyd Gang, as it came to be known. Edwin Alonzo Boyd headed up the troupe of thieves.

Edwin Alonzo Boyd's story is not just about crime. It is also about the broader societal context in which these events occurred. His actions were a product of the time and reflected the socio-economic conditions of post-war Canada. Boyd's ability to evade capture and maintain his mystique contributed to the enduring fascination with his exploits.

I had not yet started school when the bank robbery occurred. The stories of the people in the bank lived on. I never met Eddie Boyd, as he was popularly known, but I was reminded of his exploits for years. The tales of those who experienced the robbery were repeated over the years, even though the Colborne theft was one of the least remarkable of all the Boyd Gang's epic outings.

People had been noticing several men walking around the town streets wearing suits. That made them stand out from the ordinary folk who dressed up only when going to church, weddings, and funerals. They were the Boyd Gang. At two thirty in the afternoon, they would pull an armed robbery of the bank, and the townsfolk would tell the tale for years to come.

1 The Canadian Bank of Commerce merged with the Imperial Bank of Canada on June 1, 1961, to become what is now known as the Canadian Imperial Bank of Commerce or often simply CIBC.

Edwin Alonzo Boyd was born on April 2, 1914, one year before his policeman father enlisted to serve in World War I. In the 1930s, Boyd was a vagabond and petty thief gaining a criminal record. Boyd enlisted in the Canadian Army to serve in the Second World War. He was posted to England.

Boyd's enlistment in the Canadian Army during World War II adds a layer of complexity to his character. His service reflects a commitment to a cause greater than himself, illustrating that even individuals who later engage in criminal activities can have multifaceted lives and experiences.

While overseas, he met and married Doreen Thompson. The couple had three children: twins fathered by Boyd and another child from Doreen's previous marriage. Their first child, Edwin Jr., died before the twins arrived. During an air raid, a nurse accidentally dropped the baby on its head. The couple returned to Canada when the war ended.

Eddie attempted to support his family in Toronto by working as a streetcar driver. But boredom soon set in. He possessed movie-star good looks and had even wanted to become an actor. But instead, he returned to a life of crime, conducting solo robberies. He used a German Luger he acquired during the war and pulled off at least six holdups in the Toronto area, including the theft of $3,000 from a North York branch of the Bank of Montreal on September 9, 1949.

He needed help in the bank robbery business so he partnered with fellow robber, Howard Gault. That was his first undoing. When Gault was arrested, he snitched on Boyd, and the two were sent to jail.

Had not Gault ratted on Eddie, he probably would have stayed free much longer. Once apprehended, he was held for trial at Toronto's Don Jail. He met with two other inmates, Willie Jackson and Lenny Jackson. The two were not related.

Lenny Jackson had ridden the rails during the Depression, as had Eddie Boyd. While drifting across Canada, Lenny suffered a leg amputation from an unfortunate run-in with a locomotive. But in this instance, the amputation paid off. Before his jail placement, he had been fitted with a prosthetic. This presented him with a rare opportunity for someone destined to be sent to jail. He could use the artificial leg to hide a hacksaw blade. It was used to remove some window bars.

On November 4, 1951, Eddie, Willie, and Lenny squeezed through and dropped thirty feet to the ground and freedom. They were supposed to have been picked up by an accomplice, Val Lesso, who used the name Steve Suchan. Suchan failed to show up. He was busy with a girlfriend and missed his appointment as a getaway driver.

The publicity of the daring jailbreak just added to Eddie's thrill. He also used his flair for drama during the robberies. He would use his skills as an Army commando to leap onto the bank counters and waive his pistol around. He also dressed for the occasion in good suits and wore theatrical make-up. His meticulous planning and ability to execute high-risk operations demonstrated a level of intelligence and daring that was rare among criminals of the time.

The newspapers ate it up. The three Toronto daily newspapers, the *Toronto Telegram*, the *Toronto Star,* and the *Globe and Mail*, tried to outdo each other by publishing scoops about the "Boyd Gang" even though Lennie Jackson considered himself the true leader.

Only two weeks after the jailbreak, the Bank of Toronto was robbed of $4,300. Then, on November 30, $46,000 was stolen from the Royal Bank of Canada in Leaside. The *Toronto Daily Star* dubbed it "the biggest hold-up in the history of Toronto." The four had engaged in robberies totalling about $75,000 in four months. A *Toronto Telegram* headline proclaimed a $26,000 reward for the gang's capture, dead or alive.

When Willie was caught and arrested in Montreal, Eddie and his wife went into hiding. Despite the gang's criminal activities, some moments showed Eddie's humanity. His devotion to his wife and ability to elude capture for a time highlighted his resourcefulness and determination to protect his loved ones.

Things turned deadly serious on March 6, 1952. Lenny Jackson and Steve Suchan were captured after a gunfight with police. Bullets were fired at Sergeant of Detectives Edward Tong and his partner, Sergeant Roy Perry. Tong died 17 days afterward. The search was put on overdrive to capture the escaped criminals. Willie was already in custody. Lenny and Steve were picked up in separate altercations with police.

Police had been following Eddie's brother. When it was discovered that the brother had rented an apartment, police concluded they could find Eddie there. They were right. Edwin Alonzo Boyd surrendered without incident.

Authorities at the Don Jail decided it would be easiest to manage the gang if they could be kept together. They were placed in a former hospital ward that had been turned into a cellblock, complete with audio monitoring.

The four seemed to get along well with the staff, laughing and joking and presenting themselves as well-behaved inmates. On one occasion, Willie Jackson grabbed the keys secured to a guard's waistbelt. It seemed harmless. Jackson squeezed tightly. When the guard was out of sight, the impression of the key was left on Jackson's hand. The men then outlined the impression left on the hand onto a cell wall.

With material scrounged from various sources, they fashioned a makeshift key. They also observed that the jail was short-staffed, with no one doing patrols between 5 and 7 a.m. They used this time to exit their cells and, again, saw at the window bars. They covered the cut marks on the bars with soap and dirt to hide their work. They also covered the microphone with a pillow so the sound of the cutting would not be detected. Once again, they managed to escape.

The men holed up in a deserted property. It was only when some residents of North York complained of homeless men in an abandoned farm that police became involved. The Boyd Gang surrendered without a fight. Even before the days of rock and roll, they were treated as rock stars. The *Globe and Mail* reported on the arrest: "Teenage girls, screaming and clapping their hands, gathered near the North York station and chanted, 'We want Boyd.'" The public's fascination with the gang, particularly with Boyd, reflected a complex mix of fear and admiration. Their ability to captivate the public's imagination demonstrated a charisma that transcended their criminal acts.

Once again, the four were locked into cells at the Don Jail. This time, there was 24/7 surveillance. After the trial in the fall, Willie Jackson was sentenced to 20 years consecutive to a seven-year term previously imposed, and Boyd was sentenced to eight concurrent terms of life imprisonment. Suchan and Lennie Jackson were hanged at the Don Jail on December 16, 1952. Despite the grim end, the legacy of the Boyd Gang remains a fascinating chapter in Canadian history, illustrating both the darker and more intriguing aspects of human nature.

Eddie Boyd was paroled in 1962, but his parole was suspended until he was released in 1966. The press continued to seek Eddie out for interviews. Dale Brazao of the *Toronto Star* was the first to find his whereabouts and wrote extensively to satisfy the thirst of the avid folk hero following. CBC producer Brian Valee tracked Boyd down, and during an interview in his Vancouver home, Boyd admitted a murder for which he was never charged. Eddie divorced Doreen while imprisoned but remarried once released. He worked as a driver for disabled individuals and cared for his wife and another woman under an assumed name until he died of pneumonia in British Columbia on May 17, 2002. He was 88 years old.

Although Eddie had aspired to be an actor, it can be argued that he achieved more fame as a bandit. Two books were written on the Boyd Gang, and an award-winning musical, *Girls in the Gang*, based on the story of the Boyd Gang, debuted in 1987 at Toronto's Factory Theatre. Eddie was also profiled in a 1998 CBC documentary, *Life and Times*.

In 2011, a movie titled *Citizen Gangster* was made based on Eddie Boyd's life, starring Scott Speedman as Boyd. There was even an episode of *Law and Order: Special Victims Unit* in which Brian Dennehy, playing the Eddie Boyd character, confesses to a murder shortly before dying.

In 2023, the art gallery in Colborne devoted one room to display press releases of that little town's contribution to the legend. No one was ever shot in the robberies Boyd committed.

I never met Eddie Boyd or had any dealings with his partners, but I did assist another man in prison for a career that paralleled that of Boyd. That man was Gilbert Galvan, the so-called Flying Bandit.

Gilbert Galvan was born in Los Angeles in 1958. His criminal career started (or was discovered) when the person known to police as Gilbert William Galvan, Jr. was seventeen. He rang up a string of convictions for robbery, attempted robbery, disorderly conduct, and obstructing a peace officer. In 1984, Galvan was imprisoned in St. Joseph County, Michigan, for embezzling Western Union. He took advantage of the minimum security and escaped from the institution. He understood most escapees are caught shortly after their prison break, but Gilbert Galvan was not one of the ordinary inmates going AWOL.

Galvan enlisted the help of a friend to smuggle him into Canada. He settled in Pembroke, about a hundred kilometres north of Ottawa. He also telephoned his former jailers to wish them well. The handsome, clean-cut, and quick-witted young man stood out from the crowd. Galvan realized that could be a problem. He had to reinvent himself. He had to manufacture a new identity. He assumed the alias Robert Whiteman. It has yet to be determined for sure how he was able to obtain a government ID listing the alias as his name. There was speculation that he purchased a health card from a vagabond, assumed his name, and used that identity to obtain a driver's licence.

A problem in representing oneself as another is that Galvan needed a Social Insurance Number to gain employment. Receiving small amounts of cash under the table would not lead to the long-term stability the newly invented Robert Whiteman sought. While looking for work in Vancouver, he returned to perfecting the bank robbery. A $600 score whetted his appetite. This is something he was good at. He was amazed that Canadian banks lacked armed security guards. He disguised himself for his first few efforts and became adept as a quick-change artist, pulling a heist and transforming himself into Robert Whiteman's character. This endeavour provided him with ready cash. However, there were a limited number of banks in the Pembroke area.

Robert Whiteman needed seed money to harvest an expanded field of activity. One well-known source of funds was an Ottawa-based fence named Tommy Craig. To his peers, Tommy Craig was affectionately known as The Fat Man. Tommy and his crew preferred driving Chrysler Fifth Avenues. This earned them the nickname The Chrysler Gang.

Tommy bought and sold jewellery. He was constantly seen wearing thousands of dollars worth of expensive rings, watches, and bracelets. When asked by CBC News why he adorned himself so lavishly, he said, "If you're going to sell it, you gotta flash it." Police suspected Tommy Craig of reselling the loot from jewellery store robberies throughout the region. Proving it was an ongoing problem.

Gilbert met a woman in Pembroke. Her name was Janice. To her, he was always Robert, as Gilbert did not disclose his real name, his American citizenship, criminal past, or ongoing livelihood. They married and had two children. After that, Janice called herself Janice Whiteman.

With the money Galvan initially received from Tommy Craig, he purchased airline tickets. Janice would drive her husband Robert to the Pembroke Airfield and kiss him goodbye as he headed for another "business trip."

As far as Janice knew, her husband was employed by a Calgary-based company and couriered stocks and bonds. Janice was never let in on why his trips were so frequent. He would travel first class and would eventually build up 160,000 Aeroplan miles. He would fly across Canada, commit a robbery, and return the same day. He robbed banks in every Canadian province except Prince Edward Island and Newfoundland.

At that time carry-on baggage was not checked at airport security so Galvan would stash two handguns in his travel bag along with a costume change. Upon arrival at a chosen destination, he would case the site he hoped to rob, work out the details, and return to carry out the robbery when he was satisfied that all precautions were taken to avoid arrest.

His *modus operandi* was to travel to distant cities to rob one or two banks. Ontario Provincial Police (OPP) Officer George Snyder, who eventually arrested Galvan, said, "He would be impeccably dressed in the best suits. As he approached a bank, that's what you would see, a businessman carrying an attaché case." When about to enter and rob a bank, he would wear work clothes over his suit and put on a facial disguise. When the robbery was over, he would remove the work clothes and facial adornments again, becoming the wealthy businessman. Sometimes, he would walk back to the bank he had robbed dressed in his suit and carrying a briefcase in his business attire and ask the police what was happening.

On his return home, Janice would pick him up at the airport. She only suspected anything might be unexpected when she requested five dollars to pay for a taxi. He directed her to reach into the pants pocket of some trousers hanging nearby. Inside was a money clip. Her eyes widened as she counted out 18 one-thousand-dollar bills. "She just about had a heart attack," Galvan commented. He said the money was from two paycheques and a bonus his employer had paid him. She instantly believed him and cautioned that such a large sum should be deposited in the bank. He complied.

Galvan never fired a gun in any of his robberies. He later told CBC News, "My only motivation for a life of crime is money. I mean, I was fully cognizant of what I was doing. I understand the concept of right and wrong. I did it for the money, period."

Tommy Craig was also greedy. He encouraged Galvan to expand his horizons and target jewellery stores as well as banks. Galvan stole merchandise from across Canada, and Craig fenced the goods in the Ottawa area. Galvan successfully robbed six Birks jewellery stores. The Vancouver armed robbery was the biggest the city had experienced. At one point, two million dollars of merchandise had been lifted. It also became Galvan's undoing.

Craig had encouraged Galvan to bring along one of Craig's crew. The partner left behind the disguises and a sawed-off shotgun that had been used during the robbery. The gun had been stolen during an Ottawa jewellery store robbery. Police were able to trace the weapon back to Craig. OPP Officer George Snyder began surveillance on all of Craig's contacts. One of those was Galvan, previously unknown to Canadian police. Photos eventually led to the facial recognition of an escaped American prisoner. The man everyone was calling Robert Whiteman was Gilbert Galvan. Police further matched Galvan's travel with the locations of robberies. They coincided.

On June 12, 1987, Janice dropped Robert off to fly to London, Ontario. Once again, he successfully secured $22,000 from the London bank. He flew home.

Janice, who was pregnant with Robert's second child, and their daughter were waiting for his arrival. So were the police. Robert Whiteman deboarded the aircraft and moved confidently towards his wife and child. According to Officer Snyder, "As he walked through the airport, two members of our tactical squad passed by him, one on either side and grabbed him and put him down on the ground." Searching the briefcase, the police found the stolen London cash, two guns, a wig, false skin, and a removable mustache.

The scene shocked Janice. She called out, "This is a mistake. That's my husband. You obviously don't mean to arrest him." Then, Janice discovered that the man she knew and loved was not Robert Whiteman, but Gilbert Galvan.

Gilbert describes the confrontation between Gilbert and Janice: "She comes in, and she sits down, and she looks at me, and she goes, 'Your name's not Robert Whiteman. You're not even Canadian,' and I say, 'Well yeah, yeah, that's true.'" But despite the lies, Gilbert admitted he loved Janice and always provided for her. "To me, that was my definition of a good husband," Galvan said. Despite his criminal activities, Galvan's ability to provide for his family and maintain a façade of normalcy for Janice and their children showcased his commitment to them. His cleverness and resourcefulness allowed him to lead a double life successfully, albeit temporarily. His life was a complex mix of affection and deception.

Galvan eventually pleaded guilty to 59 armed robberies that yielded about two and a half million dollars. He told CBC that he had no money, and the proceeds of crime were not hidden away. He was sentenced to 20 years in prison. He began serving his sentence at Collins Bay Institution in Kingston. Once that sentence was finished, he could expect to be deported to the United States to complete the unexpired portion of the sentence he had yet to serve there.

I met Gilbert at Collins Bay in 1994. Ever the showman, he signed a release allowing CBC to record our interview for a documentary that CBC producer George James was filming for the TV program *Man Alive*, which featured my firm.

When in prison and sentenced to 20 years, he quickly discovered that even if paroled at the earliest date, he would have to remain locked up for about seven years. Should he not be paroled and detained beyond the usual two-thirds release date, he could spend the entire 20 years in prison.

Once deported, he would still have to spend seven years in a United States prison. He was frustrated when he sat down to speak with me on what would become a televised interview.

> "We're talking 20 years in Canada. We're not talking of first-degree murder. [With additional seven years in the US], they want me to serve more than a life/25 sentence. Huh, it's crazy. I'm not going to do it."

Eventually, I convinced Gilbert to accept immediate deportation, allowing his Canadian and American sentences to run concurrently. He agreed, and in 1984, he was returned to the United States. In 1996, Robert Knuckle published a book, *The Flying Bandit: Bringing Down Canada's Most Daring Armed Robber.* The book was later adapted into a 2022 movie, *Bandit*, starring Josh Duhamel as Gilbert. In 2005, a Canadian true crime series, *Masterminds,* focused on Galvan's exploits. He had become a star.

Once deported, he completed his American sentence at a prison in Wisconsin in 1988. He then robbed a bank in McHenry, Illinois, in December 2000, for which he was sentenced to fifteen years the following April. He was released from federal custody in 2014.

On release from American custody, broke and unemployed, it seemed Gilbert Galvan's life was on a downhill trajectory. On a Saturday in mid-May 2015, a man was spotted in a supermarket in Barrington, Illinois, a suburb of Chicago. He was wheeling a shopping cart loaded with liquor and exited the store without paying. When approached by store security, he abandoned the cart and fled. The following Monday, he returned and loaded the cart with 24 bottles of whiskey and rum, two greeting cards, and three floral arrangements. A man who had stolen more than two and a half million dollars in cash and more than two million dollars in jewellery over a three-year spree was now impoverished and nabbed for nine hundred dollars worth of booze. Once again, he bypassed the cashier. This time, the police were waiting. He was taken to the police station and fingerprinted.

Barrington Police Chief Dave Dorn commented, "This time, he made it out the door where we were waiting for him. He was extremely cooperative with the officers. He was polite and very laid back. Then, the search for fingerprints turned up something the police were not expecting. Dorn was surprised. "We didn't expect to have one of the most prolific bank robbers in the history of Canada stealing from our local grocery store."

Despite his fall from grace, Galvan maintained a calm and cooperative demeanour, reflecting a degree of acceptance and resilience in the face of his circumstances. His life, marked by audacity and cunning, also demonstrated an underlying adaptability and resourcefulness, traits that, if channelled differently, might have led to a more positive and lawful path.

The shoplifting charge resulted in another fifty-day sentence. However, by this time, Gilbert, by outward appearances, was a changed man. His mug shot displayed a chubby, not-well-groomed older man who compared unfavourably with his past handsome, well-groomed, athletic appearance in Canada. He continued his hunt for fame. Gilbert Galvan portrayed a bar patron as a background performer in the movie about him, *Bandit*, which was shot in Georgia. He was photographed alongside the star, Josh Duhamel.

Why are we so fascinated with people like Eddie Boyd and Gilbert Galvan? We certainly seldom see such people portrayed as heroes or anti-heroes when the crime is murder or sexual misconduct. But bank robbers? That's a different story. Perhaps it's because their crimes, while clearly illegal, seem rooted more in acts of mischief than acts of darkness. They become folk heroes, even pop culture icons, with movies made about their daring escapades and nicknames that roll off the tongue like characters in a caper film.

The answer lies, in part, in revisiting the ideas of economist and political theorist Mancur Olson, discussed at the beginning of this chapter. We, as citizens, may accept that we need the stationary bandit—the structures of law, order, and governance—to preserve civil society. But in reality, our sympathies often drift toward the roving bandits like Boyd and Galvan, whose antics allow them to thumb their noses at the very systems that most of us feel powerless to challenge. We would never dare stand up to bureaucracy or major financial institutions ourselves. But so long as no one gets seriously hurt, there's a certain vicarious thrill in watching those who do. They can enjoy their fifteen minutes of fame—their small, rebellious spotlight. And we, comfortably on the sidelines, can watch our news feeds with fascination, proclaim our disapproval of lawbreakers, and vote for politicians who promise to get tough on crime—all the while secretly delighting in the sheer audacity of those who got away with it, even if only for a little while.

12

Martin, Simpson, LaKing, and Carriere

Gladiators

Whatever comes out of these gates, we've got a better chance of survival if we work together. Do you understand? If we stay together, we survive.

—Maximus, from the film *Gladiator*

WHEN A PERSON is sentenced to a penitentiary term, the impression left with the judge, the lawyers at trial, and spectators is that, for a period of time, Canada's harshest punishment—the deprivation of liberty—will be endured in a place where boredom is likely to be the greatest hardship. Few, however, realize that a penitentiary term also condemns the convicted person to a harsh and often violent environment, where survival depends on navigating a dangerous and unpredictable social hierarchy. In this world, even a seemingly minor insult—like being called a "goof"—can spark a fight to the death, evoking the dark and brutal contests of the Roman Colosseum.

On February 3, 1999, *Kingston Whig-Standard* crime reporter Rob Tripp received a most unusual call. Tripp knew that a Kingston Penitentiary inmate, Alfie Martin, had been stabbed and died. What the Correctional Service of Canada had not told the media were the suspects' names in what was considered a prison murder.

The caller identified himself as Robert Simpson, a former inmate of Kingston Penitentiary. But Simpson wasn't just calling on his own behalf—he was also speaking for his fellow KP inmate, Donald LaKing.

After January 26, Simpson and LaKing had been involuntarily transferred to maximum-security Millhaven Institution. At the time the call was made to Rob Tripp, a third suspect's name had not been added to the list. That inmate was Pierre Carriere.

"I told [authorities] that I did it, and they still haven't come and charged me," Simpson told Tripp. "I didn't hide anything…I made a full statement to police [on videotape]." Both Simpson and LaKing were spending twenty-three hours a day in solitary confinement when the call to the Kingston newspaper was made.

Murders were nothing new to the penitentiary system. A 1986 article by the *Toronto Star's* Kathleen Kenna listed examples of murders that had taken place in the previous three years.

- August 10, 1983 – Peter Campbell, 27, beaten with a weight-lifting bar;
- January 12, 1984 – Gerald Stewardson, 25, was strangled with a parka cord in the exercise yard at Millhaven Institution;
- February 27, 1986 – Niki Rivard, 23, stabbed to death in his cell at Millhaven;
- May 30, 1986 – James Harvey, 24, stabbed at Joyceville Institution;
- July 20, 1986 – Mark Shannon, 26, fatally injured in a knife fight at Kingston Penitentiary by Terry Fitzsimmons;
- October 5, 1986 – Larry Parney, 27, stabbed in his cell at Collins Bay Institution.

The Campbell murder noted above was a situation where the inmate was in a segregation cell, spending twenty-three hours a day in solitary confinement. He refused to leave his cell for a one-hour exercise period because he feared he would be injured or killed. He had passed a note to the prison nurse for delivery to the prison doctor expressing his fear. The doctor was not in, and the notice was placed in the doctor's mail slot. Campbell did not go into the yard but remained quietly in his cell.

When the hour-long exercise period ended, and inmates returned to their cells, Campbell's solitary cell number was called out to be unlocked. The guards failed to notice that Campbell had never left his cell but triggered the unlocking mechanism anyway. This allowed Campbell's inmate adversaries to gain entrance and do him in.

The case went to court in March 1985. Four inmates pleaded guilty to the murder or to being accessories. One of those inmates was Donald LaKing. He was sentenced to five years for being an accomplice. It meant nothing. The sentence would run concurrently with the three life sentences he was already serving. This was a grim reminder of the cycle of violence that often perpetuates within the prison system. However, it also provided an opportunity for reflection and a realization that systemic changes were necessary to prevent such tragedies.

When I read Rob Tripp's *Toronto Star* article, I was undoubtedly unaware that I would later be representing Donald LaKing on another charge of murder. Representing LaKing allowed me to gain a deeper understanding of the complexities of the criminal justice system and the challenges faced by those who are incarcerated. It also reinforced my commitment to seek justice and advocate for reforms that would create a safer and more humane environment for all inmates.

Most people who have been law-abiding citizens their whole lives think that justice is served when an accused is sentenced and led out of the courtroom to begin a penitentiary term. Our punishment is supposed to be the loss of liberty. In reality, the journey of justice does not end with sentencing; it merely transitions into a different phase, where the focus should shift towards rehabilitation and ensuring the safety and dignity of incarcerated people, but seldom does.

Few realize that after being transported from the courtroom, life becomes much more fragile than if one were sitting on a cot wiling away the time until the warrant of committal expires. Few entering the correctional system for the first time have any suspicion of the amount of sexual and physical violence they will observe and perhaps experience in their new surroundings. The situation becomes worse when there is little hope of release. For those who have used brute force to achieve their goals, prison offers little disincentive. It becomes a modern-day school for gladiators.

Crime is said to be a young man's disease; birthdays are the only cure. The list of people murdered in prison listed earlier is notable in that the victims were all young adults. At the time of Simpson's call to the *Whig-Standard*, he was 36. Donald LaKing was 42.

Back in 1978, LaKing, then twenty-one years old, had been charged along with two others with willfully setting fire to the Saint John provincial jail. Both Simpson and LaKing had their body count. Simpson was in prison for stabbing a man outside a Quyon, Quebec bar. He was serving an eleven-year sentence for manslaughter and robbery. Carriere had been sentenced to two life sentences for the murders of two men in Quebec.

Alfie Martin had also had a list of convictions, making him an unsympathetic victim, as he had run up numerous convictions in his 38 years. He followed an 81-year-old woman, broke into her house to steal her purse, and sexually assaulted her. Along with a few others, Martin then broke into the home of a 66-year-old man, where they beat and robbed him. He also stabbed two unarmed brothers.

People with such records are simply assumed to be killers, and little time is spent evaluating an explanation as to why a fatal assault took place. When an inmate injures or kills another inmate or a guard, the expectation is that the incident becomes the prisoner's ticket to a Special Handling Unit (SHU), where years of solitary confinement are the norm. The first step in this transition was having Simpson and LaKing relocated to another prison where they would be in solitary confinement.

Admitting murder to reporter Rob Tripp was extraordinary. Simpson urged the reporter that he wanted his story told because he feared that once shipped off to a SHU, the true story of how correctional officers shirked their duties would never be said. He believed a coverup was underway to protect those whose job it was to defuse prison violence.

Simpson feared any presumption of innocence would be lost and that the Correctional Service of Canada would impose the punishment without hearing the accused's side of the story. He wanted to be charged and go to trial. He was adamant that he and LaKing had acted in self-defence.

Simpson told Tripp that inmate Alfic Martin was running amok on the cellblock, assaulting and threatening to assault Simpson and other inmates. Martin appeared to be high on alcohol and narcotics. There had been a ten-minute knife fight on the range where Martin tried to kill LaKing. Simpson described his involvement in the incident:

> He [Martin] put his hand in his pocket to get a knife or something, and then I defended myself, and as soon as he moved two feet away from me, I dropped [my] knife and walked away. I want this to come out in court. I want to know why no one came to help me, and I want it shown that I did not hurt anyone with intent. This was self-preservation.

The reporter then contacted the Correctional Service of Canada (CSC) to ask about their reaction to the unusual story he had just been told. Kingston Penitentiary assistant warden John Odie told him:

> Certainly, there's no coverup. Two investigations are ongoing. Police and the Correctional Service are investigating. If there are any deficiencies or recommendations that are contained in either one of the reports, we certainly will react accordingly.

Simpson told Tripp that he believed the videotapes of activities in the cell block would show Martin had repeatedly accosted him. It started as playful jousting but rapidly turned ugly. Simpson recalled:

> Then he started to get really serious and started punching me really hard, real hard, and I said, 'Look, I don't want no trouble. I don't want to play around like that. Sorry. Stop it'.

Martin looked at Simpson and said, "You want to mess with me? You don't know me. I'll murder you." Martin then punched Simpson again. There were 29 inmates locked in this range, and tensions were building. LaKing tried to play peacemaker. He stepped in to tell Martin to back off. Martin walked away briefly, but only so long as it took him to retrieve a knife. He then confronted Simpson and LaKing again, and all hell broke loose.

Simpson said he was unprepared for the attack. He never sought to bait Martin or insult him. "I wasn't upset," Simpson remembered, "just scared to death." When he stabbed Martin, it was in self-defence. "I defended myself, and as soon as Martin moved two feet away from me, I dropped the knife and walked away," Simpson repeated, stressing his belief he acted in self-defence.

Reporter Tripp also contacted Detective Sergeant Rick Myers, head of the Ontario Provincial Police-led penitentiary squad investigating criminal activity within Ontario's prisons. "There's no coverup." Myers maintained. "We're doing a thorough investigation, and we want all the evidence to be gathered before we lay any charges."

Assistant Warden Odie did not deny that Martin had a violent past but made no comment on Simpson's allegation that Martin was hated by the authorities in the prison. There would be no admission that the staff did not care if Martin was taken out by his fellow cons. Odie did confirm that just before five in the afternoon on the day Martin was killed, staff saw an altercation on the cellblock and observed that Martin was not "acting normally." Staff suspected he was under the influence of some contraband substance. Odie recalled that Martin was eventually removed from the cellblock at about eight that evening. He suffered from stab wounds. Other inmates returned to their cells peacefully. Odie also confirmed that police had seized video tapes but would not speculate what those tapes would reveal.

Donald LaKing also served up a telephone confession of his involvement in Martin's slaying. LaKing said that Martin had cornered him in LaKing's cell the day Martin went on a drug and alcohol-fuelled rampage. "I fully believed this man intended to kill me," LaKing stated. As Martin tried to close in on LaKing, LaKing found a metal shelf bracket and slammed the object down on Martin's head. "I hit him three or four times on the head, repelling him. There was blood, all from the top of his head." Like Simpson, LaKing blamed the situation on the prison staff, who were supposed to maintain order and not let things get out of control. "I believe they are responsible for this individual's death," LaKing stated.

LaKing accused prison staff of failing to isolate Martin earlier in the day when they knew Martin was intoxicated and out of control. Martin was said to have become abusive to staff at about one in the afternoon, continuing his belligerent behaviour well into the afternoon. In the late afternoon, he shouted and threatened in the prison dome area, the central hub for access to the various cell block areas. Most inmates who acted out in this manner would be immediately restrained and moved away to isolation.

But Martin, according to LaKing, was not an ordinary inmate. Staff hated and feared Martin, LaKing believed. The inference was that staff foresaw the possibility that inmates would quell Martin's obnoxious behaviour without risking staff safety. LaKing felt no hesitancy in stating his position.

> They figured he either is going to come up into the range and stab somebody and that way end up transferred to a special handling unit or somebody's going to take care of him...as did happen.

LaKing expected the more than 20 inmates caged along with him in the cell block area where the stabbing occurred—and the video camera that recorded happenings on the range—would back him up.

It wasn't until the beginning of August that Simpson and LaKing were advised of the decision that both men would be charged with second-degree murder. A third man was also implicated. Pierre Carriere was 36 years old and had been one of the 28 inmates residing on the range where the Martin stabbing occurred. The men were not new to being involved in the human loss of life.

As noted previously, LaKing had pleaded guilty to the Millhaven incident. Simpson was in prison for stabbing a man outside a Quyon, Quebec bar. He was serving an 11-year sentence for manslaughter and robbery. Carriere had been sentenced to two life sentences for the murders of two men in Quebec. The men had nothing to lose in taking the matter to trial. A deal for less time and a reduction of charges would be meaningless.

Simpson and LaKing had contacted me before the actual laying of the charges. Both had been granted Legal Aid. I advised that it would be improper for me to represent both men on an expected murder charge. I urged that another lawyer be retained. Simpson and LaKing wanted me to name a colleague who would not be afraid to stand up to the system. I suggested several names and outlined the backgrounds of the colleagues I recommended. In the list of names I put forward, I mentioned that Toronto criminal lawyer Edward Sapiano was known to compile a list of Toronto police officers who had been caught, as Edward put it, "testilying." He would raise the issue whenever possible to shatter any credibility the police officer would have when involved in his clients' trials. This satisfied both Simpson and LaKing. It was agreed that I would act for LaKing and contact Sapiano, asking that he represent Simpson.

Once retained, Sapiano and I made several court appearances protesting that police were dragging their feet on the investigation while the prisoners were confined under severely restrictive prison conditions.

When the murder charges were laid, it was somewhat surprising to Simpson and LaKing that Pierre Carriere would be included as one of Martin's killers. The Ottawa press was unsympathetic in describing the man who had been raised in the Lowertown area of the city. An August 6, 1999, edition of the *Ottawa Citizen* described Carriere as a "career criminal." It recounted how he had gunned down a corner store owner in front of the businessman's son and then killed and dismembered his partner in the crime.

On August 6, 1999, Robert Simpson, Donald LaKing, and Pierre Carriere entered a Kingston courtroom wearing handcuffs and leg shackles. This would be a routine appearance before a justice of the peace, but it marked the beginning of the judicial process. No pleas were taken; no disclosure of the evidence the Crown prosecutor would rely on had been disclosed to defence counsel. There was uncertainty as to why Carriere was with the other two co-accused. Simpson and LaKing continued asserting that Carriere had not been with them when Martin was stabbed.

While it was promising that the three would eventually be heard and their positions known, there was a more immediate crisis. Simpson and LaKing had been held in solitary confinement at Millhaven Institution since an involuntary transfer to that prison had been ordered when Martin died. I had brought an application to the Federal Court seeking their release, noting in the court brief that they were to be presumed innocent until proven guilty and commencing punishment for a crime only alleged to have happened, violating their rights as citizens of Canada. The governing legislation of Canada's prisons clearly states that all prisoners retain the same rights as free Canadians, except those rights necessarily constrained by their incarceration.

I had always been critical of the use of solitary confinement. In an earlier case, I had brought to the court's attention for the first time the psychological torture that solitary confinement entailed. I had hoped that my representation of Kingston Penitentiary inmate Terry Fitzsimmons, who had spent six years in solitary before being released directly to the streets, would become a test case that could see that a regressive form of punishment was unconstitutional.

After his release, Terry had gone on a spree of bank robberies and murders that resulted from the mental torture imposed on him. The defence would have put the prison system itself on trial. However, Terry Fitzsimmons did not have the mental stamina to continue the fight and begged that the judicial process be cut short. He ended up pleading guilty to lesser charges of second-degree murder. Perhaps the Simpson and

LaKing cases would allow me once again to bring the research of Harvard Professor and Psychiatrist Dr. Stuart Grassian to the courts' attention. I would ask if turning men into monsters was in society's long-term best interest.

In the federal court claim, I sought, on Simpson and LaKing's behalf, a permanent injunction barring the Correctional Service from transferring the pair to an out-of-province SHU. They could not instruct counsel and make full answer and defence to an expected murder charge. The claim also noted that there were incompatible inmates at the SHU where the possibility of their being killed was exceptionally high.

The Federal Court case was adjourned when the police promised the charges would be forthcoming in May. Meanwhile, Sapiano and I continued to fight for the release of Simpson and LaKing from solitary confinement in the provincial Superior Court. In his remarks to Justice Paul Cosgrove, Edward Sapiano noted the extreme concern of the inmates' lawyers. "These two men are being held like animals in a cage. Animals at the Humane Society are being treated better than our clients," Sapiano asserted. Crown Attorney Jack McKenna told the judge there was no reason to rush to have the court interfere with how corrections officials maintained the situation. He let the court know he had spoken with the police recently and was told that a decision to charge the inmates would be made within three weeks. Courts are always reluctant to second-guess correctional officials. Accordingly, Justice Cosgrove adjourned the move for release from solitary to later in the month.

Even after charges were laid on August 4, more procedural wrangling occurred. Edward Sapiano filed documents in a Kingston court in late August to force a September 2 review before a judge to explain why full disclosure of the Crown's case about the three men charged has not been made. The court application did not go as expected. Justice Helen MacLeod held this was not an unusual or exceptional case where the circumstances would require a review of the adequacy of the Crown's disclosure by a justice other than the trial judge (*R. v. Simpson et al.*, 2000). The problem was that a trial judge would not be appointed until the parties signalled their readiness to go to trial.

The Crown suggested it was common for a delay in providing full disclosure. Sapiano continued by describing the delay as foot-dragging. "This case is different," Sapiano charged. He noted that the police had seven months to collect evidence before laying charges. "I am absolutely confident that the Crown and the OPP are going to be dragging their feet every step of the way," Sapiano said. Both Defence counsel for Simpson and LaKing were particularly anxious to review the videotapes of the images recorded on the day of the stabbing. Defence counsel believed the production of the tapes would vindicate their clients' positions that they were acting in self-defence.

While these preliminary skirmishes were ongoing, I continued seeking funding to attack the issue of solitary confinement. I applied to the newly restored Court Challenges Program, whereby the federal government offered five thousand dollars in funding to lawyers interested in bringing cases seeking to create new laws enhancing citizens' civil liberties.

When I appeared before a panel to decide if a work-up of a case to challenge the transfer of inmates to Special Handling Units before being convicted, I argued that the question to be asked was if such a transfer would amount to psychological torture. "I'd like to challenge the constitutionality of the practice of that kind of a review that does not allow for any discretion," I maintained. The argument worked. The five thousand dollars was for the development of the position paper. Further funding would be provided if a test case went to trial.

The Court Challenges Program had been eliminated by a Progressive Conservative government but restored when the Jean Chrétien Liberal government was returned to power. It did not sit well with the Conservative Minister of Correctional Services of Ontario, Rob Sampson.

Although my work challenging the Correctional Service practice focused on civil liberties, I was astounded that it created a political firestorm in Ontario. I was arguing about a federal power that had no application to how Ontario ran its jails. The division of powers was irrelevant when it served a politician's instinct to play a "get tough on crime" card.

Sampson wrote a letter to the editor of the *Kingston Whig-Standard* saying he was "fed up" with governments paying more attention to criminals' rights than to victims' rights. Rob Sampson wrote:

> Rather than funding make-work projects for defence lawyers and being apologists for offenders, the Liberals would be wise to follow our government's lead in recognizing who the real victims are!....As far as the Ontario government is concerned, it's the victims of crime, and not the criminals, that are placed in a disadvantaged and vulnerable position.

The Correctional Service also agreed to release the inmates from solitary confinement, making the Federal Court application moot. The court application in that action was discontinued.

The trial began in Kingston on April 18, 2001. Assistant Crown Attorneys Ross Drummond and Gerard Laarhuis acted for the prosecution. Toronto lawyer Douglas Usher appeared for Carriere. All three accused persons pleaded not guilty and asked to be tried by a judge alone without a jury. The accused and their lawyers agreed that having the case tried before a jury would not be advisable. It would be expected that the prosecution would try to bring out the fact that each accused was previously convicted of killing one or more people. That could leave an adverse inference that jurors might decide the case as "taking out the trash." Further, even if a motion were brought to exclude admission of their criminal records into evidence, most jurors would recognize that the defendants were penitentiary inmates and would want to know why they were in prison. The speculation could be as disastrous as having their records admitted.

Ross Drummond began the case by making an opening statement to the trial judge, Justice Bernard Hurley. Drummond decided it was preferable to admit Alfie Martin's unsavoury background upfront without being brought out in cross-examination. Drummond acknowledged Martin as a "drunk and a bully" who "used violence to get his way." He went on to advise that the 38-year-old victim was frequently intoxicated and was so on January 26, 1999, when he was killed.

Martin had been convicted in 1984 and 1989 for rape, robbery, aggravated assault and attempted murder. He committed his last two crimes three months after being released from prison. He was serving a ten-year sentence when he was slain. While in prison, Martin accumulated over 50 institutional charges. Most were for assaults and damaging prison property. On the day he died, Martin and a buddy set a fire on G-range, where he and the three accused men lived, causing the prison sprinkler and alarm systems to be activated.

Assistant Crown Attorney Drummond concluded his address by reminding the trial judge,

> Society does not throw away the key and turn a blind eye to what happens behind those walls. Even Alfie Martin deserves the protection of our law and the right to continue as a human being.

Defence counsel looked at one another, wondering how that remark would square with Minister Sampson's attitude of minimal concern for criminals.

Drummond outlined the case he hoped to prove beyond a reasonable doubt: that Simpson stabbed Martin while Carriere held him and LaKing clobbered him with a metal bracket. Drummond concluded that the evidence would show the contention that the accused acted in self-defence as a self-serving lie.

The first day of evidence looked promising for the defence. Most of the day was spent watching videotapes of the events that transpired on the day of the killing. The tapes portrayed Martin as a man who was seriously out of control. Sapiano questioned Corrections Officer John McCormack, who had presented the recordings in evidence. He answered, "Alfie Martin got drunk a lot. He was predictably volatile. Many inmates didn't challenge Alfie Martin; many feared him."

The videotapes allowed the judge to see first-hand what had happened. At 3:47 on the tape, the video showed Martin, LaKing, Simpson, and another inmate named Long leaving a cell. McCormack commented, "It looks like Alfie Martin takes his coat off and is swinging at Simpson. They're having a little boxing match of some sort." When the video camera zoomed in to get a better look at the situation, McCormack could interpret the situation better: "I don't believe it's a play fight, and I don't know who's winning." Then, suddenly, the fighting stops. The combatants appeared to be shaking hands. Martin is seen kissing him on the cheek and hugging him.

Less than an hour later, at 4:38 p.m., the tape depicts Martin, Simpson, and LaKing talking. LaKing is shown entering his cell on the tier above and leaving about 50 seconds later. LaKing descended stairs to enter the lower tier of cells and engaged in another "little boxing dance" that lasted 31 seconds.

Eight minutes later, a flurry of activity included Martin and several inmates, including LaKing and Carriere, in the stairwell on the fourth level. No audio was on the tape, but one would have expected a noisy situation. Martin was shown pushing LaKing and brandishing a homemade knife inmates call a "shiv."

McCormack testified that he called the Unit Manager to report that Martin was causing problems. Staff spoke to Martin at about six o'clock, trying to calm him down. Martin admitted that he was drunk and had shot heroin. The manager recommended that Martin go to segregation to allow himself to control himself better away from other inmates. Martin said he would agree to do so if, and only if, he had assurances he would be released from segregation the following day. The manager could not bind the institution to such terms. Martin then stormed off in anger. The institutional staff did nothing to assert control over Martin.

Right after that, there was a fire. Inmates had set the fire. The sprinklers kicked in. McCormack described his view from the control room window as "like a car wash." He could not observe what was going on outside his vantage point. The fire's first flash was at 6:05 p.m. Nineteen seconds later, the flames flared up. Nine seconds after that, the fire was out. At 6:09, the video camera was covered up. Martin was not seen on tape after that. The camera had been covered by Martin's young inmate friend, Clifford Long.

On the following day of trial, the prosecution called an inmate witness. It is a violation of the "con code" to testify at trials with the publication of the inmate's name. Should other inmates learn that an inmate was testifying against one of their own, there could be severe, indeed lethal, consequences. Therefore, the trial judge imposed an order barring the publication of the inmate's name.

This inmate witness was a career criminal transferred to Kingston Penitentiary after escaping from a minimum-security institution and recaptured several months earlier. He came to know Martin but denied their relationship was particularly close. He was just someone he had used drugs with and occasionally played cards with. The inmate was resentful that his security level had increased to maximum. He did not like being at KP. He said during cross-examination that he thought it was "inappropriate" that he had been sent to that prison and that he requested to transfer out of it three days after his arrival.

Although he agreed that Martin could be irritable at times, he disagreed with Officer McCormack that Martin was out of sorts that last day of his life. He recalled the incident he witnessed. It was LaKing, he insisted, who pushed Martin. LaKing knocked Martin off balance, and then Simpson moved in and stabbed Martin repeatedly. He said the knife used was the same one he had seen in LaKing's hand earlier, when LaKing had the tussle with Martin. He described the weapon as having a cylindrical blade, like an ice pick. It was made of yellow metal and had a handle wrapped in white tape. It was probably made of copper or bronze since inmates believed those metals do not set off the metal detectors should an inmate be subject to a scan when moving from one prison area to another. After the stabbing, Simpson washed the blood from the knife while using a sink near the washers and driers on the lower tier. He then threw the blade through an open window nearby on the range.

He also said that he observed Martin trying to get away after he was stabbed. However, LaKing pursued him along the range catwalk and beat him on the head with a heavy object about a foot long and four to six inches wide.

This witness blamed Martin's death on Simpson and LaKing. Should he be found credible, it could be vital to convict Martin and LaKing of murder. It was crucial to the defence to raise doubt about the accuracy of his testimony. A vigorous cross-examination was needed.

When it came time to challenge this witness, it was decided it would be most fruitful to suggest that the witness had reason to lie. That reason was his resentment of being transferred to Kingston Penitentiary and his desire to get out.

Therefore, the witness needed to state in his own words how he came to reside at the institution, his dislike for having his security rating enhanced, and the steps he had taken to be transferred out of KP. He willingly shared this information.

He also acknowledged that should he return to Kingston Penitentiary after giving the explosive testimony he had just provided, it would not sit well with other inmates who abided by the con code. He again acknowledged that he fully understood the danger he had just exposed himself to. He was then asked if giving evidence for the prosecution was an easy way to get a transfer to a lower-security institution. He said, "I'm not sure how to answer that." He then agreed that it would be possible that having incompatibles in the same prison would assist in securing a transfer.

Right after Martin's death, this inmate agreed to talk with the police. Transferring him to lower security was approved 15 days later, on February 11. The transfer was brought about on February 17, two days after he gave his statement to the police. Having this brought out in evidence crushed the inmate witness's credibility.

Douglas Usher must have felt gratified that during the first few days of trial, no evidence was led that implicated his client, Pierre Carriere, in the killing. That all changed when another inmate, a 32-year-old who was serving time for manslaughter, told the court that Martin was making his way along the upper tier of G-range toward the control room where the guards were located when Carriere suddenly appeared and blocked his path. At this time, Martin had been mortally wounded. He was about the width of eight cells from where the stabbing had occurred, and LaKing chased him down, beating him with a heavy object.

The witness described what he observed as leading up to the stabbing. He said the fatal encounter between Martin and

Simpson occurred a couple of hours after the knife fight with LaKing. The confrontation that led up to Martin's death started when Simpson was standing at the railing of an upper tier looking down at Martin on the tier below. The witness stated, "I could see he [Martin] was getting upset." Martin then proposed that if he was to fight Simpson, they should get at it.

Martin extended his hands to prove they were empty. He stated that the men should either fight or drop the animosity. "I know you're paranoid about my having a knife. You know I got no knife."

The witness was unclear if Martin had ascended the stairs to put himself close to Simpson, but that is the only logical inference. If the witness told the truth, that could explain what happened next.

Simpson moved to the front of LaKing's cell and placed his arms on it. His back was to Martin. As Simpson turned around, the witness observed that Carriere, seated on the railing, dismounted and moved toward LaKing's cell. Carriere grabbed Martin as Simpson inflicted the stab wounds, and Carriere must have also hit Martin, maybe even stabbing him. According to this witness, Martin retreated toward the control post while LaKing continued the beating with a bent bar.

That witness was a significant setback for Douglas Usher. Unlike Simpson and LaKing, Carriere made no statements about himself in the incident. If this witness were believed, Usher's client would be a co-conspirator in the murder.

Carriere's chance rested on the cross-examining skills of his lawyer. Usher did not disappoint. He challenged the sequence of events the witness described and secured the admission that he may not have the order of events quite right. He also agreed with Usher that it would have been foolhardy for Carriere to perch on the catwalk railing four metres above a concrete floor. Usher continued to snipe at the witness's sworn facts, causing him to back down on the certainty with which he had delivered his testimony. The cross-examination concluded with an attack on the proposition that Carriere had been involved in the stabbing. The witness' final answer was, "I'm not sure."

When Simpson and LaKing had first spoken with Rob Tripp, the newspaper reporter, after the event, they claimed that the Correctional Service had mishandled the situation and put their lives in danger. With the inmate witnesses being subject to attacks on their credibility, the testimony of the prison staff would be able to resolve any lingering doubts about the accused men's liability.

Sherri Lynn Crisp had been the unit manager the evening when Martin died. She admitted that Martin's unruly behaviour had escalated over the afternoon, but she waited for the right time before ordering officers onto the range to apprehend him. Later, she had a chance to speak with Martin. She suggested he go into segregation, but he refused. He claimed other inmates would call him a "goof" if he agreed. She understood that being called a goof in prison was the worst insult imaginable. There was also a plan to remove Martin involuntarily after the inmates were locked down for the supper count. But the inmates refused to lock up.

Corrections Officer Earl Young was posted to watch Levels 3 and 4 of G Range on the day of the altercation. He remained unconvinced that Simpson and Martin's fight was other than play or that the "shoving match" on the stairs was severe, notwithstanding the glint of metal.

The Crown also called two inmates from F Range. Their credibility was also challenged in cross-examination. One of those inmates was forced to divulge that he had repeatedly traded information about fellow prisoners with the Preventive Security Officer at KP and other institutions, no doubt in exchange for perceived benefits. On one such instance, he had reported that another inmate had been muscling him for medications. It was later discovered that the inmate had been profiting from selling the drugs to other inmates in the prison's black market.

By the time the trial ended its tenth day, Usher could be pleased that a headline in the Kingston daily newspaper read, "Carriere's role in slaying still unknown." The inmate witnesses were unable to link Usher's client to the killing. However, the best shot of tying this third accused to the crime would be by forensic evidence.

The Crown called Dr. David Dexter to give expert evidence. Dexter was director of autopsy services and the forensic unit at Kingston General Hospital. On examining the wounds inflicted on Alfie Martin, his expert opinion was that three different weapons created the wounds. This lent credence to the allegation that Carriere was involved. This evidence was the backbone of the Crown's case.

However, Usher had a witness to counter Dexter's testimony. Usher drew upon the case involving another pathologist, Dr. James Ferris. Dr. Ferris had been a critical witness in the murder trial of Louise Reynolds. She had been charged with causing the death of her young daughter, Sharon. One expert had provided an opinion that Sharon's injuries were caused by stabbing, but Ferris had concluded the wounds were equally consistent with dog bites. Charges were withdrawn. Usher explained that reliance should not be rooted in one opinion.

Since no murder weapons were found, Usher argued, variations in the type of wounds could account for a belief that more than one weapon had been used. Dr. Dexter's evidence that the shape of the stab wounds suggested two weapons were used. As for LaKing, the doctor testified that although there were contusions to the scalp, there was no brain injury. Martin did not die because a metal wall bracket pummeled his head. The injury that resulted in death was a stab wound slightly above Martin's navel that pierced the mesenteric artery, causing a massive hemorrhage.

When Dr. Ferris was called, he questioned Dr. Dexter's analysis. Having reviewed Martin's autopsy report and photographs, Ferris swore a single weapon could have caused the wounds. When cross-examined, the uncertainty of the number of weapons was amplified by Dr. Ferris' response to the question asking if more than one weapon may have been involved. He replied, "Can they all be caused by one weapon? Absolutely. Can they be caused by more than one weapon? Yes."

Assistant Crown attorney Gerard Laarhuis hoped he could strengthen the Crown's case by calling the person the court ordered could only be identified as Martin's young friend. The "young friend" was not as helpful as Laarhuis had hoped.

This witness was only 19 when sent to prison two years earlier for manslaughter in 1995. He had stabbed a man five times during a robbery when he was 16, and three years later, stabbed an inmate for calling him a name. An additional year was added to his sentence. He trashed his cell once because he did not want to eat liver. He had also assaulted guards. At Kingston Penitentiary, his disciplinary infractions totalled 138.

He denied witnessing Martin getting stabbed. He also denied seeing blood on Martin, although the two were together frequently. He denied he was assisting Martin in any respect. He understood Martin was a big man (180 lbs.), standing six feet tall, sporting a shaved head, and a menacing look. "He was a warrior. He could handle himself."

None of the accused took the stand to give evidence. Defence counsel had given each of their clients the view that the evidence presented by the Crown had not proven the case beyond a reasonable doubt. The accused agreed and signed instructions to their lawyers not to call evidence. Closing arguments were made, and the matter adjourned for delivery of Justice Hurley's decision.

The first sentence of the June 23, 2001 *Globe and Mail* summed up the result: "The killing of one of the nastiest and most unpredictable kingpins in Kingston Penitentiary remained a mystery yesterday after three fellow inmates were acquitted of the killing." The key finding made by Justice Hurley was that Martin's assailants acted in self-defence:

> A person defending himself against an attack, reasonably apprehended, cannot be expected to weigh to a nicety the exact measure of necessary defensive action.

The judge reviewed the various assaults that had taken place during the afternoon of the killing and wrote on each case; "I concluded that Martin was the aggressor. In each case, the other party sought peace and declared that he didn't want to fight." As for Carriere, Justice Hurley concluded that the Crown's case against him was "contradictory and confusing" and that the two inmates who gave evidence against him were "extremely unreliable."

My exhilaration of having my client acquitted of a murder charge was short-lived. A few days later, I received another call from LaKing. He and Simpson (but not Carriere) had received a notice that the Crown was seeking an appeal to the Ontario Court of Appeal. It would be possible for the Court of Appeal to overturn the acquittal and order a new trial. I wanted to assure LaKing that I wished to have every aspect of the defence examined, and if I had made any mistakes, I certainly did not want any error on my part to be hidden at LaKing's expense. I, therefore, recommended that he hire Toronto lawyer Daniel Brodsky to act on his behalf at the appeal. He did precisely that. Toronto lawyer James Lockyer acted for Simpson.

The appeal came on for hearing in February 2004. The Crown's position was that the trial judge erred in finding that the position the accused parties advanced at trial lacked an "air of reality." It maintained that life inside that range on the day of the stabbing was not much different from any other time. There was no atmosphere of "extreme fear." Simpson did not testify at trial. The Crown argued that Justice Hurley concluded that Simpson was also fearful because a reasonable person would have been afraid.

The three-judge panel of the Ontario Court of Appeal reserved its decision regarding Simpson. However, the appeal challenging the LaKing acquittal was dismissed after oral argument when the appeal was heard. The panel accepted Brodsky's argument that LaKing and Simpson were not acting in concert. The only crimes for which LaKing should have faced were for assault. The Crown had never appealed the trial judge's finding that Simpson and LaKing were not acting as a team. Any blows inflicted on Martin by LaKing were not part of the alleged murder of Martin.

The appeal court issued written reasons for dismissing the appeal regarding Simpson in April. Madam Justice Janet Simmons wrote for the unanimous court that it was entirely open for the trial judge to conclude that Simpson feared for his life. The Court said that when Simpson chose not to testify, as he had every right not to do so, and the evidence was entirely circumstantial, a trial judge had no option but to ascertain what a reasonable person would do in the circumstances and use that inference to reach a verdict.

Simpson and LaKing achieved the decision they wanted when they spoke with a reporter shortly after Martin's death. The claim that the Correctional Service acted improperly was not raised at trial. However, that complaint was later dealt with at a coroner's inquest about Alfie Martin's death in 2005.

Why had the guards allowed the violence to escalate? At the time, defence lawyers for Simpson and LaKing had suggested that Martin was a troublemaker, and the correctional staff hoped for fellow inmates to do him in. Another theory was that the Martin stabbing occurred at a politically sensitive time. An inquest in Kingston had recently looked into the 1993 death of Robert Gentles, who had been asphyxiated by a team of guards sent to Upper G Range to restrain him. Three years before Martin's death, Madam Justice Louise Arbour had written a scathing report on abuses that had taken place at the Kingston Prison for Women in which she described the federal correctional service as a lawless entity in need of judicial control.

The guards' union was granted standing at the inquest, and those claims were disputed. The union maintained that frontline workers were hampered by a bureaucracy limiting their actions until management approved them.

The coroner's jury also heard how Martin's friend Long had covered the lens of the surveillance camera and set a fire on the range.

After a week-long hearing, the jury concluded that Martin died from stab wounds. The jury could not assign criminal liability; its function is merely to determine the cause of death and make recommendations to prevent similar situations in the future. In this case, the recommendations focused on installing more security cameras with colour and sound capabilities on the range. Before the inquest began, the prison had installed a second surveillance camera. However, the jury found that insufficient because "all areas of the range must be visible at all times on camera," and it is "imperative that guards in the control post have an unobstructed view." Other recommendations suggested reconstruction of the prison's layout to give better visibility to happenings on a range, the installation of loudspeakers to ensure commands are heard, and giving lower-ranking staff more authority to act in a crisis. These were recommendations only, and the jury's analysis was predictably ignored.

Serving a prison term should not be a recruitment drive for warriors facing mortal combat. Some inmates are so dangerous that they can never be reasonably expected to live life peaceably once released. Instead, we have enacted dangerous offender laws to keep the most dangerous individuals away from those of us on the outside and never to become a threat to us. Yet, keeping them inside, very dangerous people continue to prey on their fellow inmates.

Is it any wonder that the prison experience hardens an individual such that the imprisoned individual must constantly be on guard? By continuing present modes of operation and neglecting meaningful reforms to ensure that our prisons are no longer gladiator schools, any prison sentence can result in the unexpected imposition of the death penalty. It may be time to examine our laws to ensure that they aim to provide peace inside and outside the institutions.

Most criminologists would accept the notion that the function of Canada's correctional system is rehabilitation. But when is it time to give up and find that some offenders cannot be rehabilitated? It is a common phrase at Parole Board of Canada hearings: "The best predictor of future behaviour is past behaviour." When is it time to admit that some criminals are not salvageable? In Canada, courts can impose an indeterminate sentence if one is found to be a dangerous offender.

In the United States, several states have enacted "three-strike laws." The three-strikes laws significantly increase the prison sentences of persons who have been previously convicted of two or more violent crimes or serious felonies and limit the ability of these offenders to receive a punishment other than a life sentence. It is a shift from the concept of rehabilitation as a goal in corrections. It has been called the McDonald-ization of punishment. Instead of focusing on meting out a penalty specially tailored to the individual offender, the aim is to control high-risk groups based on aggregations and statistical averages. Three-strikes laws achieve uniformity in the punishment just as a fast-food chain advertises uniformity of its products.

What laws such as Canada's dangerous offender law provisions do is to ensure the continuation of the status quo. Such laws remove hope of eventual release and an incentive to abide by institutional rules. They harden people in ways the public rarely sees, returning them to the streets shaped by acts of darkness both suffered and committed, and no longer fearing the worst punishment our courts can impose.

13

Paul Bernardo

Open and Honest Inmate Expression

Public opinion is a compound of folly, weakness, prejudice, wrong feeling, right feeling, obstinacy and newspaper paragraphs.

—Robert Peel

VERY FEW would dispute that in Canada, we live in a country that recognizes the Rule of Law. The laws by which we are governed apply to all. No one is above the law. Everyone has the right to be treated equally by the same standards. We also live in a democracy. That system of government recognizes that the will of the majority is the basis on which we enact laws, although respect for minority interests must be considered. Sometimes, a seeming majority of the public can be convinced that our laws should not be applied equally. When political considerations enter the public forum, one faces the problem that perhaps democracy and the Rule of Law cannot coexist.

Thankfully, that discord rarely erupts. Yet, the visible fault line can be seen when we deal with prison issues. The Rule of Law says prisoners should be treated humanely and fairly according to established practices. Yet, we see the public becoming enraged when a criminal is seen benefitting from the laws requiring fair treatment, and they conflict with the public notion that greater punishment not conforming with the rules is warranted. That tectonic friction was evident when the public saw the lenient treatment of one of Canada's most notorious criminals.

When *Toronto Sun* reporters Scott Burnside and Alan Cairns released their book *Deadly Innocence* in 1995, most Canadians were familiar with the name Paul Bernardo. The authors maintain that Bernardo would score 33 out of a possible 40 on the Psychopathy Checklist developed by Dr. Robert Hare. He also shared the profile of a serial sex killer based on FBI studies. The reporters noted,

> As so many sexual sadists tend to be, Paul Bernardo is a psychopath. During his time in court, he exhibited nothing like traditional emotion. He appeared puzzled whenever Crown attorney Ray Houlihan confronted him with the moral aspects of his forced sex. He described cutting up Leslie Mahaffey's body as clinically as he would have analyzed a balance sheet at Price Waterhouse.

There was no appreciation of the terrible sense of loss experienced by the parents of the slain women, Doug and Donna French, and Dan and Debbie Mahaffy. Their lives were forever changed by Paul Bernardo's unforgivable acts of darkness. The change, Paul Bernardo experienced, insignificant in comparison, was his removal to a segregation cell at Kingston Penitentiary. He lived isolated in a cell with a plexiglass shield to prevent other inmates from spitting or throwing excrement at him. Although the death penalty was no longer administered in Canada, life imprisonment meant that he would continue in isolation indefinitely. He would have to fear for his life lest other inmates carry out the retribution the courts were prevented from administering.

It's a wonder that Bernardo was ever arrested. There had been various sightings of a person suspected of being the rapist. Still, of 11 people who came forward to police, all except one witness identified the car the suspect drove as being a Camaro. There was another witness, a mechanic, who identified the vehicle as a cream-coloured Datsun. Police had no faith in this second witness and discounted his account.

Police conducted a time-consuming and costly check on all Camaros in Ontario in the hopes of identifying the sex offender. A Toronto-area private detective, Mike O'Brien, was conducting surveillance on another suspect on another case—a man thought to have been involved in the abduction of three-year-old Kayla Klaudusz.[1] The little girl had been abducted on July 10, 1991 and was later found dead in Toronto's Ashbridge's Bay.

During the surveillance, the detective spotted his suspect leaving a Toronto swingers bar and noted the plate numbers. The man he suspected of involvement in the Klaudusz abduction climbed into a cream-coloured Datsun driven by Paul Bernardo, who was with his wife, Karla Homolka. The detective's confirmation of the mechanic's description allowed police to reopen their search. Once the vehicle was correctly identified, police were able to identify and prosecute Bernardo as the sex offender they were looking for.

Bernardo's sentence began on September 1, 1995. He was taken to Kingston Penitentiary and classified as a maximum-security inmate. His convictions were for first-degree murder (x2), kidnap-unlawfully confine (x2), aggravated sexual assault (x2), and indignity to a dead body. These index offences were for his treatment of Kristen French and Leslie Mahaffey. Other charges had been stayed connected to the death of Tammy Homolka, the sexual assaults of "Jane Doe," and other sexual assaults attributed to Bernardo, who was identified as the "Scarborough Rapist." The Correctional Service of Canada (CSC) listed Bernardo as a High-Profile Offender according to the operational guidelines of the CSC, which are known as Commissioner's Directives.

1 The suspect O'Brien was observing was not David Wayne Snowden, who was convicted in 1996 for the murder. He has remained in prison since his conviction and was denied parole in 2023. O'Brien believes Snowden was not alone in the abduction, but the man he observed was never arrested.

A high-profile offender is described as "an offender whose offence dynamics elicited or have a potential to elicit a community reaction in the form of significant public or media interest."

Bernardo's security was reviewed approximately every two years. CSC used a statistical tool called the Security Rating Scale (SRS). They developed the SRS to determine the proper level of security needed for each offender. When the SRS score was calculated, it invariably produced a number that translated to a "medium security" rating as the level required for this inmate. In every instance, at least until the SRS review conducted on November 8, 2022, the tool indicated that Bernardo should be considered a medium-security inmate.

Despite the statistics, CSC imposed an "override" to maintain Bernardo in maximum-security lockup. Bernardo's incarceration was marked by highly restricted and controlled interactions with other offenders. It was more a fear for the offender's safety than for behavioural concerns that prompted using the override.

Once sentenced and confined to a federal penitentiary, Paul Bernardo remained primarily out of the public eye. It was only when news came that once again aroused public interest that his name appeared on newspaper pages. When Karla Homolka was released, another wave of resentment toward Bernardo erupted.

On another occasion, it was written that a 30-year-old woman from London, Ontario had fallen for Bernardo, tattooed his name on her body, and announced they would be married. Yet, again, public interest in Bernardo was piqued, and he was made the scapegoat for those upset with the criminal justice system. How could he lure such women into his dark web of cruelty and murder? No newspaper attempted to discuss the psychiatric condition of hybristophilia—a term applied to people who become sexually exhilarated by those who commit crimes.[2]

Even when the press reactivated memories of Paul Bernardo, few were aware of the daily boredom Bernardo would have experienced. There is emotional pressure to lash out occasionally to relieve the monotony of prison life. Sometimes, prison rules must be broken for one's self-defence.

Paul Bernardo's segregation from the general population began on November 8, 1995, a week after his conviction and the day he arrived at Kingston Penitentiary (KP). Even though H Block at KP was home to some of Canada's most dangerous and notorious criminals, it was a solitary place with little camaraderie between inmates. Boredom was maximized.

Breach of prison rules routinely resulted in the inmate being charged institutionally. Institutional charges are not criminal but can affect one's chances before the Parole Board. Yet, H Block became the scene of a minor inmate revolt on October 5, 1998. Inmates on Lower H Block tossed their food trays from their cells and threatened to smash them up. Some inmates lit fires. Even though they were confined to their cells, a mob mentality took over. One inmate even tossed the television he had bought, considered by all as precious property, into the corridor to emphasize the frustration and boredom the inmates were experiencing. Activity such as this could not be ignored. Institutional charges were laid. Paul Bernardo was handed an Inmate Offence Report and Notification of Charge. It alleged that Bernardo had been part of the group that set cell fires. But even institutional charges must be proven. In

2 Kristin Canning, "There's Actually a Reason Why So Many Women Were Obsessed with Ted Bundy," *Women's Health*, May 7, 2019. Canadian author Elliott Leyton has been quoted as explaining why some people are attracted to "celebrity" prisoners like groupies are attracted to rock stars: "Because we romanticize and glorify violence, it's not surprising these people who are extremely violent should be seen as romantic." (Elizabeth Payne, *Calgary Herald*, August 18, 1991).

Bernardo's case, the charge was dismissed due to reasonable doubt that he had been involved.

By 2017, Paul Bernardo had had enough. He wanted to challenge the maximum-security rating that the Correctional Service had applied and enable him to move out of segregation and into a lower-security institution where he might even be considered for parole. To challenge his security level, he would have to have the court agree that maintaining his imprisonment in a maximum-security institution was unreasonable.

One of the documents a court would likely consider would be an Assessment for Decision (A4D). One such report, dated January 11, 2016, noted that, by that date, Bernardo had remained in segregation for 17 years due to his high-profile status and the constant threat to his safety from other offenders. Although the A4D confirmed that Bernardo was not in segregation, he had been placed on the "Sub Population Range as a no-contact offender." The report further noted that although other prisoners had targeted Bernardo, "he has never engaged in any institutional violence."

Bernardo never brought the challenge. Existing jurisprudence established that a Warden's decision to refuse association with general population inmates would not be disturbed by the court (*R. v. Olson,* 1987). In that case, child killer Clifford Olson challenged the legality of an order to transfer him from Kingston Penitentiary to a Special Handling Unit (SHU), a prison within a prison located out of his home province, where he would be segregated for years on end. A legal procedure known as habeas corpus is the means to challenge an illegal order. Olson suspected his transfer to segregation was on orders of the Solicitor General of Canada (now re-named The Ministry of Public Safety) the Minister responsible for Canada's penitentiaries. The heart of the case Olson brought was to determine the legality of a Minister intervening in the operations of a prison.

The Ontario Court of Appeal denied Olson's motion. It found that Olson was imprisoned in the penitentiary based on a valid warrant, and it was also clear that he was confined correctly in administrative segregation. It was the Warden's duty to make such orders. In Olson's case, there was abundant evidence to justify the Warden exercising that option. Had Olson been correct, the Appeal Court held that the Solicitor-General had neither the authority nor power to order an inmate to be segregated since the statute and regulations give that decision to the institutional head. The governing legislation recognized that the Solicitor-General had overall ministerial responsibility. Still, it did not authorize the Solicitor-General to segregate a particular prisoner from the general population in a penitentiary. It does not confer authority or power on the Solicitor-General to interfere with the rights or liberty of a specific prisoner. If the appellant was held in segregation because of the order of the Solicitor-General, the appellant's segregation was unlawful. However, the evidence was clear that the head of the institution decided whether or not the appellant should remain in administrative segregation. The fact that the Solicitor-General made an illegal order cannot place in doubt the appellant's confinement in administrative segregation, which was otherwise lawful.

A further argument by Olson was that such a transfer would be unconstitutional because it denied Olson his fundamental freedom not to be treated with cruel and unusual punishment. His continued confinement in administrative or protective segregation was not treatment that was so excessive as to outrage standards of decency. Most right-thinking people would agree that segregation from the general population in prison in the circumstances authorized by the regulations is necessary and acceptable. Olson was a dangerous man, and in light of his previous experience in the penitentiary, there were excellent reasons to fear the maintenance of order and discipline in the institution where he must serve his sentence of life imprisonment. Segregation to a prison within a prison is not per se cruel and unusual treatment, although it may become so if it is so excessive as to outrage standards of decency. Many years later, the concept of solitary confinement being unconstitutional would be accepted. Olson's case was dismissed. An appeal to the Supreme Court of Canada was denied. While this decision would demoralize Bernardo in applying, it would prove useful when he received a transfer in 2023.

Besides the Olson case, Bernardo could consider other decisions for his benefit. Another decision, *R. v. Musitano,* (2006) set out that ongoing media attention is likely to invoke reactions from the public, and it is not a legal basis for refusing a transfer to lower security.

In June of 2022, Bernardo applied for a transfer to the medium-security Bath Institution. Although he qualified with an SRS score indicating medium security, the CSC again used the override to keep him at maximum. This time, however, he worked with senior management and the Security Intelligence department at Millhaven Institution to develop a plan for institutional integration. This led to Bernardo becoming one of several inmates who would be compatible with others to attend health care, programs, school, and yard as a cohort. By July 2022, the integration program was deemed a success.

This marked a turning point since his previous failure to integrate had led prison officials to believe his safety could not be assured.

Bernardo then consulted with his Case Management team and applied to transfer to La Macaza Institution in the Quebec region. La Macaza was deemed an appropriate receiving institution because it could accommodate high-profile offenders and offenders serving time for sexual offences. The Office of the Correctional Investigator initiated informal discussions concerning Bernardo's security classification to ensure that he would be safely kept under the least restrictive conditions to ensure both his own and institutional well-being.

With the integration issue now resolved, there was no basis for overriding Bernardo's security rating. His designation as a medium-security inmate was now approved. In November of 2022, Bernardo obtained the support of his case management team to be transferred to the Quebec prison. Security would not be a concern. Bernardo would be housed behind a secure, controlled perimeter. His movements and associations would be regulated and monitored. Moreover, La Macaza Institution offered a Sex Offender Maintenance Program to bolster Bernardo's rehabilitative efforts.

The transfer was initiated on May 29, 2023. A "heads up" phone call went out to victims. Not all registered victims were immediately reached. In the afternoon of the same day, CSC once again reached out to victims, saying the transfer was complete. Victim notification was done by a directive describing the scope and timing of releasing such information.[3]

Not surprisingly, the news of the Bernardo transfer started a political firestorm. Toronto lawyer Tim Danson revived his position as spokesman for the Mahaffy and French families and raged against the transfer in Toronto media. During CBC's *Metro Morning* on June 5, Danson once again lashed out at CSC, saying that a decrease in security for Bernardo causes revictimization for the families of the murdered girls. He also claimed the transfer made it harder for the families to attend scheduled parole hearings due to the increased distances.

Most shocking was the suggestion that CSC was manufacturing a scenario that would justify the Parole Board of Canada releasing Bernardo. Danson argued that these underhanded moves jeopardize Canadians' faith in our institutions.

3 Commissioner's Directive CD-784 and the associated "Transfer Notification Tool".

Perhaps Danson cannot accept that such moves are not out of the ordinary and are to be expected as long-term offenders age in the system and complete correctional programming. Danson's concerns would not be so disturbing, except that Canada's Minister of Public Safety, Marco Mendicino, played the political card and undermined officials in his department. He told the press:

> [The decision to transfer Bernardo out of maximum was] shocking and incomprehensible. Our thoughts are with the families of Kristen French and Leslie Mahaffy and all those affected by these horrific crimes. We stand with them and all Canadians who are rightfully appalled by this move. Having devoted my career as a federal prosecutor to protecting our communities, I have reiterated my firm expectation that CSC take a victim-centred and trauma-informed approach in these cases.

It would be proper for the minister to question his top officials to ensure there were no mistakes in what happened. However, it would be nothing short of political interference should the minister direct the decision-making authority vested in his officials. If CSC decision-makers are abiding by the rule of law and acting within their limits in ordering the transfer, political interference by the minister is far more problematic than any complaint of Danson.

The Correctional Service of Canada thoroughly reviewed the Bernardo transfer, a significant event. On June 26, 2023, CSC issued a comprehensive report, a document of utmost importance, that upheld the decision-making that resulted in Bernardo's transfer. Canadians should be "rightfully appalled" about turning what appears to be a justifiable administrative decision into a political football. If we allowed the Minister of Public Safety to interfere as he seemed willing to do, we would live in a society no longer governed by the rule of law but in a police state obliging the whims of the powerful for political popularity. The review undertaken by the Correctional Service of Canada would seem to exonerate that branch of government from bowing to political pressure. Yet, on October 25, 2023, CBC News reported that CSC stopped Paul Bernardo from having his lawyer make a statement to the media concerning the transfer. The CBC report was based on documents uncovered through a *Privacy Act* application that there had been a flurry of messages between prison staff and the Privy Council Office. The gist of the communications involved a concern that Bernardo would speak publicly. One email is quoted in the news report as saying:

> We are told that Bernardo had talked to his lawyer about speaking up publicly to media on his behalf. However, we have since intervened and spoke to him about victim considerations and are told he would advise his lawyer.

The CBC report also quoted Canadian Prison Law Association president Tom Engel as indicating the transfer did not warrant a blackout to prevent safety concerns at an institution. He said:

> I'm at a loss to understand where [CSC] would think that part of their role is to shield victims from statements a prisoner might make to the media....I don't know where they think they get the authority to do that. To me, it's exceeding their role as being in charge of the custody, rehabilitation, and that sort of thing for prisoners.

Engel's quote underscores the need for transparency in treating prisoners and the importance of respecting their rights. Catherine Latimer, president of the John Howard Society of Canada, echoed Engel's words. She commented that it is fair that prisoners have an opportunity to explain what is happening to them in custody. This reiterates the importance of prisoners' voices and the need to ensure they are heard and respected.

On the one hand, the CSC took great pains to issue a report showing the transfer system was working efficiently and according to the law. Secretly, it was cooperating with the Privy Council Office to quelch the political firestorm that erupted by illegally suppressing an inmate's constitutionally guaranteed right to free speech. In this case, political considerations trumped the Rule of Law.

Another area where law and politics collide is balancing the public's right to know the workings of our institutions with laws protecting an individual's privacy. That conflict was central to an appeal brought by, among others, the French and Mahaffy families to gain access to documentation used during Bernardo's parole hearings, which were denied because of Canada's privacy laws (*Fraser et al. v. Canada, Minister of Public Safety and Emergency Preparedness et al,* 2023).

Toronto lawyer Tim Danson argued it is illogical that parole hearings are accessible to the public, but the evidence used during the hearings remains secret. The presentation to the Federal Court of Appeal equated the view that an offender's incarceration and parole records should be disclosed just as trial records are made public, and the parole process is integral to carrying out the sentence.

The argument was a more formalistic approach to the notion that a prisoner loses all his rights after being sent to prison. The court noticed that the files CSC kept contained large quantities of what might be ordinarily considered "private information." These files included:

- Admission and discharge records (i.e., personal effects, valuables);
- Case management reports (i.e., police reports, offender applications);
- Discipline and disassociation reports (i.e., disciplinary and segregation records);
- Education and training (i.e., employment records);
- Health care (i.e., medical and surgical, dental and psychiatric assessments);
- Preventive security (i.e., incident reports, modus operandi);
- Psychology (i.e., psychological assessments, treatment records);
- Sentence administration (victim information, community contacts); and
- Visits and correspondence (i.e., lists and contact information of visitors, declarations of common law unions).

Such files contain a tremendous amount of personal information on an offender. It is understood that the constant supervision of a prisoner implies that a certain amount of individual privacy is necessarily relinquished because of incarceration. However, the Court of Appeal said that, nonetheless, the CSC must operate by the law that states that prisoners retain all the rights enjoyed by members of society, limited only by those rights that are necessarily removed or restricted because of their imprisonment.

Yet, in an application heard at the same time the victims were arguing for prison records, the CBC applied for access to the audio tapes of parole hearings. In a separate judgment, the same panel of judges authorized the release of the audio recordings of the hearings (*Canadian Broadcasting Corporation v. Parole Board of Canada*, 2023). The decision provided:

> A declaration that the open court principle entrenched under s. 2(b) of the *Canadian Charter of Rights and Freedoms* ("Charter") applies to the Parole Board, that its proceedings are presumptively open to the public, and that records from its proceedings, including audio recordings of hearings, are public in the same way that court records are public.

Armed with this declaration, the CBC obtained and listened to the hearings involving three dangerous offenders who had appeared before the Board, including Paul Bernardo. The hearings dealt with Paul Bernardo, Craig Munro, who had murdered a Toronto Police Officer and Ethan MacLeod, also known as William Shrubsall, who had committed a series of violent crimes and sex assaults in Nova Scotia. The Parole Board required CBC to sign an undertaking promising not to record or broadcast the audio-taped hearings.

On October 30, 2023, CBC News reporter Ashley Burke published her account after hearing the hearings. Her account suggests one reason for the hesitancy in releasing documentation. The news report quotes Bernardo as saying:

> I didn't agree with my victims using the considerable victim status power.... This has caused me... extra pain and suffering over and above the sentence. I do not like my victims for this. But everyone else who only wishes me the worst, I otherwise don't care about them.

When this passage was read to Bernardo during his hearing, he agreed with the Board that his words sounded "absolutely horrible." It was undoubtedly proper for Bernardo to be asked about his writing after sixteen years of solitary confinement to gauge his present point of view. It is essential for his psychological treatment and rehabilitation that inmates express themselves openly and honestly so programs can be addressed or adjusted to meet the inmate's needs. If inmates felt their communications would eventually be made public without the context in which they are created, it would be a disincentive to speak the truth and thereby foil possible treatment opportunities.

Furthermore, for high-profile inmates, there would continue to be a wariness that such statements would be published and place their safety in danger lest other violent inmates try to administer "prison justice." Inmate Selva Subbiah was stabbed after his parole documents were obtained and published online.

In my experience assisting with hundreds of parole hearings, I struggle to recall any instance where non-public information influenced the decision-making process. Both the Correctional Service and the Parole Board diligently ensure that decisions align with proceedings open to public observation. The confusion highlighted in *Fraser et al v. Canada* (2020) stems from misunderstandings that are familiar primarily to those specializing in prison law.

The first issue is encapsulated in a quote from the families' lawyer, Tim Danson, as published in the *National Post* on August 13, 2021:

> In my view, when people convicted of first-degree murder apply for parole and seek to be released from the consequences of their life sentence and criminal acts, they forfeit their privacy rights.

This perspective overlooks the fact that, under Canadian prison legislation, inmates retain certain privacy rights. Moreover, it misconstrues parole as a release from the sentence, whereas it is, in fact, a modification in its administration.

The second issue arises from the misconception that the parole process mirrors the criminal process, necessitating an open court policy. In the Fraser decision, Justice McVeigh painstakingly establishes that Charter section 2(b)—which guarantees Canadians the right to freedom of expression and the press—does not apply to parole hearings, as they are neither judicial nor quasi-judicial proceedings.

Canadians and Canadian lawyers frequently go to court arguing a violation of rights. There is a right to privacy and freedom of expression, and our trial system is to be seen as open and above board. But rights are not absolute. One person's right to one thing must compete with another person's right to something else. We can live peacefully in a society by applying the rule of law and understanding that our rights and freedoms are not absolute. Rather, rights and freedoms must be balanced, ensuring that equal enforcement of the law applies to everyone, even prison inmates, who do not enjoy the popularity the "get tough on crime" politicians crave.

Upholding the rule of law and understanding that our rights and freedoms require balance ensures equal enforcement for all—even Paul Bernardo, who may not garner public sympathy but is nonetheless entitled to the same legal protections.

14

Robert Wilson (Rosie) Rowbotham

Cheech and Chong Moments

It felt good turning everybody on to a spiritual thing with the smoke. I wasn't a criminal. I was a pothead. I was a hash man.

—Robert "Rosie" Rowbotham

Rosie was a catalyst for all of this change.

—Alan Young, Osgoode Hall Law Professor

Rosie was a child of the sixties. The Vietnam War was raging. Robert Wilson Rowbotham (everyone called him Rosie) was an early proponent of peace, love, and weed. When he was about fifteen years old, he smoked his first joint at his friend's house in Belleville, Ontario. He described the experience as the "coolest thing ever." It was challenging to get weed in Belleville. One needed to go to Toronto to find more. That's what Rosie did. With his long curly locks, he could be spotted on Highway 401, the main four-lane thoroughfare, hitchhiking from his hometown to Toronto. He would return home with a supply to be sold locally.

In March 1967, Rosie was arrested for the first time for possessing an ounce of cannabis and sentenced to 30 days. He had not reached the age of maturity when the local police arrested him for possession of the substance. He spent his 30 days not in a group home but in jail.

The local newspaper covered the bust. Much to his and his parents' embarrassment, he was named in the news stories. When he had completed his sentence, he dropped out of school, not completing grade 10. He moved to Toronto, where he would be unknown and have ready access to his favourite recreational drug. He soon found Rochdale College, or maybe it found him.

Rochdale was the centre of the hippie universe in Toronto. Although the eighteen-story building on Bloor Street was intended to be an alternative educational and cooperative living experiment, it diverged from its purpose to become a centre for drugs with a Canada-wide reputation. It was not a degree-granting institution. It was a free art school where acceptance was granted to anyone with non-judgmental thinking. Rosie called the drug-fuelled atmosphere a "mosaic of culture, art, music, expression and inspiration."

Despite the illegal activities that flourished in Rochdale, the community fostered a unique environment of creativity and countercultural expression. Many of its residents, including Rosie, were drawn to the ideals of peace, love, and artistic freedom that defined the era. For all its flaws, Rochdale was a space where young people could explore new ideas and challenge societal norms.

It also became a financial opportunity. In the ordinary course, cannabis (weed) and hash could be obtained from street gangs in Toronto or from armed bikers. That could be scary. Dealing with Rosie, an upbeat hippie, was much more fun. He started small. He was making ends meet, selling up to ten kilos of weed over an extended time. Then, he had a chance meeting that would change his life.

Rosie was smoking a cigarette outside Sam the Record Man's store on Yonge Street in Toronto when a Lebanese businessman approached him.

"Are you Rosie Rowbotham, the guy who sells hash at Rochdale?" the stranger asked.

"If you're looking for a confession, you got the wrong guy," Rosie replied, expecting that to end the conversation. But the businessman pressed on. He told Rosie to look for a car parked outside Varsity Stadium at the University of Toronto. The keys were in the ashtray, and there was a ton of hashish in the trunk. "Don't worry about getting a hold of us," Rosie was told. "We'll get a hold of you." There were no visits to a lawyer, no negotiations, and no signed contracts. The deal was made.

After getting a taste of success, Rosie imported hashish from Lebanon and weed from all over the world. By 1972, a drought in supply was bridged by Rosie establishing a link between bikers and hippies, and soon, convoys of vans bound for Toronto established Rochdale as an international hub for the supply of weed.

Rosie rented six apartments at "the Rock," the unofficial name for the Rochdale complex. He used the premises as a stash house. He was becoming well-known as the go-to dealer. He was making money hand over fist. It was not the money Rosie enjoyed; it was the wine, women, and song that accented his hippie lifestyle. He also appreciated the notoriety of his illegal profession. He once proclaimed that if a person smoked a joint anywhere in North America, it probably came from his supply. "If you bought hash in the seventies, I don't care if you were in California, Boston, or Chicago; you got it from me," he boasted.

With a constant supply of cash, finding ways to launder it was essential. Rosie set himself up as a concert promoter and established other businesses so the illicit funds could be banked as legal tender.

Rosie's entrepreneurial spirit extended beyond the illegal drug trade. His ventures into concert promotion and other legitimate businesses reflected his ability to adapt and innovate, capitalizing on opportunities within the burgeoning counterculture of the 1970s. This ability to pivot between business models demonstrated a keen understanding of market dynamics, even if the underlying activities were illicit.

Rosie's feats were gaining such notoriety that *Rolling Stone* magazine dispatched an American writer and journalist, Richard Stratton, to visit Rosie in Toronto to conduct an interview and write about the Toronto scene for the publication. Stratton became fascinated with Rosie. Stratton understood the financial opportunity that Rosie's empire provided. The two men decided to go into partnership. Rosie would remain in Toronto, and Richard would establish an operation in New York.

Stratton also had influential friends. Stratton introduced Rosie to the Pulitzer Prize-winning writer Norman Mailer. The three men occasionally met at Mailer's country home in upstate New York.

The year 1974 marked the time of historic endings. United States President Richard Nixon stepped down from his office in light of the Watergate scandal. Richard Stratton was busted in New York City, and Rosie Rowbotham was arrested in Toronto. Rosie's arrest was for possession of over a ton of hashish and cannabis.

The trial took place in Toronto. He was no longer the youngster picked up by the cops in Belleville. This time, it was for conspiracy to import a ton of hashish into Canada. Rosie pleaded not guilty. He retained Toronto counsel Moishe Reiter to act on his behalf. The preliminary hearing was long and contentious, extending over some 18 months—the transcript of the proceedings contained over 2,400 pages. During the preliminary hearing, counsel called 41 witnesses for the accused. The hearing spawned several appeals.

These legal challenges resulted in multiple rulings unfavourable to the accused. In *R. v. Rowbotham,* 33 C.C.C. (2d) 411, the court addressed the admissibility of intercepted telephone conversations. In *R. v. Rowbotham* (No. 2), 36 C.C.C. (2d) 303, the defence sought permission to examine Richard Stratton and Frank Grasso in Boston and obtain their testimony in transcript form, as they could not attend the trial in Canada; this application was denied, and the subsequent appeal was also unsuccessful. Additionally, in *R. v. Rowbotham* (No. 5), 2 C.R. (3d) 293, an attempt to exclude wiretap evidence obtained by an RCMP officer—allegedly in violation of RCMP protocols—was rejected by the court.

While out on bail for his first trafficking trial, Rosie picked up new charges. However, he was eventually acquitted when the trial judge directed a verdict of not guilty following a motion for nonsuit at the end of the Crown's case.

With the preliminary hearing concluded, Rosie was committed to stand trial. It was also a lengthy procedure, drawing significant interest from the press. His trial was remembered by Rosie, who had his friend Norman Mailer take the stand and offer character evidence for the accused. Mailer compared Rowbotham to Errol Flynn, who portrayed the swashbuckling pirate in *Captain Blood*. He told the court that imprisoning Rosie would be a mistake and would be "bad for the cosmos."

When it came time for Rosie to speak, he was unapologetic. He stood up in court and told the judge he'd continue dealing weed because there was nothing wrong with a hippie selling flowers; he'd eaten a quarter ounce of hash that morning in a Brampton jail.

"I felt good turning everybody on to a spiritual thing with the smoke. I wasn't a criminal. I was a pothead; I was a hash man," he said. Neither the judge nor the jury was impressed with the statements of the accused or his witness. He stated bluntly that if he is released from prison, he will do the same thing again. His remarks were not uttered in contempt. He believed that it was wrong to send a peace-loving hippie and subject him to the violence of prison just because he was selling a plant that did not harm anyone. But the police were listening and took Rosie's hour-long proclamation seriously.

Rosie entered the maximum-security Kingston Penitentiary in 1978. He was sentenced to 14 years, later reduced to nine years on appeal. While awaiting his appeal, he used the four-year wait in prison to his advantage. He completed high school and obtained a degree in psychology from Queen's University and a business certificate from Sheridan College.

When he was released in 1982 on day parole, his involvement with police and the courts was the beginning of a new phase of investigation and prosecution. The Drug Squad tapped his phone, and he was busted again with about 7,000 kilograms of Lebanese hash. The police called the new trap laid for Rowbotham, "Operation Rosie." It was a massive, and costly police investigation involving over a hundred police and Drug Enforcement Agency personnel from the United States. Once again, there was extensive use of wiretaps. Rowbotham told the cops he'd keep dealing weed, and he did. He said, "I was General Patton in the War on Drugs."

Stratton and Rowbotham had arranged the delivery of eight tons of hashish. Police were alerted, but only a ton and a half of the product was seized. About a dozen individuals were arrested in this drug sweep. One of those charged was Bob Young, a brother of Neil Young of Crosby, Stills, Nash, & Young fame. At this trial, Rosie had Neil Young speak up for him as Norman Mailer had done previously.

The trial before Justice Eugene Ewaschuk began in April 1984 and took a year to complete, with six days of jury deliberation. Eleven people were found guilty on May 8, 1985 in a drug conspiracy involving as much as $54 million worth of hashish and cannabis smuggled into Canada from the United States. Rosie Rowbotham was named the group's ringleader; sometimes, he was called "chairman of the board." The prosecutor, Chris Amerasinghe, said Rowbotham was "Canada's largest importer of soft drugs." He alleged a general scheme to import and traffic in hashish and cannabis conducted generally by

Rowbotham and a co-accused named Skryzdlo. It was alleged that they were at the heart of all conspiracies charged and joined in from time to time by the other accused in lesser or more significant parts.

Rowbotham was described as the chairman of the board and Skryzdlo as the president. Skryzdlo placed orders in the United States on an ongoing basis under Rowbotham's direction, and Rowbotham would set the prices and was in charge of distribution. Skryzdlo and another co-accused, Goldstein, operated a legitimate business called Sprout House, producing and selling alfalfa sprouts. The case for the Crown was that Sprout House was the headquarters of the conspiracy and that Goldstein was aware of and participated in the illegal activities at the premises.

There were three significant seizures in the course of the investigation: one in Huntsville on November 15, 1981, involving 988 lb. of hashish and 43.75 lb. of cannabis, alleged to have been imported from the United States at Sault Ste. Marie, Michigan, and emanating from Rosie's friend Stratton, who was alleged to have been the principal supplier of Rowbotham and Skryzdlo; one in Maine on March 21, 1982, involving 1,126 lb. of hashish and 220 lb. of cannabis also involving Stratton; and one at the Chelsea Inn in Toronto on April 17, 1982, involving 271.7 lb. of hashish all seized in a car at the Chelsea Inn, the vehicle being registered to the girl-friend of a man named Stone. Stone was alleged to be the new supplier of Rowbotham and Skryzdlo, whom Young had recruited after the arrest of Stratton.

Despite Moishe Reiter's best efforts, Rosie was once again convicted. The court was reminded that Rosie never used violence in committing his crime. There was no evidence of importation of cocaine, heroin, or other hard drugs. Nonetheless, Justice Ewaschuk sentenced Rowbotham to 20 years imprisonment. It was the longest sentence ever handed out in Canada for cannabis and hashish offences. Still, defence counsel for the various co-accused lodged appeals claiming the trial judge erred by making several legal errors, including excusing a juror who had been appropriately impanelled (*R. v. Rowbotham*). The Appeal Court struck the verdict and ordered a new trial.

All the co-accused applied for bail pending the commencement of the retrial. All were successfully released on posting sureties ranging from $25,000 to $250,000. That is, except for Rosie Rowbotham. Michael Code, the prosecutor, was not so insistent that Rowbotham be granted bail. "He's cramming for his finals," Code told the *Toronto Star*. "If he passes, Rowbotham will become one of few inmates to have earned a B.A. while serving a prison term," Code said. Michael Code proposed that if bail is granted, terms of release should include daily reporting to the police. Since Rowbotham was indigent, he could only post $75,000, representing the equity in Rosie's parents' home. Justice Allan Goodman reserved the decision on bail.

When Justice Goodman's decision was handed down on April 14, 1985, the news for Rosie was not good. The judge refused to grant bail. He took into account that Justice Ewaschuk had imposed a 20-year sentence. The prospects of conviction following a new trial were good. Further, Rowbotham was arrested while on parole for a similar crime and continued to serve a nine-year sentence. He remained unsatisfied that Rowbotham would appear for trial even if a substantial amount with deposit and sureties were required.

Nonetheless, on appeal, Supreme Court Justice Patrick Galligan granted bail. Rosie was released from jail to face a second trial. Rosie, while out on bail, incurred new drug charges. Both "the chairman of the board" and "the chief executive officer" were convicted of importing and trafficking vast amounts of hashish and cannabis between 1981 and 1982. Justice Patrick Galligan sentenced Rowbotham and

Skryzdlo to 17 years and 12 1/2 years in prison, respectively. Others involved in the scheme had entered guilty pleas and were sentenced to lesser terms.

Justice Galligan rejected the prosecution's recommendation of imposing a life sentence on Rosie. He seemingly expressed that seeing him released on bail had been a mistake. "I, too, was convinced that he would not return to the drug trade," the judge said. But he added that he foresaw a return to such activity when released the next time. He characterized Rosie as the worst possible offender but said the 17-year sentence was appropriate because life sentences should be the penalty for those who traffic in hard drugs. Galligan quoted Rowbotham's words from the 1977 trial in which Rosie said, "I am not remorseful for anything I've done. I believe I have helped society. I cannot be rehabilitated. I don't believe in it."

Rowbotham would be Galligan's last case before his appointment to the Ontario Court of Appeal. Besides praising both Crown and defence counsel for handling the case, Justice Galligan praised Sergeant Gary Carter, who was in charge of the police investigation. "You supervised a brilliant investigation," Galligan said[1].

Even though Justice Galligan found the 17-year sentence appropriate, defence counsel did not. An appeal was taken, and Justice J. A. Doherty of the Ontario Court of Appeal ultimately substituted a sentence of 13 years for Rowbotham and 8 years for Skryzdlo.

Rosie saw the money and time spent on his prosecution as "a tragic and disproportionate waste." He was forceful in his belief that he "didn't break God's law" and that authorities had wasted millions of dollars pursuing him for selling harmless weed.

1 In September 2002, Gary Carter, a 28-year veteran of the Toronto Police Force who retired in 1995, was sentenced to one year of house arrest after pleading guilty to stealing $47,000 from a fund established to investigate organized crime.

There needed to be more clarity between how legal authorities viewed lawbreaking and how Rosie viewed his actions. Law enforcement and judicial institutions see laws as imperatives deserving to be obeyed. Those who do not abide by the law deserve punishment. Rowbotham's concept of right and wrong was not based on obedience to a superior authority but on the notion that laws should exist to prevent harm. In his view, he did not harm his fellow man; indeed, he offered a product to enhance one's enjoyment of life.

Rosie still had to stand trial for drug offences incurred while he was on bail awaiting his second trial. This time, Rosie Rowbotham and David Roblin were charged with conspiring to traffic in a narcotic in Toronto and Austin, Texas. This trial ended when the trial judge agreed to order a directed verdict of acquittal. Both Rowbotham and Roblin appealed. The issue on this appeal is whether the Crown was entitled to rely on the general conspiracy provisions of the *Criminal Code* or whether the Crown was required to prove that trafficking in a narcotic was an offence under the law of Texas to benefit from the presumption of territoriality and prosecute the offence here. The Crown appealed this acquittal.

The Appeal Court handed down its decision on October 16, 1992. It held that, given the trial judge's finding, it was clear that there was evidence of conspiracy to traffic a narcotic in Canada. That being the case, there was no need to consider s. 465(3) of the Code or whether trafficking in narcotics was an offence under the law of Texas.

There was evidence for a jury to consider. The motion for a directed verdict of acquittal should have been dismissed. The appeal was allowed, the respondents' acquittal was set aside, and a new trial was directed.

On December 7, 1994, a jury found the appellant guilty of conspiracy to traffic in cannabis. On December 19, 1994, he was sentenced to 18 years imprisonment to be served consecutive to a 13-year sentence he was then serving imposed in June 1989, as reduced by the court. This resulted in a 31-year sentence with an expiration date of May 19, 2020.

Once again, it was for the Ontario Court of Appeal to review the propriety of this sentence. However, an Appeal Court must have a trial transcript to appeal. The problem was set out in the Court of Appeal's February 26, 1999, decision:

> From the materials before us, we are satisfied that it is impossible to obtain a transcript of the trial proceedings, particularly the instructions delivered by the trial judge to the jury. Most of the appellant's grounds for appeal from his conviction related to purported errors in the jury charge. With respect to one of the errors—the failure to charge on the co-conspirator's exception to the hearsay rule—the trial judge rejected requests by the Crown and the defence to include a [specific instruction]. In this regard, counsel for the respondent conceded that this amounted to a fatal non-direction.

Despite the Crown's and the defence's efforts to cancel the prosecution, the Appeal Court ordered another new trial *(R. v. Rowbotham)*.

Meanwhile, Stratton won his appeal in the United States and wrote a book on the adventure. He married a former Texas police officer who also got into writing. Her book *Rush* was made into a movie. Stratton and his wife started *Prison Life Magazine* to advocate for those serving time. Stratton reunited with Rosie, who was named Canadian managing editor. The magazine covered topics such as Terry Fitzsimmons' ordeal with solitary confinement in a feature article titled "A Short Brutal Life."

Stratton would go on to develop and be a consulting producer for the TV series *Oz*. Stratton and Rosie kept in touch, and the creative juices flowed. While serving a sentence in Collins Bay Institution, Rosie answered an ad to become the new host of a TV talk show produced by Kingston Cablenet and piped weekly into all area prisons. Rosie renamed the show *Prison Life Television* and invited guests to be interviewed by Rosie on topics of interest to the inmate population. Rosie continued to write for *Prison Life Magazine*. He achieved fame through local TV appearances and magazine writing for an international audience.

Rosie wanted to interview a prison law lawyer for his television show. He asked me to be a guest on one episode, and I was impressed with the professionalism with which he conducted the interview. Even the TV crew consisted of prisoners released on passes to initiate a program highlighting prison issues and analyzing wrongs within the criminal and correctional systems. For the first time, international media focused on the prisoners' perspectives on issues.

On Oct. 6, 1997, Rosie was paroled. Upon release, one of his first stops was an interview with Michael Enright on a national CBC broadcast. Rosie was so impressive that CBC hired him to focus on prison issues. The CBC also gained. CBC reporter Maureen Brosnahan wrote,

> I was assigned to oversee his journalism and ensure he didn't break "too" many CBC rules. In turn, he opened doors for me by letting inmates know that I was "solid" and trustworthy. I will always be indebted to him for that.

The Court noticed a significant change. The Court of Appeal outlined the progress made in its 1999 decision:

> In joining in this proposal, counsel for the respondent acknowledged that the appellant has served a significant amount of time in custody on other charges and has achieved success in his rehabilitation, as

> evidenced by the fact that he was granted day parole on October 5, 1997, and full parole on November 13, 1998. As well, the appellant is currently employed as an associate producer for the CBC and a member of a reference group which advises the Solicitor General of Canada on issues relating to the *Corrections and Conditional Release Act*. Counsel for the respondent is satisfied, given the appellant's employment, current interests, and the obvious community response, all of which are outlined in the appellant's affidavit, that he is re-integrating himself into the community.

The Crown did not proceed with the retrial. He became very successful and was admired for his work with the CBC.

Gradually, the academic community came around to Rosie's concept of the law. Julian Roberts, a University of Ottawa professor of criminology specializing in sentencing, called the sentences meted out to Rowbotham "disproportionate" in the mistaken belief that a harsh sentence would help in the cause of deterrence. He is quoted as saying, "He got a sentence you'd normally associate with big-time narco barons. More serious crimes are punished less severely."

Osgoode Hall Law Professor Alan Young said, "When law stands on a weak foundation, that's when you see the harshest sentences." He went further in accepting Rosie's view, "Nobody in the history of humanity has been significantly harmed by marijuana."

Neil Boyd, professor of Criminology at Simon Fraser University, agreed, saying:

> He's a political prisoner in the sense that jails ought to be reserved for people who hurt others—violent crimes, or predatory property crimes, that is, people who take advantage of others—and I don't see Rosie as a criminal. He challenged the moral validity of the

> law and did so in a very confrontational way. Had he taken a much more deferential tact, I don't think he would have received the length of sentence that he did.

It was not Rosie who changed his beliefs. It was that society was relaxing its attitude to cannabis, and just a few years later, the drug was legalized. Retail stores selling the product sprouted up in almost every Canadian community. While it is true that laws often reflect societal norms, changing societal norms can see the repeal of regulations.

Rosie was released on day parole to a halfway house in Toronto in October 1997. A CBC producer, Sean Jones, read of Rosie's release and proposed that Rosie would be an unusual and exciting guest to be interviewed by CBC host Michael Enright on a show called "This Morning." The day after he moved into the halfway house, Rosie sat in a CBC radio studio in front of a microphone and was interviewed on national radio.

Michael Enright, the show host, questioned Rosie on his rehabilitation. The answer he received was unexpected. Rosie said:

> I still have the same value systems, but I, you know... if I ever had my life to live over again, I would do the same thing.

When Enright pressed Rosie about his repeated legal troubles and returns to prison, Rosie explained that after serving his initial sentence of three or four years, he found himself trying to rebuild his life, driven by ingrained habits. He described his actions as part of a lifestyle—an addiction to a certain way of living. He emphasized that he wasn't involved in violent crimes like bank robberies or causing harm to others. Instead, his activities were nonviolent and rooted in the counterculture of the 1960s and 1970s. He mentioned assisting American draft dodgers, selling drugs, and engaging in music promotion, all of which were intertwined with the era's cultural movements. This lifestyle fulfilled his personal identity, economic needs, and provided a sense of purpose, leading him to return to it repeatedly.

That interview sparked CBC producer Ira Basen to suggest something new for the radio network. Rosie was offered a job as a CBC producer and journalist. It required a significant adjustment for Rosie and those working at the broadcast centre. It was unusual for a parolee to leave a halfway house to go to work and sit at a desk with a computer and be expected to type and send emails. All that was foreign to one who had spent years in prison. It was unusual to have a parole officer visit an employee at work for updates on the progress being made on the new job.

It was also a new experience for radio staff to associate with someone who had spent years in prison and to hear tales of a side of life some had never contemplated. As Ira Basen put it, "He taught us so much. He opened up many doors to ways of thinking ... and introduced us to a fascinating cast of characters from Rochdale and prison."

However, Rosie gave the CBC listening audience a different perspective, too. In January of 1998, Alan Eagleson, a lawyer for several prominent NHL hockey players, was about to begin his sentence for ripping off his player clients. Rosie recorded his open letter to Eagleson, pointing out what the disgraced lawyer could expect. The letter, mocked Eagleson, a wealthy man, for receiving preferential treatment: "You're all alone in the holding cell. Next, there's more than 50 others crammed together like sardines, and they'll be in there for a lot longer than you." This personal point of view was new to radio listeners and offered a perspective unmatched elsewhere in the popular press.

Yet, trouble continued. In 2001, *Toronto Star* Legal Affairs Reporter Tracy Tyler broke the story that Rowbotham had been arrested by police and charged with assault causing bodily harm and uttering death threats to his common-law wife. A bogus charge led to Rosie being suspended on parole and returned to prison.

At the age of 50, Rosie was forced to occupy a cell at the maximum-security Toronto East Detention Centre. His parole had been suspended when his common-law wife, Valerie Phillips, accused him of a domestic assault. Rosie sat for two and a half months awaiting trial. The trial was held in October 2001.

Rosie retained Moishe Reiter to defend him on the criminal charge. Reiter asked me to join him as co-counsel when the matter went to trial. Rosie was acquitted, but instead of walking out of court as a free man, he was sent to the maximum-security Millhaven Penitentiary to await a post-suspension hearing before the Parole Board. His release on parole was subject to good behaviour. Even though a criminal court acquitted him, it was up to the Parole Board to determine if he continued to be a manageable societal risk.

With Rosie's newly acquired high-profile status as a CBC reporter, the media took a deeper-than-usual look into how inmates are treated.

On October 23, 2001, the *Globe and Mail* published an editorial titled "Why is he still in jail?" The piece began by highlighting public concern over Robert (Rosie) Rowbotham's continued incarceration. It noted that, like any dedicated journalist, Rowbotham delved into areas unfamiliar to his audience, such as the prison system. Ironically, his most compelling story might be his own: a legal system that knowingly keeps an innocent man imprisoned. The editorial acknowledged his past cannabis-smuggling convictions but pointed out that the new charge was different, involving an allegation of violence stemming from a 911 call in which his spouse accused him of assault. The newspaper accurately summarized the aftermath, stating that his spouse, a convicted perjurer, later testified in the Ontario Court of Justice that she had fabricated the entire story and had been unsuccessfully trying to convey this to the Crown and police for weeks.

Understandably, legal authorities accustomed to women trying to protect their men, even the ones who assaulted them, did not want to back down. It was only after she repeatedly asserted in court that she had been in a stupor of drugs and drink and had been angry at "Rosie" for threatening to leave her over her substance abuse that the Crown asked the judge to dismiss the charges. The judge told him he was free to go on these charges.

The suspension of Rosie's parole was still in place even though the court had acquitted him. He explained the situation to the Parole Board and told them he continued to be a manageable risk to society.

Rosie's treatment exposed a situation in Canadian correctional law of which few were aware. The *Globe* article said:

> The real risk is that by holding Mr. Rowbotham after his acquittal, the corrections authorities are becoming a law unto themselves and imperilling the rights and freedoms of Canadians. And according to Mr. Rowbotham's lawyer, John Hill, he is not the only one in this situation.

Even though Rosie had been granted bail on the assault charge, the suspension of his parole and placement in a provincial detention centre had more significant ramifications than simply the loss of his job and his freedom. Once acquitted and returned to a federal penitentiary, he went through the typical measures involved in "pen placement." A simple skin test was administered to detect if the inmate had tuberculosis. The TB test proved positive. Correctional institutions can be breeding grounds for TB. In 1998, a federal study found that one in five inmates entering the prison system tested positive for the bacterial infection. In the end, the skin test proved to be a false positive, but that did not remove the anguish the inmate endured, thinking he may suffer from a severe illness.

The post-suspension hearing was initially scheduled for November 23, 2001. However, when critical comments about the correctional system were made in the news media, a date suddenly opened up, allowing for an earlier review. The hearing before the Parole Board was scheduled for October 26.

I was retained to act for Rosie at his post-suspension hearing. He performed brilliantly before the board and in front of an audience of observers, most of whom were CBC luminaries. The hearing was more than to rubberstamp the finding of innocence the court had made. The report prepared by the Correctional Service of Canada urged the Board to cancel Rosie's parole. The author of the report recommended that the Board accept that the spouse's denial that an assault took place was "a classic victim posture." At the hearing, after three hours of questioning, Rowbotham denied any abuse. The parole hearing lasted longer than the criminal trial.

The Board focused on Rowbotham's relationship with Valerie Phillips. When the Board retreated to decide, the prison treated those attending the hearing with coffee and cookies. An audience at a parole hearing is quite unusual, especially an audience that includes nationally recognized radio celebrities such as Michael Enright, Avril Benoit, and Shelagh Rogers.

Board member Michael Crowley announced that the suspension was cancelled. The audience erupted in applause despite the CSC recommendation. The Parole Board agreed with the court and revoked the suspension. The Board's decision complimented Rowbotham's "outstanding" success as a parolee. "There's evidence you've become pro-social," Crowley declared. It required Rosie to attend an assessment by a psychologist to confirm that he is not in an abusive relationship and that he should seek family counselling with Valerie Phillips. His parole would continue until his warrant expiry date in June 2022.

Subsequently, I became a founder, producer, and host of a radio show on a local community radio station, Northumberland 89.7 FM. Cannabis was about to be legalized. I asked Rosie, this time, to be the interviewee. He readily agreed and invited me to his Toronto home, where he eloquently spoke of his crimes unapologetically. I recorded his conversation for a later broadcast. He continued to consider himself to be General Patton in the war on drugs.

Years later, an individual who had known Rosie during the Rochdale College era reached out to share a story suggesting that Rosie continued his involvement in drug trafficking after his release from prison. The correspondent, choosing to remain anonymous, recounted that in the late 1990s, Rosie had been released from prison and was hosting an intriguing show at CBC's downtown studio. Although Rosie invited him to visit the studio, he declined.

At that time, the correspondent was collecting a payment of approximately ten thousand dollars from Rosie on behalf of their team and delivering the product to a buyer. He was thrilled to see Rosie after many years, though Rosie didn't recognize him, as he had been a minor figure at Rochdale in 1970 compared to Rosie's significant presence. Now, he was merely the delivery person for a shipment of 20 kilograms of black hashish. Utilizing a company vehicle equipped with a concealed compartment, he parked under a tall light post in the Yorkdale Mall parking lot, near the Indigo bookstore and the Rainforest Cafe. After grabbing a tea, he encountered Rosie, who had gained considerable weight. Rosie purchased two large tarts from Indigo, offering one to the correspondent, who declined. They briefly discussed books they had read in prison, with Rosie mentioning that *Shogun* had helped him escape mentally during his incarceration, while the correspondent cited *Papillon*.

Proceeding to business, the correspondent handed Rosie the keys to his van and provided detailed parking instructions: "third row, section 87, right under the light standard." From the second-floor window of Indigo, he pointed out the blue GMC all-wheel-drive van to Rosie, who acknowledged it and headed downstairs to retrieve the goods. Concerned about Rosie's recent prison release and the nature of their clients, the correspondent took extra precautions.

Observing Rosie attempting to unlock several incorrect vehicles with the provided keys, the correspondent activated the van's panic alarm, rushed downstairs, and redirected Rosie to the correct vehicle. The parking lot was monitored by Plaza security, and any suspicious activity could have led to immediate intervention. They walked together to the blue van and then to Rosie's car. The correspondent had expected Rosie, once dubbed "Captain Hashish," to drive a luxurious vehicle, but instead, he had a rusted 1979 Pinto with a loud muffler. Upon opening the doors, smoke from a recently extinguished joint billowed out. Rosie lit another joint and drove away, creating a scene reminiscent of a Cheech and Chong moment.

While Rosie maintained his pro-cannabis stance, Canada's perspective evolved. In a *Globe and Mail* article, Osgoode Hall Law School Professor Emeritus Alan Young contended that legalizing cannabis is merely the beginning; comprehensive legislation is necessary to rectify past injustices faced by individuals criminalized under previous drug laws. He highlighted the detrimental effects of the punitive drug war, noting that many individuals endured lengthy prison sentences for minor cannabis offences, families were disrupted with children removed from caring parents due to cannabis use, and individuals faced job losses and violent police raids. Young emphasized that society as a whole suffered, as substantial resources were diverted from addressing serious crimes to enforcing drug laws, ultimately compromising public safety and security.

Rosie became a free man when his sentence expired in 2002. Because of his criminal record, he was ineligible to participate in legally selling cannabis when laws changed. He continued, I am told, to sell it in small quantities. He was unapologetic until the end; cancer took the 72-year-old's life in 2022.

Looking back on Rosie Rowbotham's ordeals with the criminal law, we see that spending years in prison for something that nowadays would be considered a legitimate commercial venture is possible because a person is out of sync with societal norms. Rosie's perceptive commentary on prison issues has led to a better public understanding of why the humane treatment of prisoners is essential. We owe Rosie our gratitude. May he rest in peace.

15

George Lovie

Nothing But Fear Itself

FRANKLIN D. ROOSEVELT's famous words during his 1933 inauguration, "We have nothing to fear but fear itself," still hold true. Fear can be a powerful driver of political concern. In the 1930s, it was the fear of economic collapse following the 1929 stock market crash.

Today, fear is being used to advocate for stricter crime policies. This fear prompted the *Sudbury Star* to publish an article on September 9, 2020, with the chilling headline, "The animal has been released from the cage."

The article highlighted the deep concern expressed by former NHL goalie Don Edwards upon learning the news that George Lovie, the individual who had been released from the minimum-security Beaver Creek Institution to reside at a halfway house in Sudbury the year before, had his day parole extended. The Parole Board of Canada can order day parole and place necessary restrictions for public protection. The offender must prove that the risk is manageable.

The conditions of Lovie's release included residing in the Sudbury community residential facility, having no contact with his victims' families, and reporting any direct or indirect contact with them. He was ordered to abstain from alcohol and report any attempt to initiate relationships with women. The Parole Board knew that his release plan included volunteering in Sudbury, starting a carpentry business, and using inherited funds to buy a home in Sudbury.

Why was this former hockey player, now living in the United States, so adamantly opposed to a Canadian prisoner having his restraints loosened? It came down to fear. Don Edwards was genuinely afraid that George Lovie might harm his Canadian relatives.

That fear stemmed from a traumatic event in 1991. At the time, George Lovie, then 33, had been romantically involved with Edwards' sister. The relationship ended when she accused him of sexual assault. Lovie denied the allegation, but soon after, he showed up armed with a gun and a knife. Although Edwards' sister managed to escape, her mother was fatally shot and her father stabbed to death. Lovie was convicted of two counts of first-degree murder. The sexual assault charge was later dropped after he received the maximum penalty of life imprisonment.

George Lovie spent years in prison before being transferred to minimum-security Beaver Creek Institution. Now, it was time to consider release. He knew the Parole Board would be sceptical of granting immediate freedom to a convicted murderer. He would need to prove he was ready. The first step would be to gain limited access to the community and return to the institution without incident. But even that required Parole Board approval. The process typically began with a request for an escorted temporary absence—an ETA, in correctional terms. For Don Edwards and his family, the idea of Lovie re-entering society wasn't just uncomfortable—it reawakened a personal history marked by violence.

The grant of an ETA would allow an inmate to go into the community for a few hours, perhaps to a store, accompanied by a correctional officer. The officer would monitor the inmate for good behaviour and signs of institutionalization, such as becoming anxious when confronted by crowds or experiencing noises common to someone who has never been held captive. Permission to go on ETAs also requires Parole Board approval.

Michael Crowley, a highly experienced member of the Parole Board of Canada, attended two of Lovie's attempts to seek this limited form of release and chaired the hearings.

Things did not go well for Lovie, as Crowley explained:

> I saw him twice and sat through about five hours of victim presentations. The first time, I called for a recess so folks could get a break. But then he chose to withdraw his ETA application, and there was no hearing. But I had everyone come back into the room, explained what happened and opened the floor up to questions about parole as a process, not about the case. I even had a reporter stay. It went well after some initial bewilderment, at least until someone asked when he could apply again. 'Immediately' was the answer from our staff, and virtually everyone exploded in anger and walked out. A few thanked me. A few years later, virtually the same scenario, except he stayed, and we had a full hearing. We denied release but encouraged him to participate in an assessment for sex offender programming, given the allegations. He said he would. We could tell that the victims are genuinely afraid of him, even though that makes no sense. But that emotion has ruled their lives for so many years it will never leave them.

Over time, George Lovie demonstrated significant progress in his behaviour and attitude, which did not go unnoticed by the institution's staff. He actively participated in rehabilitation programs, including anger management and vocational training, which helped him develop new skills and a better understanding of the consequences of his actions. These positive steps contributed to the eventual decision to grant escorted temporary absences.

The next step was to ask the Board for Unescorted Temporary Absence, or UTA. Ordinarily, a UTA takes the form of a weekend visit to a halfway house to earn an invitation to reside at the community facility. Once the inmate had proven himself to the Board, his next step would be to apply for day parole. This allows an inmate to remain at a halfway house for six months and again prove to the Board that he is ready for full release to the community.

George Lovie eventually was granted a day parole release with tightly monitored restrictions. The Parole Board extended the restrictions of his day parole in 2023, and in March 2024, Lovie was granted full parole. Although he could now live on his own and not in a halfway house, he will continue to be subject to state supervision for the rest of his natural life. Family members were able to address the Board at his hearing and begged the Board to refuse to grant full parole. They remained fearful that the man who inflicted such harm over thirty years ago may still come after them.

Statistics show that the percentage of paroled inmates who become recidivistic is few, and the number who kill again is exceedingly rare. That is of little comfort to the families. The Parole Board has done its job ensuring that the risk to the community is manageable and the victims' families have been allowed to make a victim impact statement. Yet, the families and the community are still enraged.

Part of the problem for public discontent is that the correctional system tries to solve a complex issue with simple solutions, such as allowing for reading victim impact statements. Few people understand the lengthy procedures used to see the inmate rehabilitated and cascade from maximum to minimum security. Few know the degree to which the Parole Board takes pains to ensure that full parole is granted to only the most deserving. Even though victim participation is allowed at a hearing, some see this as a meaningless exercise or, worse, a revictimization of the families.

It is time to take victims more into the confidence of the correctional authorities and allow victims to actively meet with and engage with the prisoner throughout the offender's incarceration. Such a procedure would help educate those who have been victimized into a better understanding that rehabilitation assists the whole community and is far more effective than using prisons as places of punishment. The Correctional Services of Canada offers a voluntary program called the Restorative Opportunities Program that focuses on addressing the harm caused by crime and meeting the needs of those involved. The program provides victims the opportunity to communicate with the offender who harmed them. It will enable both offender and victim to understand that people change over time and that rehabilitation is possible. It can replace fear with hope.

Still, the program is little known and too rarely used. In its absence, a louder voice often prevails: one that calls for harsher sentences, longer confinements, and a refusal to see offenders as anything but irredeemable. It is a voice rooted in fear, but also in a desire for control—a belief that darkness must be contained, not confronted. This mindset reinforces the notion that the prison cell is the only safe solution, ignoring the deeper question of what justice truly requires. When we respond to violence with inflexible severity, we risk replicating the very dynamics of harm we seek to eliminate. In that way, the desire for endless punishment becomes its own act of darkness—more insidious because it cloaks itself in the language of safety and virtue. True accountability, on the other hand, demands something more difficult: recognition, reckoning, and the possibility of repair.

Epilogue

We would all like to live in a world where truth, justice, and protection of our civil liberties are unquestioned. Unfortunately, that is not this world. One of the disruptive forces affecting our quest for the society we crave is that we often mistake truth with preconceived notions. Preconceived notions are built on stereotypes, prejudices, sexism, and racism. Whether we care to admit it or not, these obstacles to the recognition of truth may stem from unconscious biases.

Stereotypes are beliefs or assumptions about how a particular group acts or reacts because of generalized assumed characteristics based on race, gender, age, or nationality. Stereotypes may result in unfair treatment or attitudes towards people identified as belonging to such groups.

Stereotypical reactions occur most frequently when we are confronted with individuals or groups we do not know well. Our brains process information drawn from the environment in which we exist. One tendency is to believe that our present circumstances are unchanging—as they were in the beginning, are now, and ever shall be. Such an attitude enables our cognitive processes to disregard our historical past and assume that the values we now hold have always been in place.

This method of misperception is known as cognitive bias. We see the world in a distorted manner. Cognitive bias is particularly troublesome if judges or triers of fact hold such biases. We were told as children that the police were our friends. We grow up believing that it is an undeniable truth. When the police present evidence in a trial, our cognitive bias makes us less critical. That can cause us to view the evidence through a distorted lens, leading to error and misunderstanding.

Another form of bias that often exists is confirmation bias. We like interpreting information that conforms to our existing or shared beliefs and rule out anything disruptive to these preconceived notions.

One form of confirmation bias is the belief that society is hierarchical; that some people are our "betters," and others fall below us in social rank. Those people adjudged to be superior in social rank can do no wrong, and those who fall below us are the source of societal misery.

This confirmation bias is often exploited by politicians who promise to get tough on crime. Criminals, we like to think, are a subspecies undeserving of occupying a place in our day-to-day world. "Lock 'em up," and some would say, "Throw away the key." This has led to a situation where precedence in sentencing offenders is given to the concepts of denunciation and deterrence. A harsh sentence is a denunciation of the wrong that has been done and a belief that spending excessive time in prison will serve as a deterrent to like-minded individuals who might choose to participate in similar misconduct.

The problem is that there is no statistical proof that such a method of punishment works. Because of stereotypical thinking, we have built a justice system where racism has led to an over-representation of Indigenous and racialized minorities in our jails.

We often hear it said in sentencing courts and before the Parole Board that one must take responsibility for one's acts. Consider the degree of responsibility that the woman discussed in the following case study must take for becoming addicted to alcohol and drugs. It is a true story told to me by the woman's granddaughter. The woman was a young Indigenous child named Josephine. She was taken from her First Nation in Saskatchewan and placed in the Muskowekan residential school near St. Albert, approximately 20 kilometres northwest of Edmonton. At the age of twelve, Josephine became pregnant, having been sexually assaulted by a Catholic priest working at the school. It was learned that she was carrying twins. On the day she gave birth, the priest seized the babies, wrapped them in cloth, and burned them alive. Josephine suffered psychologically and emotionally and took to chronic substance abuse. She could not control her behaviour and was now expected to accept responsibility for her improper behaviour.

Josephine was never compensated, nor was any apology offered for the unspeakable abuse she suffered. Unfortunately, her story was repeated in tales of abuse delivered by other residential school survivors.

We often look to "the what" that has been done when a person acts out, not "the why" it happened. Fortunately, through legislation and court decisions, we are beginning to look at the societal precursors of crime. We are starting to understand that historical mistreatment of certain groups has created a social class preordained to fall into criminal actions and substance abuse. If we keep whipping the dog, the animal will likely become vicious. Instead of punishing the dog, maybe it is time to reconsider our guilt in how the situation arose.

The bottom line is that when we degrade a person because of skin colour or social standing and treat that person miserably, we are performing the societal equivalent of whipping the dog. Yes, those men did wrong, but let us not forget to strive to know why they did it. It is a manner of dehumanization that is every bit as wrong as the evil that men do.

But history is not destiny. It is up to each of us to be less judgmental and to strive for rehabilitation rather than punishment. Our institutions work if we allow them to work. A peaceful and safe society is everyone's goal. All it takes is our commitment and resolve to achieve it.

Acknowledgement
In Memorium

Authors customarily acknowledge the many people who have assisted in writing their work. Although unusual, I would like to devote these closing remarks to my animal friends who have stood by me throughout my legal career and admit what I emotionally perceive as a personal moment of darkness.

Being a lawyer often equates with having a stressful life. The American Psychiatric Association says pet owners are more satisfied with their lives than non-pet owners. Eighty-six percent of owners credit their pets with positively impacting their mental health.

Throughout my legal career, whenever I got bogged down in writing or research, I would turn my head to my dog and say, "Do you want to go for a walk outside?" The pet was always agreeable. Whatever pleasure that animal derived, I could calm down and carry on.

I have almost continually had a dog. Within a year of my call to the bar, I adopted Skippy, a Samoyed/White Shepherd cross; then there was Lucy and Ethel, husky/collie crosses; and later there was Judge, a terrier crossbreed. Hedy, an English Cocker Spaniel, has been at my side for 14 years.

That is until June 18, 2024. When dogs age, the decline in their health happens rapidly. Earlier this year, we accepted her blindness and what has been diagnosed as "doggy dementia."

My wife and I noticed that she was constantly licking her front paws for no apparent reason. Our veterinarian advised that this behaviour sometimes indicated internal pain. Added intestinal problems convinced us that it would be kindest to ask for euthanasia. Our vet agreed.

An appointment was made with our local animal hospital for 9:30 on the morning of the 18th. We were asked to accompany Hedy into a room where she sat on a table. I was asked to sign the consent for the process. (*I'm signing my little girl's death warrant* was my instantaneous thought!) We continued petting her while a sedative was administered. We were asked to remain in the room with Hedy while the relaxant took effect.

The veterinarian took her to another room, where a catheter was inserted in her left front paw. Hedy was then returned to us. This time, the vet took a syringe from her pocket and inserted the lethal drug into the catheter. My mind went straight away to the scene at the prison in Huntsville, Texas, and the injection given to Stanley Faulder, a Canadian on death row who had been convicted of killing a Texas oil baron's wife. A meeting to delay the execution was arranged with then-governor George W. Bush and the head of the Texas Board of Parole. It was unsuccessful. Faulder was led into a small chamber; the drugs were injected, and he coughed twice and silently passed away.

I commented to the veterinarian that this was like my experience with Faulder. The doctor did not pick up on my horror, and she commented that it was a humane and painless way to go. She then placed her stethoscope on Hedy's chest, and the next words I heard were, "She's gone."

Did the American Psychiatric Association include that sense of loss when arriving at its statistics? When my mother, who suffered for ten years with Alzheimer's and was reduced from a loving, caring, intelligent woman to one confined to a

Hedy at home

bed, unable to walk, talk or know her family or surroundings, died, my emotion was of relief. Why should I shed tears for an animal when I did not for the person who gave me life?

Two events after the 18th put things in better perspective for me. The first was a complaint I received from a former client who I had referred to a very well-respected, but elderly lawyer. His case had been dismissed because the lawyer had missed a limitation period. A check with the law society revealed that the lawyer had been administratively suspended but was later returned to practice. I suspected he had forgotten to pay his annual fees or file the necessary yearly returns. The lawyer was in his 70s. The law society does not require cognitive testing to remain in practice. Dementia can happen to anyone, but more frequently when one ages. It can have disastrous results when a client needs a lawyer's mind that functions appropriately. Has anyone ever suggested that this lawyer retire? Retirement for a lawyer is difficult because the job defines what you do and who you are. Later, I watched the American presidential debate between then-President Joe Biden and then-former President Donald Trump. Joe Biden's lapses and non-sequiturs were similar to the speech patterns of people I have encountered with dementia. The next day, political commentators, including the *New York Times*, suggested it was time for Biden to release his convention delegates and allow the Democratic Party to select another, more youthful, nominee.

Whether it be a dog's life, a successful law practice, or the American presidency, sometimes the kindest thing to say is, "You've given us your best. But now it's time to step aside."

The same comment should be considered when we evaluate the operations of our judicial system. If some aspects are not working, it may be time to forget, "That is the way we've always done things," and press for reform.

John L. Hill

John L. Hill is a retired Canadian lawyer known for his work in criminal and prison law, focusing on representing penitentiary inmates and individuals involved in some of Canada's most complex cases. He is a triple graduate of Queen's University with degrees in political science and law, and he also holds an LL.M. in Constitutional Law from Osgoode Hall. Throughout his career, Hill has handled high-profile cases, including those involving solitary confinement and wrongful convictions. He has written extensively, including the book *Pine Box Parole*, where he examines how the prison system can exacerbate criminal behaviour. He continues to write about crime and imprisonment, shedding light on the flaws within Canada's legal system. John L. Hill lives in Cobourg, Ontario.

Salvatore Caramanna

Foreword writer, **Sal Caramanna**, is a leading criminal defence lawyer in Toronto. His distinguished career has focused on defending complex, high-stakes cases. A graduate of Osgoode Hall Law School, he has represented clients in major trials, including wrongful conviction cases. From 2008 to 2013, he chaired the International Review Committee for AIDWYC (now Innocence Canada), reviewing numerous cases and assisting wrongly convicted defendants in the United States. He continues to work on wrongful conviction cases. His background in science with an Honours B.Sc. in nutritional sciences, a pre-medical school program, has been valuable in cases involving forensic evidence.